An Introduction to Education in Bible Times

From Creation through the Early Church

Christopher J. Reeves

Copyright © 2019 Christopher J. Reeves
ISBN: 9781798723821
Library of Congress Control Number: 2019936226
Published in the United States of America

All rights reserved as permitted under the U. S. Copyright Act of 1976. No part of this publication may be reproduced, distributed, or transmitted in any form or by any means, or stored in a database or retrieval system, without the expressed written permission of the author and publisher.

All scripture quotations, unless otherwise marked, are taken from the *New American Standard Bible*®, Copyright © 1960, 1962, 1963, 1968, 1971, 1972, 1973, 1975, 1977, 1995 by The Lockman Foundation Used by permission. (www.Lockman.org). All rights reserved.

Scripture quotations marked JPS are taken from *The Jewish Publication Society TANAKH.* Used by permission. Philadelphia, PA. All rights reserved worldwide.

Cover Design: Christopher J. Reeves

www.BurkhartBooks.com
Bedford, Texas

DEDICATION

In appreciation for all my godly teachers and mentors who have exemplified the teachings of Scripture in their life and teaching. And to all those who selflessly give of themselves to love and teach through word and example.

ACKNOWLEDGMENTS

There are many people who have contributed to the writing of this book. I am personally indebted to each one for their contributions, support, and guidance in this endeavor. In particular, I would like to thank:

Drs. Nicholas and Leona Venditti for their friendship, their passion for Christian education, and for introducing me to the subject of lifelong learning among the Jews (which began this project).

Rabbi Mordechai Weiss for his friendship and introduction into the heart of Judaism, and for the many recommended books to read.

Dr. Igal German for his research into the Second Temple period, his work in connecting Christians to their Jewish heritage, and for the many great book recommendations.

Dr. (Rabbi) David Edery for the many conversations about the importance of connecting Christians to their Jewish roots.

Phil Forbes, Th.M., for his constant encouragement and contributions to this book.

Dr. Wesley M. Pinkham for his insistence that Christian education be a biblically-based relational experience for teacher and student.

Dr. Mark H. Glenn for his great friendship, encouragement, contributions to this book, and his vision for Christian education in its biblical context.

Molly Reeves, my beautiful wife, for her unwavering love and encouragement, and for her questions, discussions, and edits.

Stephanie Penniman, MA., for her careful edits.

All the many scholars and teachers who have researched, studied, and written the various resources that were consulted in writing this book.

CONTENTS

DEDICATION
ACKNOWLEDGMENTS
FOREWORD — XI
INTRODUCTION — XIII

PART 1
EDUCATION FROM CREATION THROUGH THE WILDERNESS

IN THE BEGINNING	19
THE PATRIARCHS	23
THREE STORIES	26
MOSES AND THE TORAH	27
THE WRITTEN AND ORAL TORAH	31
THE WILDERNESS	34
THE SHEMA	36
THE POWER OF STORIES	39
WARNING ABOUT LEARNING FROM OTHER CULTURES	40
MOSES THE TEACHER	41
CONCLUDING THOUGHTS	43

PART 2
EDUCATION FROM JOSHUA TO THE CAPTIVITY

JOSHUA	47
SAMUEL	47
DAVID AND THE PSALMS	48
SOLOMON AND WISDOM	51
THE WRONG EXAMPLE OF JEROBOAM	54
GOD'S PURPOSE FOR EDUCATION	55
THE LEVITICAL PRIESTS	59
THE PROPHETS	61
SHEPHERDS OF GOD'S PEOPLE	63
THE RESPONSIBILITY OF PARENTS	64
OPPORTUNITIES FOR CHILDREN TO LEARN	67
CHART: OPPORTUNITIES FOR RELIGIOUS EDUCATION	70

PART 3
EDUCATION FROM THE CAPTIVITY THROUGH THE SECOND TEMPLE PERIOD

THE CAPTIVITY	73
EZRA AND THE GREAT ASSEMBLY	75
THE MASTER-DISCIPLE MODEL	80
THE WRITTEN AND ORAL LAW	82
HILLEL AND THE EARLY FIRST CENTURY CE	84
PHARISEES—EDUCATION VERSUS CULTURE	86
THE SYNAGOGUE	88
SCHOOLS	92
THE BASIC EDUCATIONAL PROGRAM	97
INTEGRATING SECULAR WITH RELIGIOUS KNOWLEDGE	99
APPRENTICESHIPS	100
COMMUNITY TEACHERS	101
STUDYING IN RELATIONSHIP	102
THE VALUE AND IMPACT OF EDUCATION IN THE FIRST CENTURY CE	103

PART 4
EDUCATION IN THE LIFE AND MINISTRY OF JESUS

JESUS'S EARLY YEARS	109
JESUS AS A TEACHER	116
HOW JESUS TAUGHT	120
CONNECTING STUDY AND ACTIONS	123
JESUS AND HIS DISCIPLES	124
JESUS'S COMMAND TO TEACH AND MAKE DISCIPLES	129
A MASTER'S CARE FOR HIS DISCIPLES	131

PART 5
EDUCATION IN THE EARLY CHURCH

THE HOLY SPIRIT	137
CONTINUING IN THE APOSTLES' TEACHING	142
THE PASTOR-TEACHER	145
THE PREPARATION OF TEACHERS	147
THE ILLUSTRATION OF PAUL AND TIMOTHY	151
TO KNOW THE LORD AND WALK IN HIS WAYS	154

Teaching – διδασκη	155
Contrasts in Teaching	158
Continuing the Patterns of Teaching and Learning	159

Part 6
The Educational Text—God's Word

Introduction	163
The Divine Nature of God's Word	163
Our Approach to God's Divine Word	172

Part 7
Some Overarching Educational Themes

The LORD Our God as Father and Teacher	179
Love and Discipline	185
Learning and the Heart	186
Relationships in Teaching and Learning	191
Education as an Exodus	194
The Purpose of Teaching and Learning	196
Christ Our Wisdom	199
Using Stories in Teaching and Learning	201
Lifelong Learning	204
Conclusion	207
Glossary	209
Bibliography	217

About the Author

FOREWORD

A fresh wind is blowing in Christian education. This statement is not about phraseology like the apt renaming of traditional Sunday School as "Christian education" or the more recent use of "spiritual formation" as a descriptor of what Jesus called "making disciples." Instead, the fresh breeze blowing is a holistic approach to both testaments of what Christians embrace as the Bible. This age-old, yet relatively new emphasis, if not discovery, is that from Genesis to Revelation, the Bible is a self-consistent story with instructional value in all of its styles and genres. To that end, *An Introduction to Education in Bible Times* has connected the tendons and ligaments of instructional practice to the skeletal frame of the Judeo-Christian story.

Indeed, the early church Fathers like Justin Martyr and Irenaeus understood the Bible to be a connecting narrative. Reformers like Calvin and Zwingli and theologians from Wesley to Barth saw the Bible as an internally consistent story. Nevertheless, scriptural studies are often walled-off from practical discipleship and the transformative work of the Spirit at a personal and ecclesiastical level. Chris Reeves gives us a gift in this book. He emphasizes the idea that the Bible's books and testaments are not conceptual islands in a scriptural ocean, but what Lyotard called a metanarrative—an overarching story that explains other stories. Chris informs us that this concept of Judaism as background for Christian teaching and learning cannot be fully appreciated until we see things from the beginning, as it was for our elder brothers and fathers in the faith.

The fresh breeze referred to earlier has the effect of blowing the dust off ancient Hebrew traditions and showing how God's means and purpose for education can impact contemporary spiritual formation practices. Chris's gift to us is not small if one considers along with him, that all of the educational practices in the Bible are part and parcel of a coherent narrative that connects them together. The chapters in this book will tell one consistent story—that a good God is intimately involved in the lives of His people and He "desires all people to be saved and come to a knowledge of the truth" (1 Tim. 2:4, ESV). The Truth that Chris leads us to is more than a program. It is a discipleship paradigm grounded in a relationship with God and His Word that leads to doing from a place of being rather than being from a place of doing.

Dr. Mark Glenn

Dr. Mark Glenn is a pastor, educator, and educational advocate. He is the Vice-President of Academics at Shiloh University and received his M.Ed. from Northwest Nazarine University, M.Div. and D.Min. from The King's University, and Ph.D. from Trinity Seminary.

INTRODUCTION

Hear, my son, your father's instruction and do not forsake your mother's teaching; indeed, they are a graceful wreath to your head and ornaments about your neck.

Proverbs 1:8–9

The purpose of this book is to tell the story of education from the dawn of creation through the formation of the early church. The story of biblical education is interwoven into the plan of God for all people; the plan that men and women would come to know Him and walk with Him, keeping His ways in justice and righteousness.

Beginning with the Hebrew Scriptures and continuing through the Second Temple period and into writings of the New Testament, we will examine the purpose for God's educational plan. This study begins with creation and continues through the time of the Patriarchs, Israel's deliverance from Egypt, and the giving of the Torah in the wilderness. It then traces the history of Torah education from Moses to Joshua, from Joshua to the Prophets, from the Prophets to the men of the Great Assembly, and from the men of the Great Assembly to the Jews of the first century CE. In the latter part of the Second Temple period and the first century CE, we will examine the attitudes toward biblical education and the educational opportunities afforded to the Jewish people. Finally, we will turn to the Torah education of Jesus, His own ministry of teaching, and the teaching ministry of the early church.

From childhood and on through adulthood, we are constantly learning. Our learning shapes our thoughts and actions. Vital to our relationship with God as His people is having an educational text to study, teachers devoted to that sacred text, and a commitment to teach successive generations. Through God's educational program we see His intent to have a people who would not be influenced by the cultures surrounding them. Instead, they would be a light to the nations, illustrating the blessing of God on a people who know Him and are faithful to walk in His ways. As such, God's people would demonstrate the great wisdom and creativity that comes from a mind and heart filled with His words. They would be an illustration of the righteousness and justice that comes from loving God and loving one's neighbor.

Biblical education began in the home and community. It started with parents who loved their children and taught through example. This education expanded into a community that studied together during Sabbaths and at other times with teachers who were trained in understanding and applying the sacred texts. Over time, there were schools focused on teaching children and young adults. Colleges were also available for those with the aptitude and means to continue their studies. Additionally, the local synagogues offered continual study opportunities for everyone. For the Jewish communities, the priority of education continued to grow in its importance.

Jesus also grew up in a Jewish home and community that taught the Torah and how the members of the community should walk in its requirements. He would have studied the written text of the Torah, the Prophets, and the Writings. He would have learned the Oral Law, the traditions handed down from generation to generation of dedicated teachers and disciples. Jesus taught as a Jewish teacher, having the words of His Father in His heart and mind. He also taught with God's authority and gave that authority to his disciples to teach and make disciples of the nations.

When we think of biblical education, we might recall the words of Moses in Deuteronomy, "These words, which I am commanding you today, shall be on your heart. You shall teach them diligently to your sons and shall talk of them when you sit in your house and when you walk by the way and when you lie down and when you rise up" (Deut. 6:6-7). While this book will review the commands for teaching and learning, it will also explore the purpose, means, content, and results of education throughout biblical times.

It should be noted that this study can be used as an introduction to the larger conversation regarding the Jewish foundations of early Christianity. The reason for this perspective is that the context for the New Testament is the Jewish-biblical backgrounds seen in the Hebrew Scriptures and also in the Second Temple period writings. The story of biblical education is rooted in God's revelation to the Jewish people and the further revelation that was made available to all peoples through God's Son.

A challenge in writing this book was that much of the information about the means, content, and development of biblical education and the thought behind this topic is spread amongst and within many different sources. In each source are important pieces of the puzzle—time periods, topics, historical data, traditions, theological insights, and scholarly research. Since the content of this study is broad in its scope, covering thousands of years of Jewish and Christian biblical education, a wide variety of sources were drawn upon. Jewish sacred literature, biblical texts, Rabbinical and Christian theological writings, and scholarly studies have helped tell the story of biblical education through history.

Since this study is broad in its scope, the framework used to weave together the various interrelated pieces of the puzzle is the story and chronology of the Bible (the Hebrew Scriptures and the New Testament) and the story and chronology of the intertestamental period. Because of the breadth of the subject being described, and because it is presented chronologically, the author recommends that the chapters in this book be read in sequential order. The ideas presented in each time period draw from and build upon the previous ones. The sequential structure of the book will highlight various themes and practices as they appear in the biblical and historical records.

Some of the timeless themes presented in this study include:

- Education in God's Word is a priority in life.
- Education should be a continual lifestyle.
- Education should begin in the home.
- Education should lead one to the knowledge of God and the ability to walk in His ways.
- Education should prepare one for all of life's endeavors.
- Only learning and walking in His ways can produce a culture with justice and righteousness.
- Biblical education includes both the written and spoken Word.
- Education happens through the interpersonal relationships of parents and children, masters and disciples, teachers and learners.
- The LORD our God, our Heavenly Father, is also our Teacher.

The reader will quickly understand that education in the Bible was more than an intellectual pursuit. Education centered on knowing God, on learning His ways and keeping them. Education in the Bible was not something disconnected from real life; it was integrated with life itself, giving it direction and meaning. It brought God's claims upon His people and gave them His divine wisdom for all of life's relationships and endeavors.

So what is biblical teaching and learning, and why is it so important? Why are children to be taught the Word of God? Why are we to continually study and meditate day and night on what we have learned? Why did Jesus tell those who believe in Him to abide in His words? Is there still a necessity for biblical education? These questions will be addressed throughout the pages of this study, *An Introduction to Education in Bible Times: From Creation through the Early Church*.

Part 1

EDUCATION FROM CREATION THROUGH THE WILDERNESS

It shall come about, if you listen obediently to my commandments which I am commanding you today, to love the LORD your God and to serve Him with all your heart and all your soul ...

Deuteronomy 11:13

In the Beginning

Genesis is a book of beginnings. It tells of the beginning of creation, of man, and of sin entering creation. It tells of the first human race and of the flood that destroyed them, and the new beginning of the human race through Noah's family. These are all recorded in the first eleven chapters of Genesis. The next thirty-nine chapters deal with Abraham and his descendants, the beginning of the nation of Israel.

Instruction is central to God's dealings with His creation. This is implied in various ways in the first three chapters of Genesis. Jewish literature proposes that the Torah, God's word of instruction, was present at the creation of the world.[1] This is based on an interpretation of Proverbs 8:22-31 and the fact that God used His Word to bring creation into its existence (Gen. 1:3, 6, 9, 11, 14, 20, 24). Psalm 33:6 says that by the "word of the LORD" the heavens were made. The New Testament writers also confirm this view by stating that the Word of God was a participant in the creation of the world (John 1:1-3, 10; Heb. 1:1-2; 11:3).

The Torah is seen as both the architect of creation as well as the instruction for how to live in and steward creation.[2] Proverbs 8 says that "The LORD possessed me at the beginning of His way, before His works of old ... Then I was beside Him, as a master workman; and I was daily His delight, rejoicing always before Him, rejoicing in the world, His earth, and having my delight in the sons of men" (Prov. 8:22, 30-31). Again, it is important to emphasize the idea that God's Word was instrumental in creation as well as providing His instruction for how man was to live in His creation.

It was on the sixth day of creation that God made man in His own image and likeness (Gen. 1:26). According to Rashi's commentary on Genesis, "in our likeness" refers to the power to comprehend and discern.[3] Man was created with the ability to comprehend and discern the words of instruction that God would speak to him. Rashi also had this to say about the sixth day of creation.

---
[1] Abraham Cohen, *Everyman's Talmud: The Major Themes of the Rabbinic Sages* (New York: Schocken Books, 1995), 131-132.
[2] "Genesis Rabbah 1, *Sefaria Community Translation*, accessed January 25, 2019, https://www.sefaria.org/Bereishit_Rabbah.1?lang=bi
[3] Rashi (Rabbi Shlomo Yitzchaki) was an outstanding Jewish Biblical commentator of the Middle Ages. His commentary on the book of Genesis can be found at https://www.sefaria.org/. Accessed January 19, 2019.

> "The letter ה, the numerical value of which is 5, is added to the word ששי ["sixth," for the sixth day] when the work of Creation was complete [therefore making the spelling הששי], to imply that He made a stipulation with them that it [creation] endures only upon condition that Israel should accept the five books of the Torah (Shabbat 88a). Another interpretation of יום הששי THE SIXTH DAY [is that] the whole Creation (the Universe) stood in a state of suspense (moral imperfection) until the sixth day—that is, the sixth day of Sivan which was destined to be the day when the Torah would be given to Israel (Avodah Zara 3a)."[4]

The implication is that God's laws, His Torah ("instruction"), is the only basis by which the world can exist in its correct order,[5] and that these laws can be comprehended and discerned by man, who was created in God's own image and likeness.

The second chapter of Genesis expands on the story of the creation of man. It is in this chapter God begins to be referred to as the LORD God. This is a combination of the personal divine name *YHVH* with the more general name of *'elohim*. As Sarna states in his commentary, "The repeated use here [of *YHVH* in chapters two and three of Genesis] may be to establish that the absolutely transcendent God of Creation ('elohim) is the same immanent, personal God (*YHVH*) who shows concern for the needs of human beings."[6] Once God created man, He began to reveal Himself as the personal God who is engaged in a relationship with His creation. In this personal relationship as a Father, He begins to provide His instruction to Adam.

The second chapter of Genesis says, "The LORD God commanded the man, saying, 'From any tree of the garden you may eat freely; but from the tree of the knowledge of good and evil you shall not eat, for in the day that you eat from it you will surely die'" (Gen. 2:16-17). According to Benjamin Blech, the phrase "the LORD God commanded

---

[4]Rashi on Genesis 1:31, Sefaria, accessed January 19, 2019, https://www.sefaria.org/Rashi_on_Genesis.1.31.1?lang=bi&with=Sheets&lang2=bi.
[5]Cohen, *Everyman's Talmud*, 131. In Jewish thought, the Torah "was considered the only secure basis of the entire cosmic order. Without Torah there would be moral chaos, and for that reason, Torah must have existed always, even before the creation of the world."
[6]Nahum M. Sarna, *The JPS Torah Commentary: Genesis* (Philadelphia: Jewish Publication Society, 1989), 17.

the man "מֵאֱלֹ'ר" is more appropriately rendered: "the LORD God commanded the man to say, to mention, or to command."[7] Adam was asked to also teach others by repeating what he had been taught by his LORD God. This command spoken to Adam "refers to the mitzvah of transmitting the law to our children, as the Torah will subsequently teach us ... 'and you shall teach your children.'"[8] In other words, the LORD God, our Heavenly Father, was asking Adam to also be a father and teach his family.

The LORD God's instruction to Adam provides valuable insights. It was the beginning of an instruction manual for living in and managing His creation. Learning His ways and obediently following them were essential. There are two kinds of knowledge upon which man can base his decisions and actions: the objective knowledge of what is good and bad that comes from God, and the subjective knowledge that relies on human reasoning. In the third chapter of Genesis, Eve was tempted by the serpent to disobey God's command by subjectively reasoning that it was desirable to eat of the tree of the knowledge of good and evil.[9]

> *Now the serpent was more crafty than any beast of the field which the LORD God had made. And he said to the woman, "Indeed, has God said, 'You shall not eat from any tree of the garden'?" The woman said to the serpent, "From the fruit of the trees of the garden we may eat; but from the fruit of the tree which is in the middle of the garden, God has said, 'You shall not eat from it or touch it, or you will die.'" The serpent said to the woman, "You surely will not die! For God knows that in the day you eat from it your eyes will be opened, and you will be like God, knowing good and evil." When the woman saw that the tree was good for food, and that it was a delight to the eyes, and that the tree was desirable to make one wise, she took from its fruit and ate; and she gave also to her husband with her, and he ate.*
>
> Genesis 3:1-6

It is interesting to note the emphasis on Eve's distancing herself from her relationship with the LORD God and His command, which

---
[7] Benjamin Blech, *Understanding Judaism: The Basics of Deed and Creed* (Northvale: Jason Aronson, 1992), 191.
[8] Blech, *Understanding Judaism*, 191-192.
[9] Blech, *Understanding Judaism*, 76-77.

was then in conflict with her desire for what seemed good for food, and what was a delight to the eyes, and what was desirable to make one wise (Gen. 3:6). When the serpent approached Eve and asked, "Has God said?" he not only questioned the instruction, but it is the first time in this section that the more personal "LORD God" is only referred to by the general name of "God" (*'elohim*). This shows a distancing of the personal relationship. In the conversation that followed between the serpent and Eve, both parties referred to the intimate Creator by only the general name "God."[10] Perhaps this distancing made it easier for Eve to develop a rationale for disobeying the LORD's command.

Sarna highlights that the serpent proposed the idea to Eve that "the woman and the man will have the capacity to make judgments as to their own welfare independently of God. The insidious nature of its discourse lies in the implication that defiance of God's law constitutes the indispensable precondition for human freedom."[11] Human rationale was elevated above the learning and keeping of God's instruction—His laws to ensure that the world exists in its correct order. Blech adds:

> "Not eating the Tree of Good and Evil would have ensured that morality remain independent from human rationale. So, too, there is only one way to make certain that the commandment 'You shall not murder,' as well as the other categories [of commandments] remain inviolate: by accepting the higher, God given source of the laws governing relations between one human being and another."[12]

So rather than keeping and teaching the LORD God's command(s), Adam and Eve disobeyed Him. The result was their expulsion from the garden (Gen. 3:22-24). Although the LORD provided a way back to a restored relationship, there emerged a society that possessed a very low esteem for human life. The fourth through sixth chapters of Genesis describe the development and accomplishments of the pre-flood society. However, a society, no matter how far advanced, that does not observe

---

[10]Herbert E. Ryle, *The Book of Genesis in the Revised Version with Introduction and Notes*, The Cambridge Bible for Schools and Colleges (Cambridge: Cambridge University Press, 1921), 49.
[11]Sarna, *Genesis*, 25.
[12]Blech, *Understanding Judaism*, 78.

and teach the ways of God has no set moral compass to guide it.[13] Their disobedience eventually led to the moral corruption of the human race and its destruction in the flood (Gen. 6:11-13). But in the midst of man's decline, there were individuals like Enoch and Noah who did seek to walk in the ways of the LORD—God took these men and women to be with Himself and used them to preserve the human race (Gen. 5:21-24; 6:8-22).

The Patriarchs

How would the LORD God raise up a people who would belong to Himself out of all of the peoples of the earth? How would He instill in them His ways so they would be a witness to all other peoples of His righteousness, His lovingkindness, and His testimonies?

The LORD began the creation of His people through Abraham. The LORD appeared to Abraham, calling him out of his family and culture. He gave Abraham a promise that his descendants would be as numerous as the sands of the sea and that they would possess the land of Canaan. Through his offspring all of the families of the earth would be blessed. Abraham believed the LORD that through the miraculous birth of his son Isaac, a people would be raised up to be a witness of the one true God (Gen. 12:1-9; 13:14-18; 15:1-21; 17:1-22).

Regarding Abraham's faith, the Bible says that Abraham believed in the LORD, and it was counted to him as righteousness (Gen. 15:6). His life became an example of a walk with God, and he is called the father of all who believe (Rom. 4:16-22). Abraham was also known as a friend of God (Isa. 41:8; James 2:23), a prophet (Gen. 20:7), and a great teacher (1QapGen 19.23-24).[14]

Everything Abraham learned in his walk with the LORD he was faithful to observe and to teach his children. The LORD said, "For I have chosen [known] him, so that he may command his children and his household after him to keep the way of the LORD by doing righteousness and justice, so that the LORD may bring upon Abraham what He has spoken about him" (Gen. 18:19). There

---

[13]Blech, *Understanding Judaism*, 73-75.
[14]Rhea Reyes, "The Genesis Apocryphon: A More Divine Abraham," in *Prandium: The Journal of Historical Studies* 2, no. 1 (Spring 2013), 39.

are three important points in this statement. First, God called Abraham into a close personal relationship—one of knowing Him.[15] Second, the LORD imparted knowledge of His ways, expressed in relationship with Himself and in relationship with others (in righteousness and justice). The third point is that Abraham would teach the knowledge of God and His ways to his children. In this Abraham would become a mighty nation and all the nations of the earth would be blessed through him (Gen 18:18).

Rashi's commentary on Genesis 18:19 defines the translated phrase "I have chosen [known] him" as "none other than an expression of knowing, for if one loves a person, he draws him near to himself and knows him and is familiar with him. [So God says] Now why do I love him? 'Because he commands' … for he commands his sons concerning Me, to keep My ways."[16] The word for command is in the present tense denoting a continual action of Abraham teaching his household.

Abraham had a personal experiential knowledge of God and faith in Him. An example of Abraham's faith occurred when God asked him to offer up his son Isaac. When God told Abraham to sacrifice Isaac, Isaac did not yet have any descendants. Isaac had a promise over his life that through his descendants all the nations of the earth would be blessed (Gen. 22:18); but God told Abraham to kill Isaac before he had even started to fulfill that promise. Abraham's obedience to God's unthinkable command was with faith, faith that God was able to raise Isaac from the dead in order to fulfill His promise (Heb. 11:17-19). An angel of the LORD stopped Abraham from offering up Isaac and provided instead a ram for the sacrifice. Through this experience, God revealed Himself as *YHWH-jireh*, the LORD Who Will Provide (Gen. 22:11-14). He also taught Abraham and his descendants that they would not be like the other nations around them that sacrificed their children to the gods of this world. Instead they were to love their children and instruct them in the ways of the LORD.

Abraham knew the LORD and walked with Him (Gen. 26:5). Abraham was faithful to instruct his son Isaac in the knowledge of the

---

[15] Sarna, *Genesis*, 31. "'Knowing' in the Bible is not essentially intellectual activity, not simply the objective contemplation of reality. Rather, it is experiential, emotional, and, above all, relational. Thus, in [Gen.] 18:19, when God says of Abraham, 'I have singled him out' or to Israel, in Amos 3:2, 'You alone have I singled out of all the families of the earth,' the true connotation is 'I have entered into a special relationship with you.'"

[16] "Bereishit—Genesis—Chapter 18," in *The Complete Jewish Bible with Rashi Commentary*, accessed on January 19, 2019, https://www.chabad.org/library/bible_cdo/aid/8213/jewish/Chapter-18.htm#showrashi=true&lt=primary.

LORD and to instruct him in keeping the ways of the LORD (Gen. 18:19). This must have been why Isaac had faith to sacrifice his life in obedience to God.[17] Later, after the death of his father, the LORD appeared to Isaac and renewed the covenant that He had made with Abraham (Gen. 26:1-5).

Isaac taught his son Jacob. And the LORD revealed Himself to Jacob confirming the covenant He had given to his fathers, Abraham and Isaac (Gen. 28:12-15; 35:9-12). Jacob, according to Jewish tradition, gave himself to the study of the teaching that he received from his fathers, and to the instructive experiences he received from the LORD.[18] So why was Jacob blessed and not his brother Esau? Isaac most likely instructed both of them as they grew up in his household. As George Robinson conveys, according to the Sages of the Rabbinic period, "Jacob was clearly the son favored by Adonai, the one who studied Torah (although it hadn't been written yet!), the one whose line would become the Israelite people. There are numerous midrashic texts that describe Esau variously as an idolater and killer, one who disdained his birthright and the responsibilities of the covenant."[19] From this we can infer that Jacob paid attention to the instruction of his father and Esau did not.

The *Ethics of the Fathers* 1:2 proposes that "the world stands on three things: Torah, the service of G-d, and deeds of kindness."[20] The lives of the patriarchs exemplified these three attributes. They are expressed in the Law that God would give to His people over four hundred years later through Moses: the love and service to others (Abraham), the love and service to God (Isaac), and the love and building up of one's self by the study of God's words (Jacob).[21] The lives of the Patriarchs would become examples for future generations to study and to learn from.

---

[17]Blech, *Understanding Judaism*, 116.
[18]Blech, *Understanding Judaism*, 108-109.
[19]George Robinson, *Essential Judaism: A Complete Guide to Beliefs, Customs and Rituals* (New York: Atria Books updated edition), 270-271, Kindle.
[20]*Ethics of the Fathers* 1:2.
[21]Blech, *Understanding Judaism*, 108-109.

Three Stories

The stories of the Patriarchs demonstrate the importance of parents instructing their children in order to create and preserve a people who would walk in God's ways. "The Jews have long known that they and their religious heritage would perish from the earth if they neglected to pass its teachings on to their children."[22] The book of Genesis also provides stories that are in contrast to Abraham's walk of faithfulness to learn, to keep, and to teach his children the ways of the LORD. Three such stories are related here.

The first story takes us back to the earliest civilizations. In the days before the flood, mankind grew exceedingly wicked until God destroyed all but Noah and his family. Genesis 6:11 says, "Now the earth was corrupt in the sight of God, and the earth was filled with violence." While they may have acknowledged God, they were not interested in keeping or teaching His ways. There was no service to God, nor was there any service to others. Instead, there was only a prevailing violence and corruption where no one cared about his neighbor.[23]

The second story introduces Lot and his family. Lot, Abraham's nephew, had a good heart but he did not follow in the way of Abraham. Rather than keeping and teaching God's ways, Lot's family became influenced by the culture surrounding them. When the citizens of Sodom wished to have relations with the angels who had come to his house, Lot did everything possible to dissuade them. But after his arguments failed, he offered his daughters in place of the visitors (Gen. 19:8). When it was time to leave Sodom, Lot hesitated to leave. The angels had to forcefully remove Lot and his family from the city before it was destroyed (Gen. 19:15-16). Why did the atmosphere of Sodom influence Lot and his family? According to Jewish Wisdom, "An ignorant person's insufficient piety is not necessarily due to a lack of good intentions. Rather, true piety demands right action, not just right intentions, and that requires study and knowledge." [24] It is inferred that Lot did not give himself to the study of God's commands and did not teach them to his family.

---

[22]Marvin R. Wilson, *Our Father Abraham, Jewish Roots of the Christian Faith* (Grand Rapids: Eerdmans, 1989), 278.
[23]Blech, *Understanding Judaism*, 55.
[24]Joseph Telushkin, *Jewish Wisdom: Ethical, Spiritual, and Historical Lessons from the Great Works and Thinkers* (New York: HarperCollins e-books, 1994), 342-344.

The third story illustrates that "righteousness and justice" (Gen. 18:19) can only be found where God's ways are taught and observed. Even the advances of civilization do not assure this (as evidenced by the Holocaust and other horrors of modern-day societies). During the time of Abraham, Gerar was a dominant and advanced Canaanite city. However, Abraham's encounter with the city of Gerar led him to become fearful and say that his wife, Sarah, was his sister (Gen. 20). God warned Abimelech the king of Gerar in a dream not to touch Sarah. Abimelech confronted Abraham saying, "What have you encountered here in Gerar, that you have done this thing?" Abraham answered him, "Because I thought, surely there is no fear of God in this place, and they will kill me because of my wife" (Gen. 20:10-11). Abraham recognized that a culture, no matter how advanced, that does not observe and teach the ways of God has no set moral compass to guide it.[25] Ethics become situational and people rationalize and excuse their actions. Abraham did not feel safe in this kind of community. (As a point of emphasis, this same storyline is repeated two other times in the accounts of the Patriarchs—in Genesis 12 and in Genesis 26).

All three of these stories illustrate the necessity of biblical education: the learning, keeping, and teaching of God's ways. Only in this can individuals and societies maintain a moral compass that is in-keeping with God's righteousness.

Moses and the Torah

The Israelites went down into the land of Egypt in the days of Jacob because of a famine in Canaan. They remained in Egypt for 430 years (Gen. 46:6–7; Exod. 12:40–41). During those years in Egypt, they were enslaved by the Egyptians and grew to be a numerous people. God saw the affliction of their slavery and delivered His people out of Egypt.

God performed miraculous judgments through Moses and Aaron on the Egyptians and delivered Israel out of their bondage. He brought them out of Egypt and made them a people for His own possession. He revealed Himself to them as the LORD their God, renewing the covenant He had made with their fathers, Abraham, Isaac, and Jacob.[26]

---

[25] Blech, *Understanding Judaism*, 73-75.
[26] J. Barton Payne, "484 הָוָה," ed. R. Laird Harris, Gleason L. Archer Jr., and Bruce K. Waltke, *Theological Wordbook of the Old Testament* (Chicago: Moody Press, 1999), 211-212. Note that wherever the name "LORD" is used, it refers to the underlying name YHWH, I AM—the eternal, self-existent, and ever present one. Note that wherever the name "God" is used, it refers to the underlying name Elohim—God Almighty.

As a loving Father He dwelt in their midst, leading them, caring for them, and disciplining them. God taught them through their experiences and through Moses, giving them His commandments, His good statutes, and true laws.

God taught Israel through powerful experiences as He led them out of Egypt, through the Red Sea, and into the wilderness. Through all their experiences, the LORD was teaching them and disciplining them just as a father disciplines his son (Deut. 1:31, 8:5). He led them by a pillar of cloud by day and a pillar of fire by night. They saw His glory descend on Mount Sinai as He gave them His commandments. They witnessed His judgments on those who rebelled against His servant Moses. The Israelites were always to remember the experiences of God dwelling with them, leading and providing for them. They were to remember how He humbled them and let them be hungry and fed them with manna to help them understand that man does not live by bread alone, but man lives by everything that proceeds out of the mouth of the LORD (Deut. 8:2–5).

After Israel's initial experiences with the LORD, He taught them through giving them His words. Nehemiah described these events saying, "Then You came down on Mount Sinai, and spoke with them from heaven; You gave them just ordinances and true laws, good statutes and commandments. So You made known to them Your holy Sabbath, and laid down for them commandments, statutes and law, through Your servant Moses" (Neh. 9:13-14).

Moses is considered to be the father of Jewish learning.[27] Moses was faithful to teach the people all the commandments, statutes, and laws that he received from the LORD. He was faithful to record their sacred history, the revelation of the LORD to them, examples to learn from, their promises and covenant, and the Mitzvot by which they would live. He wrote these in the Torah to be studied and passed on from generation to generation. Every person was to study the Torah, and every family was to teach their children. They were to love the LORD, always remembering His lovingkindness toward them and remembering His ways to walk in them.

The Torah was the foundation for education in Israel. Deuteronomy 6:6-7 says, "These words, which I am commanding you today, shall be

---

[27]Israel M. Goldman, *Life-Long Learning Among the Jews: Adult Education in Judaism from Biblical Times to the Twentieth Century* (New York: Ktav Publishing House, 1975), 1-2.

on your heart. You shall teach them diligently to your sons and shall talk of them when you sit in your house and when you walk by the way and when you lie down and when you rise up." God's words were to be studied daily during fixed periods of time. Adults were required to study Torah in order to teach it to their children.[28] Every occasion was to be considered an opportunity to teach and learn. What would be the result of the children of Israel loving God and keeping His ways? They would become a mighty people by whom all of the nations would be blessed. God would dwell in their midst and walk among them. They would be His treasured possession, a kingdom of priests, and He would set them high above all the other nations (Exod. 19:4-6; Lev. 26:3-13; Deut. 26:16–19).

God's commandments, statutes, and laws were to be their wisdom and understanding for everything they encountered in life. And when the peoples of the earth heard of them, they would say, "Surely this great nation is a wise and understanding people." Moses expressed this thought by saying, "For what great nation is there that has a god so near to it as is the LORD our God whenever we call on Him? Or what great nation is there that has statutes and judgments as righteous as this whole law …?" (Deut. 4:5-8). The Torah represented God's faith and hope in His people, that "He entrusted them with the creation of a society that would become a home for His presence and an example to the world."[29]

In every generation, all the people of Israel were to understand that their well-being was dependent on their relationship with God—loving Him and keeping His Word. If they listened to His instruction and walked in it, He would give them rains in their season, so that the land would be fruitful. They would have plenty to eat and live securely in the land. They would prevail over their enemies and have peace. God would make them fruitful and multiply them and confirm His covenant with them (Lev. 26:3–13; Deut. 6:1–3).

Therefore, universal education with all the people learning and keeping God's statutes and commandments was essential for Israel's well-being. So Moses conveyed God's instruction to the children of Israel and wrote it down in a book (Deut. 31:24-26). The Levitical priests were to continue to teach the people, and the families were to teach their children. In every seventh year the Law was to be read to all the men, women, and little ones (Deut.

---

[28]Goldman, *Lifelong Learning Among the Jews*, 1.
[29]Jonathan Sacks, *Essays on Ethics: A Weekly Reading of the Jewish Bible* (New Milford: Maggid Books, 2016), 216.

31:9-12). The well-being and success of the nation of Israel depended on their faithfulness to God and His Word—to learn it, teach it, and to observe it.

The Jewish historian Josephus noted, "For ignorance he [Moses] left no pretext. He appointed the Law to be the most excellent and necessary form of instruction, ordaining, not that it should be heard once for all or twice or on several occasions, but that every week men should desert their other occupations and assemble to listen to the Law and to obtain a thorough and accurate knowledge of it, a practice which all other legislators seem to have neglected."[30]

Israel was the first society that valued universal education.[31] Learning the words of God was the right of the entire people. It belonged to them. It was their inheritance. Deuteronomy 33:4 says, "Moses charged us with a law, a possession [an inheritance] for the assembly of Jacob." The Law was the possession of every Israelite. It was not just the possession of a priestly class as in the other nations of antiquity where the knowledge of God was kept from the masses. Everyone, young and old, was to be instructed about God and His ways. They were all to be educated in their rights and duties as well as those of their leaders and the priesthood.[32] Israel Goldman explains, "Jewish life is, therefore, unique from the very dawn of its history in [that] the revelations of God, as contained in the sacred Scriptures, were made the possession of the whole people, whose duty it was, for the sake of their own well-being and for the sake of the welfare of the nation, to study it the whole of their lives."[33]

The following passage from *Ethics of the Fathers* conveys the blessings of studying and keeping the Torah that God gave to His people through His servant Moses:

> "Great is Torah, for it gives life to its observers in this world, and in the World To Come. As is stated (Proverbs 4:22): 'For they are life to he who finds them, and a healing to all his flesh.' And it says (ibid. 3:8): 'It shall be health to your navel, and marrow to your bones.' And it says (3:18): 'She is a tree of life for those who hold fast to her, and happy are those who support her.' And it says (1:9): 'For they shall be

---

[30] Josephus, *The Life, Against Apion*, ed. T.E. Page et al., trans. H.J. Thackeray, vol. I, The Loeb Classical Library (London; Cambridge, MA: William Heinemann Ltd; Harvard University Press, 1966), 363.
[31] Thomas Cahill, *The Gifts of the Jews: How a tribe of desert nomads changed the way everyone thinks and feels* (New York: Anchor Books, 1999), 144.
[32] Jeffrey H. Tigay, *The JPS Torah Commentary: Deuteronomy*, (Philadelphia: Jewish Publication Society, 1989), 498.
[33] Goldman, *Lifelong Learning Among the Jews*, 7.

a garland of grace for your head, and necklaces about your neck.' And it says (4:9): 'She shall give to your head a garland of grace, a crown of glory she shall grant you.' And it says (9:11): 'With me, your days shall be increased, and years of life shall be added to you.' And it says (3:16): 'Long days in her right hand; in her left, wealth and honor.' And it says (3:2): 'For long days, years of life and peace, they shall add to you.'"[34]

The Written and Oral Torah

The Written Torah was given by the LORD to Moses for His people. It contains the revelation of the LORD, the God of Israel. In it are the narrative stories that reveal the greatness of the LORD who dwelt in their midst. The Torah conveys the Jewish history and beginnings as God's holy people and provides examples (both positive and negative) for sound instruction. The Torah recorded the commandments God gave for how to live as a community in His presence. These commandments have been summarized as loving and serving God and loving and serving one's neighbor. Education in the Torah was to come to know the LORD, the God of Israel, and to learn the Jewish history and future in relationship with Him; it was to learn His ways through examples and commandments in order to keep them and to diligently teach them to future generations.

Moses most likely wrote sections of the Torah throughout the time in the wilderness, including the Decalogue, the various historical events, and the Book of the Covenant with the people's pledges to obey it (Exod. 24:3-4, 31:18, 32:15-16, 34:27-29; Deut. 31:9). Then Moses completed the writing of the Torah and gave it to Israel before his death.[35] The Torah became the primary textbook that Israel would study for generations to come. However, since it was difficult to reproduce multiple copies of the written text by hand, the teachings were primarily passed on for many years through oral repetition and memorization.[36]

---

[34] *Ethics of the Fathers* 6:7.
[35] Tigay, *Deuteronomy*, 500. Note that there has been considerable scholarly debate concerning Moses's authorship of the Pentateuch. However, the Scriptures themselves attest to Moses's authorship, including Jesus's own testimony in Mk. 12:26, Lk. 24:44, and John 7:19. Note that the written Torah is referred to as the Pentateuch and includes the first five books of the Hebrew Scriptures; Genesis, Exodus, Leviticus, Number, and Deuteronomy.
[36] Tigay, *Deuteronomy*, 501.

The word tôrâ basically means "teaching" whether it is the wise man instructing his pupil, a father instructing his son, or God instructing Israel.[37] God gave the Torah directly through Moses as instruction for His people. And while the written textbook provided the written history and laws to study, additional explanation was still required. Thus, throughout their time in the wilderness, Moses and Aaron taught the people how the Torah should be applied in various circumstances. According to Jewish tradition, it was from this teaching that the Oral Law originated. Robinson adds:

> "The Men of the Great Assembly believed that there had been oral interpretation of Torah almost from the moment Moses came down from Mount Sinai with the tablets in his hands. After all, was it not said that God had given the Oral Law to Moses on Sinai as well as the Torah, the Written Law? That the Almighty had whispered it into his ear by day, explained its meaning by night for forty days and nights?"[38]

The Oral Law was given to assist in the application of the Written Torah through varied and changing circumstances. According to Jewish tradition, it was given to show how to apply God's commands. Like the Written Torah, the Oral Law was passed on from generation to generation. It became part of the educational process of imparted knowledge from one person to another.

The same God who gave the commandments and the consequences for violating them revealed Himself as "The LORD, the LORD [YHWH] God [Elohim], compassionate and gracious, slow to anger, and abounding in lovingkindness and truth; who keeps lovingkindness for thousands, who forgives iniquity, transgression and sin; yet He will by no means leave the guilty unpunished, visiting the iniquity of fathers on the children and on the grandchildren to the third and fourth generations" (Exod. 34:6-7). Blech adds that the Jewish sages explained the difference between LORD [YHWH] and God [Elohim] as …

---

[37]John E. Hartley, "910 הרי," ed. R. Laird Harris, Gleason L. Archer Jr., and Bruce K. Waltke, *Theological Wordbook of the Old Testament* (Chicago: Moody Press, 1999), 404.
[38]Robinson, *Essential Judaism*, 313.

"... conveying the two-fold aspects of His personality as we perceive them. When the Lord appears to us as loving, kind, good, and gracious, He is Adoni the Merciful One. When we perceive Him as being strict, harsh, and unyielding, He is Elohim, the God of Law. Of course, God in essence is one and the same, always gracious and kind, loving and compassionate. It is only our perception that changes. The biblical verse "Hear O Israel" (Deut. 6:4) teaches us this truth. The "Lord" of mercy and the God of law are one ... Both aspects exist and define His essence. They gain expression in the two parts of the Torah, the Written and Oral."[39]

From this, one could infer that God counterbalances the strictness of law with compassion and love. The Written Law is the voice of strength and severity—it speaks in the language of what should be. The Oral Law tells how the Lord embraces His people in love and mercy, how He assists them in fulfilling His commands, and how He shows mercy to them after they have sinned by disobeying His commandments.

The Wilderness

God delivered Israel out of captivity and immediately brought them into the wilderness. Without the distractions of other cultural influences, the wilderness was a time of forming a new relationship with Him. God recalls the wilderness experience in this way, "I remember concerning you the devotion of your youth, the love of your betrothals, your following after Me in the wilderness, through a land not sown" (Jer. 2:2). The Song of Solomon says, "Who is this coming up from the wilderness leaning on her beloved?" (Song of Sol. 8:5).

The wilderness was an experience of God loving and forming an intimate relationship with His people. It took God's everlasting love to transform those who were once slaves into a people who would choose to love and walk faithfully with Him. Later in history, prophesying a time of restored relationship with Israel, the LORD said, "I will allure her, bring her into the wilderness and speak kindly to her. ... And she

---

[39] Blech, *Understanding Judaism*, 95.

will sing there as in the days of her youth, as in the day when she came up from the land of Egypt" (Hosea 2:14–15).

The wilderness was a place that was free from other distractions or obligations. Here God provided for the Israelites shade in the heat of the day, a pillar of fire for light and warmth at night, water that was always with them, and manna for food. They were also separated from other cultures of the day that worshiped images in the form of men, women, animals, the sun, other objects. Many of the gods that these idols represented were related to nature—to the seasons and the fruitfulness of crops and herds. It was in the desolate environment of the wilderness, that the LORD God revealed Himself beyond nature, not as a god to be seen, but as the LORD to be heard. He revealed Himself to His people, speaking to them, giving them His Word. Sacks explains, "In the silence of the desert, Israel became the people for whom the primary religious experience was not seeing but listening and hearing: Shema Yisrael. The God of Israel revealed Himself in speech." [40] He revealed Himself to Israel through His Word.[41]

While the initial relationship between God and Israel was tumultuous at times, God's covenant with Israel was a covenant of love. It was in the wilderness that God made a covenant with them and gave them the Torah. He even provided for their basic needs so they could focus their time on the study of His Word. As a result, Sacks continues, "The desert thus became the birthplace of a wholly new relationship between God and humankind, a relationship built on covenant, speech, and love as concretized in the Torah."[42] The wisdom of the Jewish fathers highlights, "Beloved are Israel, for they were given a precious article; it is a sign of even greater love that it has been made known to them that they were given a precious article, as it is stated: 'I have given you a good purchase; My Torah, do not forsake it' (Proverbs 4:2)."[43]

According to Jewish tradition, the wilderness was also an opportunity for Israel to study. Louis Ginzberg tells us:

> "[Aaron] would go from house to house, and wherever he found one who did not know how to recite the Shema, he taught him

---
[40]Sacks, *Essays on Ethics*, 218.
[41]See *Chapter Six – The Divine Nature of God's Word*.
[42]Sacks, *Essays on Ethics*, 219.
[43]*Ethics of the Fathers* 3:14.

the Shema; if one did not know how to pray, he taught him to pray; and if he found one who was not capable of penetrating the study of the Torah, he initiated him into it."[44]

Goldman adds:

> "As a result of these efforts by Moses and Aaron, the Children devoted themselves to the study of Torah even while in the desert, for the journey in the wilderness was intended as an exercise in discipline and as an encouragement for Torah study. Similarly, since the Israelites were relieved of the necessity of providing for their daily wants by being given the daily manna, they were able to devote all their efforts to acquiring knowledge of the Torah."[45]

At the end of the time of Moses and Aaron teaching the children of Israel in the wilderness, these words were spoken as Israel camped on the east side of the Jordan river:

> *"For this commandment which I command you today is not too difficult for you, nor is it out of reach. It is not in heaven, that you should say, 'Who will go up to heaven for us to get it for us and make us hear it, that we may observe it?' Nor is it beyond the sea, that you should say, 'Who will cross the sea for us to get it for us and make us hear it, that we may observe it?' But the word is very near you, in your mouth and in your heart, that you may observe it."*
>
> Deut. 30:11-14

The wilderness was used as a time to learn the commands of the LORD. Teaching and learning at that time was done primarily by oral teaching, by hearing and repeating, which remained the primary means of instruction in Israel even after the spread of literacy.[46] For forty years in the wilderness Moses taught a new generation. Therefore, it was said to that generation as they prepared to enter Canaan, "But the word is very near you, in your mouth and in your heart, that you may observe it" (Deut. 30:14). Jeffrey Tigay makes the observation:

---
[44]Louis Ginzberg, *Legends of the Jews* (Global Grey, 2017), 769.
[45]Goldman, *Lifelong Learning Among the Jews*, 8.
[46]Tigay, *Deuteronomy*, 78.

> "This manner of speaking reflects a predominantly oral culture in which learning and review are accomplished primarily by oral recitation [repetition]. Compare Joshua 1:8, "Let not this Book of the Teaching cease from your mouth, but recite it day and night, so that you may observe faithfully all that is written in it." Since Moses taught the Instruction to the people by heart, that (and not writing the copy that he gave to the priests and elders) constituted its publication."[47]

This implies that in the wilderness, the people not only received the Torah, but they learned it through repetition so that its commandments were in their hearts and in their mouths to remember, teach, and to keep.

The Shema

Jewish tradition has emphasized the importance of the Shema prayer. This tradition suggests that the Shema was one of the main prayers given by Moses to the people.[48] It was to be rehearsed every morning and every evening. In later Jewish tradition it was also to be the last words that a person would utter before he or she died. It affirmed for all that the LORD was their God and they would love Him with all their being.

The Shema was instructive. Since it was repeated upon waking in the morning and before retiring in the evening, the prayer was committed to memory. The Shema contained the nucleus of Israel's relationship with the LORD their God. The repetition allowed an individual to consider the depth of its personal and national meaning and its intimate relationship to life as one of God's called out people.

The Shema is made up of three passages from the Torah: Deuteronomy 6:4–9, Deuteronomy 11:13–21, and Numbers 15:37–41. The first passage includes the primary declaration of the Jewish faith—the LORD is our God, the LORD is one. The Shema continues with the ways in which that faith should be lived: to love God with all your being, teach it to your children, recite it when you awake and lie down to sleep, and bind it as a symbol on your body.

---

[47]Tigay, *Deuteronomy*, 285–287.
[48]Joseph Telushkin, *Jewish Literacy: The Most Important Things to Know About the Jewish Religion, Its People, and Its History* (New York: HarperCollins, 2008), 746-747.

The second passage specifies what would happen if they kept God's Word. Then to help ensure that these commands were remembered, the third passage provides for a daily reminder to help the people make daily choices to follow in God's commands.

It is significant that the prayer begins with "Hear (Shema), O Israel! The LORD is our God, the LORD is one!" It begins by declaring that the LORD is their personal and national God, and that the God of law and the Lord of mercy are One.[49] It was a consistent reminder and an opportunity for teaching and learning. What does it mean that the LORD is our God? Who is the LORD? And why love Him with all your heart and with all your soul and with all your might?

Long before the covenant between the LORD and His people was beautifully summarized in the Shema, the LORD had been introducing Himself to Israel. It began with knowing Him as the God of their fathers, Abraham, Isaac, and Jacob. He had been known as God Almighty and the LORD who Provides. He then introduced Himself as YHWH, "I AM," their ever-present God who cares for them. He was not a God of the past, nor One who was distant from them. He became their Deliverer, their Sustainer, their Healer, and Teacher. He was their God, living with them for all generations. He revealed Himself as "the LORD God, compassionate and gracious, slow to anger, and abounding in lovingkindness and faithfulness; who keeps lovingkindness for thousands [of generations], who forgives iniquity, transgression and sin; yet He will by no means leave the guilty unpunished" (Exod. 34:6–7).

The LORD entered the covenant relationship with His people because of His lovingkindness (*hesed*).[50] The Psalmist often speaks about the lovingkindness of the LORD. "Give thanks to the LORD, for He is good; for His lovingkindness is everlasting" (Ps. 118:1). God showed His everlasting love to Israel; their response was to love Him in return. This is similar to the writing of John the Beloved, "We love, because He first loved us" (1 John 4:19). Could this be why the Shema emphasizes that the LORD (who loves us and is ever with us) is our God and that we are to love Him?

This is the text of the Shema prayer:

---

[49]Blech, *Understanding Judaism*, 95.
[50]R. Laird Harris, "698 חסד," ed. R. Laird Harris, Gleason L. Archer Jr., and Bruce K. Waltke, *Theological Wordbook of the Old Testament* (Chicago: Moody Press, 1999), 306.

"Hear, O Israel! The LORD is our God, the LORD is one! You shall love the LORD your God with all your heart and with all your soul and with all your might. These words, which I am commanding you today, shall be on your heart. You shall teach them diligently to your sons and shall talk of them when you sit in your house and when you walk by the way and when you lie down and when you rise up. You shall bind them as a sign on your hand and they shall be as frontals on your forehead. You shall write them on the doorposts of your house and on your gates."

Deuteronomy 6:4–9

"It shall come about, if you listen obediently to my commandments which I am commanding you today, to love the LORD your God and to serve Him with all your heart and all your soul, that He will give the rain for your land in its season, the early and late rain, that you may gather in your grain and your new wine and your oil. He will give grass in your fields for your cattle, and you will eat and be satisfied. Beware that your hearts are not deceived, and that you do not turn away and serve other gods and worship them. Or the anger of the LORD will be kindled against you, and He will shut up the heavens so that there will be no rain and the ground will not yield its fruit; and you will perish quickly from the good land which the LORD is giving you. You shall therefore impress these words of mine on your heart and on your soul; and you shall bind them as a sign on your hand, and they shall be as frontals on your forehead. You shall teach them to your sons, talking of them when you sit in your house and when you walk along the road and when you lie down and when you rise up. You shall write them on the doorposts of your house and on your gates, so that your days and the days of your sons may be multiplied on the land which the LORD swore to your fathers to give them, as long as the heavens remain above the earth."

Deuteronomy 11:13–21

The LORD also spoke to Moses, saying, "Speak to the sons of Israel, and tell them that they shall make for themselves tassels on the corners of their garments throughout their generations, and that they shall put on the tassel of each corner a cord of blue. It shall be a tassel for you to look at and remember all the commandments of the LORD, so as to do them and not follow after your own heart and your own eyes, after which you played the harlot, so that you may remember to do all My commandments and be holy to your God. I am the LORD your God who brought you out from the land of Egypt to be your God; I am the LORD your God."

Numbers 15:37–41

The Power of Stories

Moses recorded in the Torah stories of Israel's history as well as the commandments to be remembered and observed. The stories were to be passed on to each succeeding generation. From these stories each generation would learn about the beginnings of their people as God's heritage. They would learn from examples, both good and bad. Throughout the centuries, Jewish teachers have brought dramatic lessons from the rich stories recorded in the Torah.

The stories in the Torah have a unique way of conveying God's relationship with His creation and with mankind. They bring to life God's special relationship with the Patriarchs and with Joseph in Egypt, revealing how He preserved the children of Israel. The stories recounted to succeeding generations God's relationship with Israel in delivering them from Egypt and caring for them in the wilderness. Israel was commanded to retell the story of Passover and to relive the experience of dwelling with the LORD in booths in the wilderness. These stories captivated the imagination of the young. They brought to life the history and context of being God's holy people. The stories inspired faith in young and old to find their personal and national relationships in knowing the LORD their God.

Warning About Learning from Other Cultures

Learning can be defined as a process that leads to change. Learning involves change in knowledge, beliefs, attitudes, or behaviors. This change unfolds over time and has a lasting impact on how learners think and act.⁵¹ This puts great importance on what is taught and what is learned. For Israel, they were to be diligent in learning and teaching God's instruction. The Torah reminds us, "Then Moses summoned all Israel and said to them: 'Hear [listen with attention and obedience], O Israel, the statutes and the ordinances which I am speaking today in your hearing, that you may [diligently] learn [and instruct] them and observe them carefully'" (Deut. 5:1). To learn the Written and Oral Torah was to elevate the people's knowledge, beliefs, attitudes, and behaviors, enabling them to walk in God's ways. They would in turn be a light and an example to other nations.

Furthermore, Robinson reflects:

> "At the heart of Jewish law are two passages from Torah; the first, a phrase from Genesis 1:27 that states that God created male and female *"b'tselem Elohim/in the image of God;"* the second, from Leviticus 19, in which God says to the people of Israel, "'You shall be holy for I, Adonai your God, am holy." If one is made in the image of the Almighty, it follows that one should behave in the manner of the Holy One."⁵²

Thomas McComiskey adds, "God is intrinsically holy and he calls his people to be holy, providing for them the standard of obedience whereby that holiness may be maintained."⁵³ By studying and keeping God's instruction Israel would learn to not be like the other nations that had profaned themselves, but they would be His holy people (Deut. 10:12-13).

Israel was to diligently follow the teaching God had given to Moses and they were not to learn the attitudes and practices of the Canaanite peoples or the surrounding cultures. "Be sure to observe what I am commanding you this day. ... Watch yourself that you make no covenant with the inhabitants of the land into which you are going, or it will become a snare in your midst" (Exod. 34:11-16). In Deuteronomy Moses continues, "When you enter the land which the LORD your God gives you, you shall not learn to imitate the detestable things of those nations"

---

⁵¹Susan A. Ambrose, *How Learning Works: Seven Research-Based Principles for Smart Teaching* (Wiley. Kindle Edition), 3.
⁵²Robinson, *Essential Judaism*, 195.
⁵³Thomas E. McComiskey, "1990 שׁקד," ed. R. Laird Harris, Gleason L. Archer Jr., and Bruce K. Waltke, *Theological Wordbook of the Old Testament* (Chicago: Moody Press, 1999), 788.

(Deut. 18:9). Rather, Israel was to destroy those nations so that they would not influence Israel and lead them into idolatry, sinning against the LORD (Deut. 20:17-18). Sadly, according to biblical history, they did not destroy those nations, but mingled with them and learned their practices (Ps. 106:34-36).

Later in Israel's history the LORD highlights again this issue of learning from other cultures. The LORD spoke through the prophet Jeremiah for Israel to not learn the way of the nations, and to "not be terrified by the signs of the heavens although the nations are terrified by them; for the customs of the peoples are delusion" (Jer. 10:2-3). Rather than Israel being influenced by other nations, God's unchanging goal was that other nations would learn His ways from Israel.

> *Thus says the LORD concerning all My wicked neighbors [surrounding nations] who strike at the inheritance with which I have endowed My people Israel, "Behold I am about to uproot them from their land and will uproot the house of Judah from among them. And it will come about that after I have uprooted them, I will again have compassion on them; and I will bring them back, each one to his inheritance and each one to his land. Then if they [the surrounding nations] will really **learn the ways of My people** ... even as they taught My people to swear by Baal, they will be built up in the midst of My people"* (emphasis added).
>
> Jeremiah 12:14-16

Moses the Teacher

Moses's role as a teacher is an important designation to highlight. Moses assumed the role of teacher at Sinai as he emphasized, "So He declared to you His covenant which He commanded you to perform, that is, the Ten Commandments; and He wrote them on two tablets of stone. The LORD commanded me at that time to teach you statutes and judgments, that you might perform them in the land where you are going over to possess it" (Deut. 4:13-14). Throughout his forty years of leading Israel, Moses was faithful to God's command to teach the people His statutes and judgments, to teach them the Torah as he had received it from the LORD.

At the end of the forty years in the wilderness, Moses told the generation that was preparing to possess the land that God had promised Israel, "See, I have taught [from the verb lâmad meaning to diligently teach, instruct, impart] you statutes and judgments just as the LORD my God commanded me, that you should do thus in the land where you are entering to possess it" (Deut. 4:5). Tigay explains:

> "The verb 'instruct' (often rendered 'impart,' as in v. 5) illustrates Moses's role as teacher of the laws. This is the role for which he is best remembered in Jewish tradition, the role encapsulated in his epithet Moshe Rabbeinu, 'Moses our teacher.' According to Deuteronomy, this role was assigned to him at Mount Sinai (see v. 14 and 5:28). The earlier books do not use 'instruct' in describing Moses's role; it is characteristic of Deuteronomy's focus on wisdom and intellect."[54]

As a good teacher, Moses taught both the understanding of God's statutes and judgments as well as the practice of them.[55] His goal as a teacher was to equip Israel to know the ways of the LORD, to keep them, and to teach them to future generations—to ensure the continued presence of God with them so that He would bring upon them all the promises spoken to them and their fathers. Through education, Moses transformed those who were former slaves into a nation whose people possessed the knowledge and ability to choose. Robinson states, "In the course of [Moses's] address, his farewell, he reminds [the children of Israel] of the foundations of their faith, their covenant with Adonai, the Ten Commandments, and other fundamentals of Judaism such as the Sh'ma. He tells them that they have a choice between blessing and curse, life and death, and that they should choose Adonai and live."[56]

---

[54] Tigay, *Deuteronomy*, 42–43.
[55] Nathan Drazin, *History of Jewish Education from 515 B.C.E. to 220 C.E. (During the Periods of the Second Commonwealth and the Tannaim)* (Baltimore: The Johns Hopkins Press, 1940), 11-12.
[56] Robinson, *Essential Judaism*, 275.

Concluding Thoughts

From the beginning, the LORD'S intention was to draw His creation into a relationship with Himself and with His Word. According to tradition the Torah, the Word of His instruction, is integrated into the very fabric of all creation. It is God's Word that possesses life, wisdom, and blessing for all who choose to love the LORD and cleave to His Word. And as a loving, ever-present Father, the LORD continues to woo His people, all people, back to a life that is in harmony with His ways. He is continually teaching His people that outside of His ways is darkness and slavery to corruption, but in the knowledge of God there is light and life. So in His love, the LORD gave His Word, written and oral; He gave teachers and He commanded parents to be like Himself— to love and teach their children. The Written and Oral Torah became God's primary curriculum for teaching and learning.

Part 2

EDUCATION FROM JOSHUA TO THE CAPTIVITY

Hear, my son, your father's instruction and do not forsake your mother's teaching; indeed, they are a graceful wreath to your head and ornaments about your neck.

Proverbs 1:8–9

Joshua

When Joshua was to lead Israel into the land of Canaan to possess it, the LORD gave him this commission, "This book of the law shall not depart from your mouth, but you shall meditate on it day and night, so that you may be careful to do according to all that is written in it; for then you will make your way prosperous, and then you will have success" (Josh. 1:8). The LORD would give Joshua good success in all that he did, not because of his leadership ability or military strategy, but because he carefully followed the Word of the LORD.

The thirty-one nations that Joshua conquered (Josh. 12:24) did not make him fearful, as they had made the children of Israel fearful forty years before. Instead, Joshua set his heart to study and believe the words that God had spoken. His continual meditation upon the book of the law, the Torah, made him successful.

During the conquest of Canaan, Joshua kept the command of God by engraving the law on the sides of a mountain. Then he read all the words of the law, the blessing and the curse, according to all that is written in the book of the law before all the assembly of Israel with the women and the little ones and the strangers who were living among them (Josh. 8:30–35). Joshua further exhorted Israel to be faithful to love the LORD and keep His commandments, according to the covenant they had made with the LORD. He passed on the book of the law, the Torah, to the next generation, with the responsibility to study it and to teach it, and to pass it on to future generations. Psalm 78 says that God "commanded our fathers that they should teach them [God's instruction] to their children, that the generation to come might know, even the children yet to be born, that they may arise and tell them to their children" (Ps. 78:5-6). This thought is also captured in the Ethics of the Fathers: "Moses received the Torah from Sinai and gave it over to Joshua. Joshua gave it over to the Elders, the Elders to the Prophets."[57]

Samuel

During the period of Judges the children of Israel turned their hearts from the teaching of the LORD. Every person did what was right in his own eyes (Judg. 13:1; 21:25). So the LORD let them be oppressed by foreign powers. And when they returned their hearts to seek Him, He

---
[57] *Ethics of the Fathers* 1.1.

raised up judges to deliver them. Near the end of this period, the young prophet Samuel was raised serving in the tabernacle at Shiloh (1 Sam. 2:18-21, 26; 3:1-21). As he grew he learned the ways of the priesthood and must have studied the Torah, for a copy of the Law was kept with the priests at the tabernacle (Deut. 31:26). The LORD appeared to Samuel through His Word and established Samuel as a prophet, a priest, and a judge in Israel.

The Scriptures compare the impact of Samuel's ministry on Israel with that of Moses (Ps. 99:5-7; Jer. 15:1). The LORD appeared to Israel again by His Word through Samuel. Samuel was faithful to teach Torah to the people, and his intercession for them impacted the course of events in Israel (1 Sam. 12:23). The result was a spiritual resurgence under his ministry. This spiritual resurgence likely impacted the education of children by their parents, the teaching of the people by the priesthood, and the LORD's leadership of the nation through Samuel.

David and the Psalms

David grew up in Israel in the territory of Judah while Israel was being influenced by the ministry of Samuel. It was during this time of Samuel's influence that David was instructed in the Law of the LORD. David learned of the mighty acts of God that He had performed throughout the history of Israel. He learned about men and women who walked faithfully before the LORD and recognized the outcome of their lives; he learned about the outcome of the wicked and foolish. He studied God's covenant with His people and the requirements for living as a community in His presence. He also observed and experienced God's response to people as they obeyed and trusted in Him or as they forsook Him. The content of David's Psalms suggests that throughout his life David continued to devote himself to learning and meditating on God's Word.

David's actions expressed his Torah education—his lifelong learning. David knew that the LORD was his God. He sought to love the LORD with his whole being. It inspired him to confront Goliath, to honor Saul as God's anointed king, and to give attention to the words of the priests and prophets. Then as king of Israel David encouraged the adherence to God's Law, promoted the national worship and service to God, and continued in the process of conquering the unpossessed land of Canaan that God had promised to Israel. The impact of his devotion to Torah education can be seen in the Psalms and in the creativity expressed in his music and worship.

David wrote many psalms about his love for the LORD and his desire to learn and keep His commandments. Thus, he exemplifies the personal impact of Jewish education. Goldman reinforces this point in his statement about David:

"Throughout the biblical period, Judaism and its great teachers sought to educate the whole people during the whole of their lives in the principles and practices of Jewish life. That the people responded to these educational endeavors is evidenced by the popular literature of the times. The poetry of the psalmist expresses, no doubt, the attitudes and feelings of many of his contemporaries."[58]

A few verses from the First Psalm convey this sentiment.

How blessed is the man ...
   [whose] delight is in the law of the LORD,
      And in His law he meditates day and night.
   He will be like a tree firmly planted by streams of water,
      Which yields its fruit in its season
      And its leaf does not wither;
      And in whatever he does, he prospers.

Psalm 1:1–3

David was a man who went through many experiences as a prophet, warrior, general, fugitive, and king. What brought David through these experiences with the blessing of the LORD upon him? In Psalm 16:8, David said, "I have set the LORD continually before me." David was taught about the LORD. Even in the days of his youth, he continually placed the LORD and His instruction in the forefront of his life (Ps. 71:5, 17). As the king of Israel, David would have possessed a Torah scroll

---

[58]Israel M. Goldman, *Life-Long Learning Among the Jews: Adult Education in Judaism from Biblical Times to the Twentieth Century* (New York: Ktav Publishing House, 1975), 4-5.

for continual study (Deut. 17:18-20). David knew that his love for the LORD and adherence to His words brought God's blessing upon his life.

Based on the Psalms that he composed, it is evident that David had a high regard for his Torah education. The following five verses in Psalm 19 highlight David's attitude toward the learning and keeping of God's words.

> *The law of the LORD is perfect, restoring the soul;*
> *The testimony of the LORD is sure, making wise the simple.*
> *The precepts of the LORD are right, rejoicing the heart;*
> *The commandment of the LORD is pure, enlightening the eyes.*
> *The fear of the LORD is clean, enduring forever;*
> *The judgments of the LORD are true; they are righteous altogether.*
> *They are more desirable than gold, yes, than much fine gold;*
> *Sweeter also than honey and the drippings of the honeycomb.*
> *Moreover, by them Your servant is warned;*
> *In keeping them there is great reward.*
>
> Psalm 19:7–11

- *The law of the LORD is perfect.* This refers to the Torah, the words given by God through Moses for His people. The words written in the Torah are perfect and restore the soul. They restore the hearts of humanity to their relationship with God. They are to be read, studied, and meditated upon.

- *The testimony of the LORD is sure.* This refers to the instruction given by God. The young and naïve will become wise through studying and keeping the testimony of the LORD.

- *The precepts of the LORD are right.* This refers to the LORD's righteous instructions or procedures for conduct; how to live as a community in God's presence. Understanding and keeping God's precepts cause the heart to rejoice through the blessing they bring.

- *The commandment of the LORD is pure.* This refers to the commandment(s) God spoke and made available to His people.

They are pure and enlighten the eyes of those who study them and keep them. They give clear reasoning, spiritual insight, and the ability to make informed decisions. This can also apply to anything that God in His lovingkindness leads and commands His people to do.

- *The fear of the LORD is clean.* This refers to awe and reverence, a feeling of profound respect for the LORD. It is morally-ethically pure and will endure forever. The fear of the LORD motivates us to learn His ways. It enables us to remain living in His presence.

- *The judgments of the LORD are true.* As the true King and Ruler and as the Father of His people, all of God's decisions and actions are faithful and true; whether they be the blessings of the covenant, discipline for instruction, or corrective judgments, they are righteous altogether—because He is righteous and true.

In Psalm 19, the psalmist declares that the words God has spoken are more desirable and necessary than anything else one could pursue in life. They provide instruction, guidance, true wisdom, and "in keeping them there is great reward" (Ps. 19:11). Certainly the prosperity of the nation of Israel under the rulerships of David and Solomon bears witness to this.

When David was near death, he spoke these words to Solomon, "I am going the way of all the earth. Be strong, therefore, and show yourself a man. Keep the charge of the LORD your God, to walk in His ways, to keep His statutes, His commandments, His ordinances, and His testimonies, according to what is written in the Law of Moses, that you may succeed in all that you do and wherever you turn" (1 Kings 2:2–3).

Solomon and Wisdom

Solomon was taught (or had his education provided) by his father David. He was most likely also taught by the priests who ministered at the tabernacle in Jerusalem. When Solomon was about to become the king of Israel, he asked God for wisdom. His education in Torah prepared him and guided him as he began his responsibilities as king.

> *Hear, O sons, the instruction of a father,*
> > *And give attention that you may gain understanding,*
> *For I give you sound teaching;*
> > *Do not abandon my instruction.*
> *When I was a son to my father,*
> > *Tender and the only son in the sight of my mother,*
> *Then he taught me and said to me,*
> > *"Let your heart hold fast my words;*
> > *Keep my commandments and live;*
> *Acquire wisdom! Acquire understanding!*
> *Do not forget nor turn away from the words of my mouth.*
>
> Proverbs 4:1–5

Education in Israel was more than just gaining factual knowledge. It was more than an intellectual pursuit. Education centered on learning God's ways and keeping them. It was not something extraneous to life. The learning of God's ways was synonymous with life. It unfolded life, giving it direction and meaning.[59] It gave practical wisdom for all of life's relationships and endeavors.

As a child grew older, he began to learn more of the details of the Law given through Moses. Through a path of lifelong learning, the learner acquired wisdom that would serve as a guide to any new situation that might arise. This wisdom was established on God's principles. It began with the ability to evaluate all of life from God's perspective. Throughout the Hebrew Scriptures we see wisdom from God applied to leadership, statesmanship, farming and tending of flocks, warfare, artisanship, administration and trade, interpersonal affairs, literature, music, and worship.

Moses admonished the children of Israel that through their diligence to study and keep God's words, the nations would see and appreciate the great wisdom they possessed (Deut. 4:6). This was evidenced at the height of Solomon's reign. The Queen of Sheba traveled to hear his wisdom and see the blessing of the LORD on his kingdom (1 Kings 10:1-13). The Scriptures further state, "King Solomon became greater than all the kings of the earth in riches and in wisdom. All the earth was

---

[59] Nathan Drazin, *History of Jewish Education, from 515 B.C.E. to 220 C.E. (During the Periods of the Second Commonwealth and the Tannaim)* (Baltimore: The Johns Hopkins Press, 1940), 12.

seeking the presence of Solomon, to hear his wisdom which God had put in his heart" (1 Kings 10:23–24).

The book of Proverbs teaches that wisdom leads to success in life, but folly leads to failure. Christine Roy Yoder summarizes the instructional goals of the book of Proverbs.

> "The instructional goals of Proverbs 1-9 and, arguably, the entire book are broadly defined at the outset (1:2-7): to teach the inexperienced how to live wisely (1:2-4, 6), to further educate the mature sage (1:5-6), and to remind everyone that knowledge begins with the 'fear of the Lord,' reverence for Yahweh, God of Israel (1:7a; cf. 9:10). Only fools ignore or despise such wisdom (1:7b)."[60]

God's wisdom is practical and provides the ability to successfully meet the challenges of life. Folly is the opposite of wisdom and is the result of intentional or unintentional ignorance of God's ways. Wise teachers sought to instruct the unlearned in the practical application of God's words. They sought to drive out folly and teach wisdom, for in the presence of wisdom folly begins to perish.[61]

Lifelong learning with the practical goal of walking in God's ways is the basis of acquiring wisdom. Proverbs 4:13 conveys this imperative for lifelong learning: "Take hold of instruction; ***do not let go***; guard her, for she is your life" (emphasis added). The idea is to strengthen and not abandon the commitment to continually study the Torah. Being educated to walk in God's ways is a lifelong commitment; it brings His wisdom and blessing upon all of life (Deut. 28:1-14). Moses reminded the Israelites, "So keep and do them, for that is your wisdom and your understanding in the sight of the peoples who will hear all these statutes and say, 'Surely this great nation is a wise and understanding people'" (Deut. 4:6). Additionally, the proverbs teach, "My son, give attention to my words; incline your ear to my sayings. Do not let them depart from your sight; keep them in the midst of your heart. For they are life to those who find them and health to all their body" (Prov. 4:20-22). God's commandments brought life and health as well as great wisdom and understanding to all who studied and meditated on them.

---

[60] Christine Roy Yoder, *Wisdom as a Woman of Substance* (New York: Walter de Gruyter, 2001), 3.
[61] Marvin R. Wilson, *Our Father Abraham: Jewish Roots of the Christian Faith* (Grand Rapids: Eerdmans, 1989), 282-287.

One final note about God's wisdom is appropriate here. When Adam and Eve disobeyed the LORD, seeking to obtain wisdom and knowledge apart from Him and were cast out of the garden, they no longer had access to the tree of life (Gen. 3:5-6; 22-24). However, divine wisdom obtained through learning and keeping God's instruction gives access to life (Prov. 3:1-22). Proverbs 3:18 says that wisdom "is a tree of life to those who take hold of her."

The Wrong Example of Jeroboam

After King Solomon died the ten northern tribes of Israel broke away from the house of David in Judah. The northern kingdom became known as Israel and the southern kingdom as Judah. The leader of the new kingdom of Israel was Jeroboam.

Jeroboam reasoned that since the temple was located in Jerusalem in the kingdom of Judah, the people of his kingdom would continue to go there for the appointed feasts and this might undermine the identity of the new northern kingdom. To remedy this Jeroboam set up idols for worship, instituted new national feasts, "and made priests from among all the people who were not of the sons of Levi" (1 Kings 12:31). Through these planned religious, cultural, and educational changes, Jeroboam created a new way of life. The people lost their unique calling as a holy nation and became assimilated into the surrounding cultures.

In the northern kingdom, the Levitical priests no longer taught Torah to the people. Those who were priests and prophets, who should have been educating God's people in His ways, profited from their promotion of idolatry.[62] Through Hosea's ministry to the northern kingdom, the LORD rebuked the teachers of Israel: "My people are destroyed for lack of knowledge. Because you have rejected knowledge, I will also reject you from being my priest. Since you have forgotten the law of your God, I also will forget your children" (Hosea 4:6). The LORD held those teachers responsible for the fate of His people. The Jewish Publication Society's (JPS) translation of Hosea emphasizes God's response:

---

[62]Douglas Stuart, *Word Biblical Commentary: Hosea–Jonah, vol. 31*, ed. Bruce M. Metzger, David A. Hubbard, and Glenn W. Barker (Dallas: Word Incorporated, 2002), 77-79.

An Introduction to Education in Bible Times

"'Let no man rebuke, let no man protest!' For this your people has a grievance against [you], O priest! So you shall stumble by day, and by night a prophet shall stumble as well, and I will destroy your kindred. My people is destroyed because of [your] disobedience! Because you have rejected obedience, I reject you as My priest; because you have spurned the teaching of your God, I, in turn, will spurn your children."

Hosea 4:4-6, JPS

Although God continued to faithfully reach out to the people of the northern tribes of Israel through His prophets, the people did not turn their hearts back to the LORD. They became more and more oppressed by their neighbors and were eventually conquered by the Assyrians and removed from the land God had given them. They were destroyed for a lack of knowledge, knowledge that would have promoted an obedience to God's ways.

God's Purpose for Education

My son, if you will receive my words
  And treasure my commandments within you,
Make your ear attentive to wisdom,
  Incline your heart to understanding;
For if you cry for discernment,
  Lift your voice for understanding;
If you seek her as silver
  And search for her as for hidden treasures;
Then you will discern the fear of the LORD
  And discover the knowledge of God.
For the LORD gives wisdom;
  From His mouth come knowledge and understanding.

Proverbs 2:1–6

God was not providing a system of education merely for the sake of becoming educated, or only for the sake of developing good productive citizens. Torah education was given as a means to grow in the knowledge of God. This is why Moses prayed to the LORD, "Let me

know Your ways that I may ***know*** You [emphasis added]" (Exod. 33:13). The Hebrew verb *yada* ("know") is used over six hundred times in the Hebrew Scriptures. It refers to God's intimate knowledge of man, the intimate knowledge between people, and man's intimate knowledge of God.[63] The prophet Hosea exhorted Israel to press on to experientially and intimately know the LORD (Hosea 6:1-3). David prayed, "Continue Your lovingkindness to those who know You" (Ps. 36:10). Ultimately, God's desire is that all men and women would enter into a relationship of intimately knowing Him (Jer. 31:34).

The knowledge of God was the primary objective for education. However, this knowledge was not intended only for the sake of "knowing." The LORD spoke through the prophet Jeremiah that to do justice and righteousness and to be concerned for the cause of the poor is to intimately know the LORD (Jer. 22:16). To know God, therefore, included an expression of faithfully walking in His ways.[64] The Torah gave instruction on how to live a life of righteousness and justice as a result of knowing the LORD and learning His ways.

Torah means instruction and teaching.[65] The Torah is the instruction of a loving Father teaching His children. Brad Young explains, "The verb *yryah*, from which the noun *torah* comes, means 'to shoot at a target with force and accuracy.' It also means 'revelation,' and primarily refers to a revelation of the nature and character of God, and how to live life to its fullest measure in a way that is pleasing to God. It means to shoot and hit the target accurately based upon the revelation of God."[66] Over time, the verb *yryah* also took on the extended meaning of "to teach," "to direct," and "to point out."[67]

Two additional Hebrew words highlight the important task of Torah education and the total commitment with which it was to be approached. The verb *lamad* is usually translated in the Hebrew Scriptures as "teach" or "learn," and basically means "get accustomed to," "exercise in," or "train."[68] Biblical education included the focused

---

[63]R. Laird Harris, Gleason L. Archer Jr., and Bruce K. Waltke, ed., *Theological Wordbook of the Old Testament* (Chicago: Moody Press, 1999), 366.
[64]Wilson, *Our Father Abraham*, 287-289.
[65]Harris, Archer Jr., and Waltke, ed., *Theological Wordbook of the Old Testament*, 403.
[66]Brad H. Young, *Meet the Rabbis: Rabbinic Thought and the Teachings of Jesus* (Grand Rapids: Baker Academics, 2007), 39.
[67]Young, *Meet the Rabbis*, 39.
[68]Wilson, *Our Father Abraham*, 297.

discipline of learning knowledge and being trained in its application. This is further seen in the verb *shânan*, translated as "to teach" and comes from a source meaning "to be sharp," "to pierce," or "to prick" as in the case of sharp instruments such as arrows or swords.[69] Deuteronomy 6:7 uses this verb to impress upon the people to "diligently teach" their children—that is, to intentionally instill the knowledge of God and His ways by persistent-repetitive instruction. Wilson emphasizes this concept: "For the teacher, God's Word is to be an instrument which 'cuts' and 'pierces' as he drills his points home to his pupils. The very finest points of Scripture are to be imprinted upon the life of the learner."[70]

Through the Torah, God taught His people about Himself and their own unique identity as His people. He taught them how to live and conduct themselves in relationship with Himself and with each other. Torah education instilled the ideal of holiness, of separation from other peoples and cultures to belong wholly to God.[71] In other words, only through the knowledge of the Torah could God's people, the Jews, truly know themselves.[72] Education, the passing on of God's Word from one generation to the next, was the means of individual enlightenment and national preservation.

God's relationship with His people was one of faithfulness and lovingkindness. His presence dwelling in their midst was the centerpiece of His relationship with them. When the children of Israel sinned against the LORD in the wilderness with the golden calf and through their unbelief about possessing Canaan, Moses's primary concern was for God's presence. He interceded for God to forgive His people and for His presence to remain with them. Similarly, when David sinned against the LORD, His primary concern was for God's presence to remain with him. He prayed, "Do not cast me away from Your presence, and do not take Your Holy Spirit from me" (Ps. 51:11). Later in Israel's history we read that Israel forsook the ways of the LORD which they had learned through the Torah and through His prophets and teachers. God finally responded by withdrawing His presence from their midst (Ezek. 10:18-19; 11:22-23). When they lost the blessing and favor of the LORD's presence, the temple and Jerusalem were destroyed and the people were taken away into captivity.

---

[69]Wilson, *Our Father Abraham*, 296.
[70]Wilson, *Our Father Abraham*, 296.
[71]Wilson, *Our Father Abraham*, 289.
[72]Goldman, *Life-Long Learning Among the Jews*, 4-5.

God's purpose for education was to enable His people to love Him and keep His ways and for one generation after another to live with His presence abiding in their midst. Education in Torah was intended for all God's people. It was concerned for the whole person and for the life of the whole community. Adhering to God's instruction would bring wisdom and a blessing upon all aspects of life.

Through education in the Torah, God empowered His people to choose life. He instructed them on what choices to make. However, He did not interfere with their choices; they were truly free to choose. The Torah taught that His people were responsible for their choices and for the consequences of those choices. God would always be faithful to love them but within the terms of the covenant. The outcome depended on their choice.[73]

> *"I call heaven and earth to witness against you today, that I have set before you life and death, the blessing and the curse. So choose life in order that you may live, you and your descendants, by loving the LORD your God, by obeying His voice, and by holding fast to Him; for this is your life and the length of your days."*
>
> Deuteronomy 30:19–20

Education also had a global purpose. Israel was to become a light and an example to the nations (Deut. 4:4-8). People were to witness their relationship with the LORD, see their relationships with each other, and desire to learn God's ways. The peoples of the earth would say, "Come, let us go up to the mountain of the LORD, to the house of the God of Jacob; that He may teach us concerning His ways and that we may walk in His paths. For the law will go forth from Zion and the word of the LORD from Jerusalem" (Isa. 2:2–3). God's ultimate plan was for Israel to teach the nations to know the LORD and walk in His ways.

The Levitical Priests

Aaron and Moses were descendants of the tribe of Levi. It was the Levites who had remained faithful to the LORD when Israel rebelled in

---
[73]Jonathan Sacks, *Essays on Ethics: A Weekly Reading of the Jewish Bible* (New Milford: Maggid Books, 2016), 211.

the wilderness. The LORD chose the Levites to belong to Himself and serve Him in the tent of meeting. Then from within the tribe of Levi, Aaron and his sons were further commissioned as priests to the LORD.

It was the responsibility of the Levitical priesthood to teach and instruct the people in the knowledge of God. The LORD spoke to Aaron, saying, "Do not drink wine or strong drink, neither you nor your sons with you, when you come into the tent of meeting, so that you will not die—it is a perpetual statute throughout your generations—and so as to make a distinction between the holy and the profane, and between the unclean and the clean, and so as to teach the sons of Israel all the statutes which the LORD has spoken to them through Moses" (Lev. 10:8–11). Aaron and his sons were to teach the sons of Israel all the statutes which the LORD had spoken. According to Jewish tradition, Aaron would go from house to house in the wilderness, teaching the people the Shema and how to pray, teaching them Torah.[74]

At the end of Israel's time in the wilderness, before entering Canaan, Moses spoke to the children of Israel to be careful "that you diligently observe and do according to all that the Levitical priests teach you; as I have commanded them, so you shall be careful to do" (Deut. 24:8). Then at the end of his ministry, Moses entrusted the written Torah to the Levitical priests (Deut. 31:9), and the Levites were commissioned with the responsibility to instruct the people. In his final blessing of the tribes of Israel, Moses said of the Levites that they would teach the LORD's ordinances and laws to the children of Israel (Deut. 33:10).

Unfortunately, Israel was not always faithful to the LORD, and the priesthood did not always carry out their teaching duties among the people. The prophet Azariah reminded King Asa of Judah about these unfortunate periods of Israel's history, saying, "For many days Israel was without the true God and without a teaching priest and without law" (2 Chron. 15:3).

The priests who administered the sacrifices and the worship at the tabernacle most likely instructed the people in the parts of the Torah that dealt with religious ritual. It was therefore the task of the Levites to expound the Torah in its more general aspects.[75] During one of the great spiritual revivals in Judah, King Jehoshaphat sent throughout the land an educational delegation consisting of priests and Levites, as seen here in 2 Chronicles 17:

---

[74]Goldman, *Life-Long Learning Among the Jews*, 8.
[75]Goldman, *Life-Long Learning Among the Jews*, 3.

> *He [Jehoshaphat] took great pride in the ways of the LORD and again removed the high places and the Asherim from Judah. Then in the third year of his reign he sent his officials, Ben-hail, Obadiah, Zechariah, Nethanel and Micaiah, to teach in the cities of Judah; and with them the Levites, Shemaiah, Nethaniah, Zebadiah, Asahel, Shemiramoth, Jehonathan, Adonijah, Tobijah and Tobadonijah, the Levites; and with them Elishama and Jehoram, the priests. They taught in Judah, having the book of the law of the LORD with them; and they went throughout all the cities of Judah and taught among the people.*
>
> 2 Chronicles 17:6–9

Later in the history of the kings of Judah, King Jehoash "did right in the sight of the LORD all his days in which Jehoiada the priest instructed him" (2 Kings 12:2). And in the days of King Josiah, the Levites taught the people and explained the Torah (2 Chron. 35:3).

The role of the Levites as teachers grew to even greater importance after the exile during the time of the Second Temple. Ezra was a descendant of Aaron, of the Levitical priests. The Scriptures say that he "set his heart to study the law of the LORD and to practice it, and to teach His statutes and ordinances in Israel" (Ezra 7:10). And in the days of Ezra and Nehemiah, the Levites were described as the ones who helped the people to understand the Torah (Neh. 8:7). When Ezra read the Torah to the people, it was the Levites who explained its contents to the adults.

God's calling of the Levites to teach His people never changed. Many centuries after Moses commissioned the Levites to teach Israel the Torah, God spoke these words through the prophet Malachi:

> *"Then you will know that I have sent this commandment to you, that My covenant may continue with Levi," says the LORD of hosts. "My covenant with him was one of life and peace, and I gave them to him as an object of reverence; so he revered Me and stood in awe of My name. True instruction was in his mouth and unrighteousness was not found on his lips; he walked with Me in peace and uprightness, and he turned many back from iniquity. For the lips of a priest should preserve knowledge, and men should seek instruction from his mouth; for he is the messenger of the LORD of hosts."*
>
> Malachi 2:4-7

The Prophets

The first prophet identified by God in the Scriptures is Abraham (Gen. 20:7). The Hebrew word for prophet is *navi'*. The form of the word *navi'* could either signify one who receives the (divine) call or one who proclaims, an authorized spokesman.[76] Sarna reinforces this concept when he states, "The prophet is the spokesman for God to man; but intercession before God in favor of man is also an indispensable aspect of his function. Moses frequently acts in this capacity, and so do Samuel, Amos, and Jeremiah."[77] However, the prophet was also a teacher, as Abraham was faithful to teach God's ways to his household (Gen. 18:19).

Moses is considered the greatest of the prophets known in Jewish history and is referred to as "Moshe Rabbeinu, Moses our Teacher."[78] The last verses in the Torah state that since the time of Moses "no prophet has risen in Israel like Moses, whom the LORD knew face to face" (Deut. 34:10). In his first farewell address to the people before his death, Moses articulated the underlying purpose of his life: "Behold, I have taught you statutes and ordinances even as the LORD my God commanded me" (Deut. 4:5).

Additionally, Goldman affirms:

> "In the development of Judaism, the figure of the prophet was destined to tower above both priest and Levite as the religious teacher of adults. The prophet's life was sacrificially dedicated to the high task of spreading and deepening the divine education of the people. In the classic period of Hebrew prophecy, these great teachers of Judaism were fully aware of their prime role as teachers."[79]

When Samuel was established as a prophet in Israel, the LORD was with him and let none of his words fall to the ground. It was at this time the LORD appeared again to Israel, because "the LORD revealed Himself to Samuel ... by the word of the LORD" (1 Sam. 3:20-21). This

---

[76] Robert D. Culver, "1277 אָבַן," ed. R. Laird Harris, Gleason L. Archer Jr., and Bruce K. Waltke, *Theological Wordbook of the Old Testament* (Chicago: Moody Press, 1999), 544.
[77] Nahum M. Sarna, *The JPS Torah Commentary: Genesis* (Philadelphia: Jewish Publication Society, 1989), 142.
[78] "Torah," Orthodox Union (June 21, 2006), https://www.ou.org/judaism-101/glossary/torah/.
[79] Goldman, *Life-Long Learning Among the Jews*, 4-5.

is significant. In the wilderness God did not reveal Himself in a physical form. He revealed Himself through His Word.[80] Now through Samuel, God was again revealing Himself by His Word.

Samuel was faithful to communicate and teach God's Word throughout Israel. Later in his ministry to the people of Israel he said, "Moreover, as for me, far be it from me that I should sin against the LORD by ceasing to pray for you; but I will instruct you in the good and right way" (1 Sam. 12:23). The prophet Samuel was a teacher. He even established schools of prophets that learned the ways of the LORD under his mentorship (1 Sam. 10:5-6; 19:19-24).[81]

The schools of prophets established by Samuel were later seen during the ministry of Elijah and Elisha (1 Kings 18:4; 2 Kings 2:3, 15). They appear to have continued through the ministry of Isaiah and the rebuilding of the temple (Ezra 5:2).[82] These schools were overseen by established prophets who educated their disciples in the knowledge of Torah, the oral teaching of the prophets, and in sacred music (1 Sam. 10:5). Through their education in Torah and the ways of the LORD they "were thereby qualified to be public preachers, which seems to have been part of the business of the prophets on the Sabbath-days and festivals."[83] The schools of prophets carried on Samuel's prophetic and teaching ministry to Israel.

The prophets were unique in the history of mankind. They were divinely inspired teachers who addressed their words to the grownup men and women of their respective generations, interpreting the Torah and translating it into practical terms of life—both private and national.[84] And while the priests and Levites taught, for the most part, in the Tent of Meeting in the wilderness, and later in the temple in Jerusalem, the prophets taught in public forums, in private assemblies, and even in their own homes (Ezek. 8:1).

Malachi, the last of the prophets of the Hebrew Scriptures, summarizes the prophetic burden for Torah education: "Remember the law of Moses My servant, even the statutes and ordinances which I commanded him in

---

[80] Sacks, *Essays on Ethics*, 217.
[81] Paul, L. Redditt, "Prophecy, History of." *In Dictionary of the Old Testament Prophets*, ed. Mark Boda and J. Gordon McConnvile (Downers Grove: IVP Academic, 2012), 592. John McClintock and James Strong, "Schools of the Prophets," *Cyclopædia of Biblical, Theological, and Ecclesiastical Literature, vol. 8* (New York: Harper & Brothers, 1894), 654.
[82] See Robert Jamieson, A. R. Fausset, and David Brown, *Commentary Critical and Explanatory on the Whole Bible, vol. 1* (Oak Harbor, WA: Logos Research Systems, 1997), 14. Also see J. Barton, Isaiah 1–39 (London; New York: T&T Clark, 1995), 22.
[83] McClintock and Strong, "Schools of the Prophets," 654.
[84] Goldman, *Life-Long Learning Among the Jews*, 4-5.

Horeb for all Israel" (Mal. 4:4). The word "remember" has the meaning of audible speaking, reciting or invoking a response of hearing (Shema) the words of the LORD. Torah belonged to all Israel, and Torah education was the right and responsibility of all the people. So it is fitting that this is one of the last recorded prophetic words of the Hebrew Scriptures.[85]

Shepherds of God's People

The Israelites were a shepherding people who understood what it meant to tend flocks of sheep. God uses the imagery of shepherding in describing Himself as a Shepherd to His people (Ps. 23:1; Isa. 40:11). God also describes as shepherds those who carry the responsibility to lead, care for, and teach His people. Toward the end of the kingdom of Judah, looking forward to a time when the people of Israel would return their hearts to the LORD, Jeremiah spoke for the LORD, "Then I will give you shepherds after My own heart, who will feed you on knowledge and understanding" (Jer. 3:15).

The root word for both "shepherd" and "feed" in Jeremiah 3:15 is הָעָר which means to feed or graze. It is used many times in the Hebrew Scriptures and is translated as shepherd, feeding, pasture, graze, tend, herdsmen, and keeper. Proverbs 10:21 also used the word for "feed" saying that "the lips of the righteous feed many," implying that those who understand and keep Torah are able to feed (or teach) others "knowledge and understanding." The uses of the root word הָעָר suggest "the edification, care, and guidance that one who would impart knowledge must have for his flock. But it also implies the need to provide food and nourishment [God's Word] for growth."[86]

The Responsibility of Parents

"You shall teach them diligently to your sons and shall talk of them when you sit in your house and when you walk by the way and when you lie down and when you rise up."

Deuteronomy 6:6–7

---

[85]Harris, Archer Jr., and Waltke, ed., *Theological Wordbook of the Old Testament*, 241.
[86]Wilson, *Our Father Abraham*, 295.

Throughout Jewish history, God has used human vessels to teach His people. These individuals, like Moses, were not only teachers, they were to be examples. For ancient Israel, the parents held the primary responsibility of teaching their children (Deut. 4:9, 6:7, 11:19). To be a parent meant to teach. And in the close-knit family structure of that day, as parents became grandparents, they also became involved in teaching their grandchildren (Deut. 4:9). The parents' responsibility for instructing the children continued throughout their entire lives.[87]

The Israelite families provided a well-rounded education for their children. It included religious instruction as well as training in practical life skills they would need in their community. It is widely held that there were no formal schools for most children. Most of their learning took place in the home and in everyday life. Therefore, education in the home began soon after a child could talk.

A young boy's first significant instruction came from his mother (Prov. 31:1–9). The young son would stay with his mother when the father went to the fields to work. As the boy grew older, the father's involvement in his son's education increased, especially as the two began to work together in the fields or in the father's trade. A son would learn from his father the history of his country, the law of the LORD, and the blessing of God in the agricultural cycle. In a Jewish home the father was bound to accept the duty of the religious education of his son. The father's responsibility included providing religious instruction, teaching his son a trade, and finding him a wife.[88]

A daughter would stay with her mother and continue under her instruction. A mother's major responsibility was to train her daughters. They were trained in skills like cooking, spinning, weaving, dyeing, caring for children, managing the household, grinding grain, music, good manners and high moral standards, and reading. Some also learned to write and calculate weights and measures.[89]

Jewish education was almost exclusively religious education. The center of education was the home, and the responsibility of teaching the child was something that the parent could not evade, if he was to satisfy

---

[87] Ronald F. Youngblood, F. F. Bruce, and R. K. Harrison, Thomas Nelson Publishers, eds., *Nelson's New Illustrated Bible Dictionary* (Nashville, TN: Thomas Nelson, Inc., 1995).
[88] William Barclay, *Train Up A Child: Educational Ideals in the Ancient World* (Philadelphia: Westminster Press, 1959), 22–23.
[89] Walter A. Elwell and Barry J. Beitzel, *Baker Encyclopedia of the Bible* (Grand Rapids, MI: Baker Book House, 1988), 657–661.

God's command (Deut. 6:7). So, it was important for parents to be well-versed in the Torah in order to teach their children. A parent had to be ready, willing, and able to rehearse to the child the instruction and the great things God had done for His people Israel.[90]

The father was the primary teacher of Torah. The mother was expected to assist in teaching. It was the parents—not textbooks, audiovisuals, or brightly colored classrooms—that were the main instruments in the learning process. As teachers of their children, parents served as living and dynamic communicators of divine truth.[91]

In the instruction of their children, the Jewish parents' major concern was that their children come to know the living God. In Hebrew the verb "to know" means to be intimately involved with a person. Godly parents helped their children develop this kind of knowledge about God.[92] From this foundation the children would come to love the LORD with all their heart, all their soul, and all their might.

Parental responsibility to teach was established at the very beginning or formation of the Jewish people. After stating that Abraham would become a great and mighty nation, and that in him all the nations of the earth would be blessed, the LORD said, "For I have chosen him, so that he may command his children and his household after him to keep the way of the LORD" (Gen. 18:19). From the beginning, the education of children by their parents would preserve for all time the people that God created for His own possession, the people He would use to be a blessing to all nations.

> *Listen, O my people, to my instruction;*
> *   Incline your ears to the words of my mouth.*
> *I will open my mouth in a parable;*
> *   I will utter dark sayings of old,*
> *Which we have heard and known,*
> *   And our fathers have told us.*
> *We will not conceal them from their children,*
> *   But tell to the generation to come the praises of the LORD,*
> *   And His strength and His wondrous works that He has done.*

---

[90] Barclay, *Train Up a Child*, 16–17.
[91] Wilson, *Our Father Abraham*, 280.
[92] J.I. Packer and M. C. Tenny, *Illustrated Manners and Customs of the Bible* (Nashville, TN: Thomas Nelson Publishers, 1980), 452–455.

For He established a testimony in Jacob
   And appointed a law in Israel,
   Which He commanded our fathers
   That they should teach them to their children,
That the generation to come might know, even the children
   yet to be born,
That they may arise and tell them to their children,
That they should put their confidence in God
   And not forget the works of God,
   But keep His commandments.

Psalm 78:1–7

Opportunities for Children to Learn

Each day the children of families who kept the Torah had many opportunities to learn. They observed how their parents and others in the community practiced the Law. They heard and learned the daily, weekly, and special prayers. These prayers had a great impact on the children's minds and hearts, constantly turning their thoughts toward God. Parents would teach their children to daily recite the Shema as they bound the words on their forehead and on their arm, placing the words near to their hearts (Deut. 6:8).

Each day children encountered a mezuzah that was placed on the doorpost of their home. It was a piece of parchment (often contained in a decorative case) inscribed with the Shema. The mezuzah was affixed to the doorframe to fulfill the commandment to inscribe the words of the Shema on the doorposts of their house (Deut. 6:9). It was another daily reminder to love the LORD their God with all their heart, soul, and strength; and to remember the teaching of the Torah.

Every week children observed the Sabbath with their families. God commanded his people to keep the Sabbath. The Sabbath was the seventh day of the week. It was to be a day of rest in which Jews remembered God's creation, His mighty acts in the birth of their people through their deliverance from Egypt, and the promises of a future Messianic Age. The weekly Sabbath observance provided a rich opportunity for children to learn about their God and their heritage.

An Introduction to Education in Bible Times

The land and agricultural life provided another profound learning experience. Barclay describes this experience of living on the land God had promised His people:

"Long before there was any formal education lads and young men must have been trained in the simple processes on which food and life depend; and in that training they could not help, perhaps half-unconsciously, perhaps by a process of soaking them in rather than of learning them, acquiring these beliefs in their hearts. For the Jew to work on the land must have been to be educated continuously in the ways of God."[93]

They were reminded that if they listened obediently to the commandments of the LORD, "to love the LORD your God and to serve Him with all your heart and all your soul, that He will give the rain for your land in its season, the early and late rain, that you may gather in your grain and your new wine and your oil" (Deut. 11:13-14).

Children learned that the fruitfulness of their labors was dependent on the blessing of God. Loving God and keeping His commandments brought that blessing. They learned that the land came from God to them—it belonged to Him and they were stewards of it (Lev. 25:23-24). They learned that God was their great Provider; He was their Great Shepherd who takes care of His people as a shepherd takes care of his flock.

The various offerings brought to the priests taught the children about the relationship God had with their family and community. Tithes and offerings acknowledged the blessing of God on their land, their crops, and their livestock. Offerings for sin reminded them of their falling short of walking in God's ways and of God's grace and forgiveness. These and other offerings would have provided important teaching moments for children.

The annual feasts also taught children of the relationship between obedience to God and the fruitfulness of the land. Each of the three major feasts followed the agricultural cycle. Passover (Pesach) fell in the early spring and was connected with when the crops would have begun to ripen after the winter rains in Israel. Pentecost (Shavuot) was also an agricultural celebration during biblical times. It fell seven weeks after Passover at the time of the late spring harvest. The Feast of Tabernacles

---

[93] Barclay, *Train Up a Child*, 19.

(Sukkot) celebrated the completion of all the harvests before the onset of the winter rains. Certainly, these feasts and the offerings from the fruitfulness of the land that accompanied each feast reinforced what children learned in their daily lives about their dependence on God for their sustenance.

Children also had unparalleled educational opportunities to learn the sacred history of Israel during the required annual feasts. At Passover they celebrated God delivering their ancestors from slavery in Egypt. At Pentecost they remembered God giving the Law to Moses on Mt Sinai. The Feast of Tabernacles, with its booths made from tree branches, commemorated God's presence dwelling with Israel and His faithfulness to Israel throughout their journey to the Promised Land. The Day of Atonement reminded the people of their falling short in obedience to God and of God's abundant mercy.

For each of the three major feast times, all males were required to go up to the tabernacle, where God's presence resided; however, entire extended families would typically travel together. During the days of the temple in Jerusalem, pilgrim families would rehearse songs on their way up to the temple. The sights, sounds and activity surrounding these times of traveling to Jerusalem would have made a significant impression on the children. There was great anticipation as they traveled with their family and community. They would be captivated by the beauty and impressiveness of the temple and the feast celebrations: the sacrifices, the hospitality and the atmosphere, the ministering of the priests, the musicians and singers, and the reading of the Law. This would have been quite an impressionable experience with numerous occasions for a child to observe, learn, and ask questions.

The Sabbatical Year (described in Leviticus 25) was another powerful lesson about Israel's faithfulness to God and the fruitfulness of the land. Every seventh year the land was to be left to lie fallow. All agricultural activity including plowing, planting, pruning and harvesting was forbidden. Unfortunately, this command was not kept by Israel during their ancient time in the land.

The Sabbatical Year was also a time for the remission of debts and an occasion for parents and children to hear the Torah read to them. In the book of Deuteronomy Moses commanded that during Sabbatical Year, at the Feast of Booths, when all Israel would assemble together, they were to read from the Torah in front of all Israel. All the men, women, children, and the alien were to hear and learn and be careful to observe all the words of the Law. The children who had never heard the Torah read to them before would also hear and learn to fear the LORD (Deut. 31:9-13). According to Goldman, with this command to assemble the people, and as it was expanded over time, "Moses established an educational institution that endured from his time down to the end of the Second Hebrew Commonwealth—a period of over three thousand years."[94]

---

[94]Goldman, *Life-Long Learning Among the Jews*, 2.

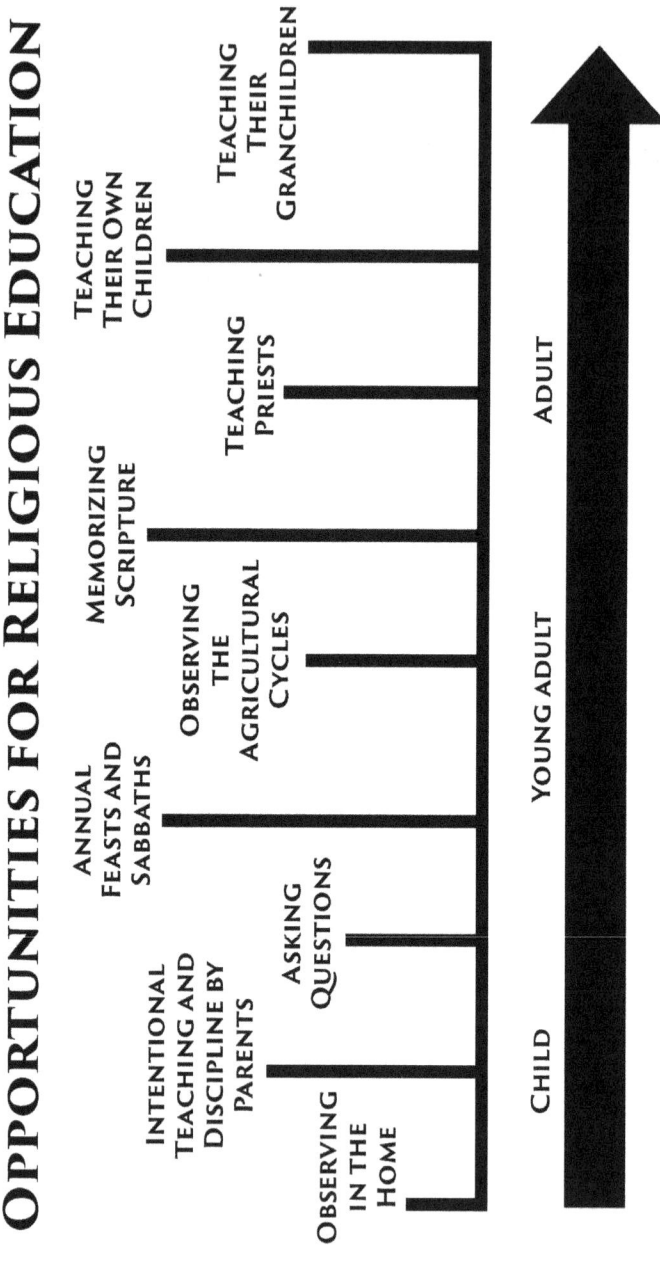

PART 3

EDUCATION FROM THE CAPTIVITY THROUGH THE SECOND TEMPLE PERIOD

The world stands on three things: Torah, the service of G–d, and deeds of kindness.

Ethics of the Fathers 1.2

The Captivity

The city of Jerusalem and the kingdom of Judah were captured by the Babylonian armies under Nebuchadnezzar in 598-597 BCE. At that time many Jews were deported into various cities of the Babylonian empire. Eleven years later in 586 BCE, after an uprising in Jerusalem, the Babylonians destroyed the Holy City and the Temple, bringing another wave of deportations.[95] These events were the fulfillment of corrective judgments spoken by God in the Torah and through the prophets.

> *"... And many times You rescued them according to Your compassion, and admonished them in order to turn them back to Your law. Yet they acted arrogantly and did not listen to Your commandments but sinned against Your ordinances, by which if a man observes them he shall live. And they turned a stubborn shoulder and stiffened their neck, and would not listen. However, You bore with them for many years, and admonished them by Your Spirit through Your prophets, yet they would not give ear. Therefore You gave them into the hand of the peoples of the lands. Nevertheless, in Your great compassion You did not make an end of them or forsake them, for You are a gracious and compassionate God."*
>
> Nehemiah 9:28–31

During the time of captivity God was still with His people. The prophet Ezekiel ministered to the exiles, teaching them from his home (Ezek. 8:1; 20:1).[96] Also the prophet Daniel ministered in the royal palace (Dan. 1:3-6, 18-21), and the intervention of Mordechai and Esther saved the Jewish nation from annihilation (Esther 7-9). The exiles in Babylon reflected on the warnings God had given them through the Torah and His prophets, so they put away idolatry and returned their hearts to the LORD.[97] In their return to the LORD, there was a great focus on the words God had spoken. Priests like Ezra diligently gave themselves to studying, keeping, and teaching Torah (Ezra 7:10). Synagogues grew as local institutions for the people to engage in Torah education and prayer.[98]

---

[95] H. H. Ben-Sasson, *A History of the Jewish People* (Cambridge, MA: Harvard University Press, 1969), 154-158.
[96] Abraham Cohen, *Everyman's Talmud: The Major Themes of the Rabbinic Sages* (New York: Schocken Books, 1995), xxxiv.
[97] Ben-Sasson, *A History of the Jewish People*, 162-163.
[98] Cohen, *Everyman's Talmud*, xxxiii-xxxiv.

Most nations of antiquity that were defeated and taken captive by foreign empires disappeared from history or had their national identities greatly altered. However, this did not happen with Israel. Removed from their country and with the temple destroyed, the Jews made prayer and the study of their reemerged sacred texts central to Jewish life.[99] Jonathan Sacks supports this notion by stating:

> "The fact that in Judaism the Torah was given in the wilderness, before the people had ever entered the land, meant that Jews and Judaism were uniquely able to survive, their identity intact, even in exile. Because the Torah came before the land, even when the Jews lost the land they still had God's Word. This meant that even in exile, Jews were still a nation. God remained their sovereign. The covenant was still in place. Even without a geography, they had an ongoing history."[100]

Because of their focus on the words God had spoken to them, the Jews were able to survive as a nation, even with their removal from the land.

During their years of captivity, the Jews witnessed the great wealth and power of several world empires. They experienced the rise, domination, and glory of the Babylonian empire. Then within a generation the Jews saw the Persians conquer this great empire and also add more lands to extend the reach of their control. In 538 BCE, the Persian king Cyrus made a decree that the Jews could return to their own land and rebuild the temple (Ezra 1:1-4). They realized that the survival of their newly reborn nation, small and weak as it was amid the great world empires, could only be assured through their right relationship with the LORD God of Israel. Their survival as a nation was not by human might or power, but by God's Spirit (Zech. 4:6). With this spiritual reawakening there emerged a parallel ideal of education.[101] Nathan Drazin describes this ideal: "A complete return to all the laws and customs of their fathers and the intensification and spread of their education would, it was felt,

---

[99] George Robinson, *Essential Judaism: A Complete Guide to Beliefs, Customs, and Rituals* (New York: Atria Books, 2000), 296, Kindle.
[100] Johnathan Sacks, *Essays on Ethics: A Weekly Reading of the Jewish Bible* (New Milford: Maggid Books, 2016), 217.
[101] Nathan Drazin, *History of Jewish Education from 515 B.C.E. to 220 C.E. (During the Periods of the Second Commonwealth and the Tannaim)* (Baltimore: Johns Hopkins Press, 1940), 15.

not only assure the survival of their people, but what was more, give the Jewish nation a high and distinct position among the nations of the world."[102] Therefore, the education of the Jewish people became a priority for their postexilic leaders.

Ezra and the Great Assembly

The first wave of Jews who returned to their land (538 through 515 BCE) under the decree of Cyrus settled in the cities of Judah and rebuilt the temple, the house of God, in Jerusalem.[103] Starting in 458 BCE, about sixty years after the second temple had been completed, Ezra and Nehemiah instituted reforms in Jerusalem and Judea and the walls of Jerusalem were rebuilt.[104] During this time, Ezra instituted a religious reformation in which the studying and keeping of Torah was made the norm for Jewish life.[105]

In the return from Persia to Jerusalem, Ezra put a great emphasis on restoring the ministry of teaching. The Bible says that he dedicated himself to study the Torah, to practice it, and to teach the LORD's statutes and ordinances to those who had returned to the land of Israel (Ezra 7:10). He also assembled other teachers for the task of instructing the people (Ezra 8:15-16).

> *And all the people gathered as one man at the square which was in front of the Water Gate, and they asked Ezra the scribe to bring the book of the law of Moses which the LORD had given to Israel. Then Ezra the priest brought the law before the assembly of men, women and all who could listen with understanding, on the first day of the seventh month. He read from it before the square which was in front of the Water Gate from early morning until midday, in the presence of men and women, those who could understand; and all the people were attentive to the book of the law. Ezra the scribe stood at a wooden podium which they had made for the purpose. And beside him stood Mattithiah, Shema, Anaiah, Uriah, Hilkiah, and Maaseiah*

---
[102]Drazin, *History of Jewish Education*, 16.
[103]Ben-Sasson, *A History of the Jewish People*, 168-172.
[104]Ben-Sasson, *A History of the Jewish People*, 172-178.
[105]Cohen, *Everyman's Talmud*, xxxiv-xxxv.

on his right hand; and Pedaiah, Mishael, Malchijah, Hashum, Hashbaddanah, Zechariah and Meshullam on his left hand. Ezra opened the book in the sight of all the people for he was standing above all the people; and when he opened it, all the people stood up. Then Ezra blessed the LORD the great God. And all the people answered, "Amen, Amen!" while lifting up their hands; then they bowed low and worshiped the LORD with their faces to the ground. Also Jeshua, Bani, Sherebiah, Jamin, Akkub, Shabbethai, Hodiah, Maaseiah, Kelita, Azariah, Jozabad, Hanan, Pelaiah, the Levites, explained the law to the people while the people remained in their place. They read from the book, from the law of God, translating to give the sense so that they understood the reading.

Nehemiah 8:1-8

Ezra's desire was for the Torah to once again be the possession of all the people. Therefore, his educational goal was for all God's people to study and practice the teachings of Torah.[106] Ezra was so zealous and efficient in this goal that it is taught in *Tosefta 4:5*, "Rabbi Yosei says: Ezra was suitable, given his greatness, for the Torah to be given by him to the Jewish people, had Moses not come first and received the Torah already (Sanh. 21b)."[107] If Moses had not already given the Torah from the LORD, Ezra would have been the one to do so. Abraham Cohen adds that other rabbis during the second century CE declared, "When the Torah had been forgotten by Israel, Ezra came up from Babylon and re-established it (Suk. 20a)."[108]

Ezra was a Levitical priest from the family of Aaron (Ezra 7:1-5; Neh. 8:2). He exemplified God's requirements, as specified in Malachi, for a Levitical priest to faithfully teach His people: "True instruction was in his mouth and unrighteousness was not found on his lips; he walked with Me in peace and uprightness, and he turned many back from iniquity. For the lips of a priest should preserve knowledge, and men should seek instruction from his mouth; for he is the messenger of the LORD of hosts" (Mal. 2:6 7).

---

[106]Israel M. Goldman, *Life-Long Learning Among the Jews: Adult Education in Judaism from Biblical Times to the Twentieth Century* (New York: Ktav Publishing House, 1975), 11.
[107]"Sanhedrin 21b," *The William Davidson Talmud*, accessed January 25, 2019, https://www.sefaria.org/Sanhedrin.21b.24?lang=bi&with=all&lang2=en.
[108]Cohen, *Everyman's Talmud*, xxxv.

Ezra was also referred to as a scribe (Ezra 7:6). He began the tradition of the scribes as religious leaders who were qualified to teach and preach the Scriptures as well as interpret them. These scribes were known as *Soferim*[109] or biblical scholars. During the last century of the Persian rule, these biblical scholars took the lead in the work of teaching the Torah to the people.[110]

Ezra is credited with starting and leading the Great Assembly in Jerusalem.[111] The original Great Assembly is thought to have been a panel of 120 prophets, scribes, and sages (wise men) including Ezra, Nehemiah, Mordecai, Daniel, Simeon the Righteous, Haggai, Zechariah, and Malachi. This assembly was the ultimate religious authority at the onset of the Second Temple period. The Great Assembly is credited with formulating the Jewish prayer service, coordinating the Jewish calendar, and establishing an education system designed to raise up further generations of Torah scholars and teachers.[112]

The opening lines of *Ethics of the Fathers*[113] say, "Moses received the Torah from Sinai and gave it over to Joshua. Joshua gave it over to the Elders, the Elders to the Prophets, and the Prophets gave it over to the men of the Great Assembly. They [the men of the Great Assembly] would always say these three things: Be cautious in judgment. Establish

---

[109] "Soferim," *Encyclopedia Judaica*, Jewish Virtual Library, accessed January 25, 2019, https://www.jewishvirtuallibrary.org/soferim. "These scribes, whose names are not known and who were active during the time of the Persian rule, laid the foundations of the Oral Law: they instituted regulations in the social and religious spheres, explained to the people the Torah and its precepts distinctly and gave the sense (Neh. 8:8). They taught the halakhot and the traditions in close connection with the study of the Bible and deduced new halakhot through the interpretation of the written text. They read the Written Law, interpreted its content, and integrated into it the traditional halakhot as well as the laws that had been derived from it. As a result of the activities of the soferim the Torah ceased to be the heritage of the priests and Levites alone. From among the many pupils they educated, scholars arose from all classes."
[110] George Foot Moore, *Judaism in the First Centuries of the Christian Era: The Age of the Tannaim*, vol. 1 (New York: Schocken Books, 1974), 308.
[111] Moore, *Judaism in the First Centuries of the Christian Era*, 31.
[112] Moore, *Judaism in the First Centuries of the Christian Era*, 32.
[113] *The Ethics of the Fathers* is a compilation that covers the time of the Great Assembly through the time of the Mishnah, around 220 CE. The first five chapters were written before the Mishnah, and they reflect the way oral teachings were preserved by studying and memorizing them and passing them on from one generation of spiritual leaders to the next. The Ethics of the Fathers begins with a statement of the chain of transmission of the Torah from the original revelation at Sinai through the men of the Great Assembly, to the disciples of these original teachers, and on through the generations of teachers who followed. By placing themselves in a line of transmission that began at Sinai, their interpretations carried the same authority as the laws God gave to Moses.

many pupils. And make a safety fence around the Torah."[114] The men of the Great Assembly realized that each succeeding generation of the Jewish people must continue to have educational opportunities readily available to them. To ensure this, they preserved the integrity and availability of both the written Torah as well as the oral interpretations. This task required teachers who had studied, memorized, and understood the Law—able to interpret and apply it for their times. These teachers also valued the importance of "establishing many pupils" by raising up future generations of teachers like themselves.

The LORD was with Ezra and the men of the Great Assembly (Ezra 7:6-7). Through their efforts, they were able to take a defeated people, a destroyed nation, and bring about prosperity and spiritual revival. They reestablished the spiritual foundation of the Jewish people that has endured to this day. Their diligent work in educating the people in Torah, in their inheritance, and how to walk in the ways of the LORD revived the Jewish religious and national identity. It created a unified focus and way of life for all Jewish people, no matter where they might be scattered.

During the Persian and Hellenistic periods, the overall population of the land of Israel grew considerably. According to the Jewish historian Josephus, toward the end of the Great Assembly under Shimon the Righteous (about 310 BCE) the Jewish people were flourishing and the population in Jerusalem reached 120,000 men (not counting women and children).[115] While these numbers are difficult to verify, the indication is that there was growth and prosperity in the land.

The *Ethics of the Fathers* contains many examples of the essential task of teaching and learning: "Shimon the Righteous was among the last surviving members of the Great assembly. He would say: The world stands on three things: Torah, the service of G-d, and deeds of kindness."[116] Drazin notes that Torah was named as the first of the three pillars upon which the entire world is founded because education and knowledge must precede the practice of well-directed activities.[117] Again in *Ethics of the Fathers*, "Antignos of Socho received the tradition from Shimon the Righteous. He would say: Do not be as slaves, who serve their master for the sake of reward. Rather, be as slaves who serve their master not for

---

[114] *Ethics of the Fathers* 1.1.
[115] Josephus, *Against Apion* 1:197.
[116] *Ethics of the Fathers* 1.2.
[117] Drazin, *History of Jewish Education*, 27.

the sake of reward. And the fear of Heaven should be upon you."[118] This admonishes the disciple who studies under a master to recognize that it is his duty before God to learn, keep, and teach Torah. Additional examples of the essential task of teaching and learning come from later teachers in an unbroken chain of masters and disciples. "Hillel [40 BCE to 10 CE] and Shammai received from them [from their masters who taught them]. Hillel would say: Be of the disciples of Aaron—a lover of peace, a pursuer of peace, one who loves the creatures and draws them close to Torah."[119] "Rabban Yochanan the son of Zakkai received the tradition from Hillel and Shammai. He would say: If you have learned much Torah, do not take credit for yourself—it is for this that you have been formed."[120]

History books are relatively silent about the religious-educational experience of the Jewish people from the time of Ezra, Nehemiah, and Malachi until the second century BCE. However, the results of the educational work of Ezra and the Men of the Great Assembly and the passing on of Torah education from one generation to the next are evidenced in later centuries within the Jewish populations of Jerusalem and Judea. Drazin supports this view by stating:

> "Aware, however, of the creative genius of the Jewish people in literature, in religious and moral law during the several centuries following the establishment of the Second Commonwealth one may reasonably conjecture that there would be a good educational system capable of producing such results. So, too, the persistence and preservation of the Jewish nationality to this day may presumably be traced to certain elements in the educational system of the Jews."[121]

H. H. Ben-Sasson continues this line of reasoning by adding:

> "Perhaps the most important of [the factors leading to the success of the Hasmonean revolt against the Seleucid rule from 167 BCE to 142 BCE] was the boundless loyalty of the Jewish masses to their religion. The ideals that had evolved in Jerusalem and Judea during the centuries preceding had penetrated the

---

[118] *Ethics of the Fathers* 1.3.
[119] *Ethics of the Fathers* 1.12.
[120] *Ethics of the Fathers* 2.8.
[121] Drazin, *History of Jewish Education*, 2.

masses of the nation. The Torah had become part of the everyday life of tens of thousands of farmers in Judea and was regarded as an essential element in their existence."[122]

Ezra and the Soferim began a religious reform through educating the people in Torah, their inheritance. This reform had a lasting and growing impact in each successive generation of Jews in the land of Israel and abroad.

The Master-Disciple Model

The men of the Great Assembly understood their responsibility to provide educational opportunities for succeeding generations, ensuring the ongoing survival and well-being of the Jewish people. Fulfilling this responsibility required raising up teachers including those like Ezra who would be able to spiritually lead the people. The master-disciple relationship was the means of raising up successive generations of teachers and spiritual leaders.

The Torah provides the master-disciple example of Moses and Joshua. Moses led and taught the children of Israel, giving God's instruction to the priests and elders. However, it was Joshua who gave himself as a disciple to Moses, serving Moses from the days of his youth (Exod. 24:13; Num. 11:28). Wherever Moses went, Joshua served him. Because he became a servant to Moses, he was the one to hear the voice of God and lead the people after Moses died. The master-disciple relationship had prepared Joshua to receive Moses's mantle to lead Israel (Deut. 34:9). Yet even after Joshua was commissioned by the LORD to lead Israel, he still held the honor of being referred to as Moses's servant (Josh. 1:1).

Another biblical example of the master-disciple relationship is that of Elijah and Elisha. Elijah ministered to the northern kingdom of Israel and presided over the schools of prophets which were likely started by Samuel. When the LORD called Elisha to serve Elijah, he left his former way of life to follow Elijah and minister to his needs (1 Kings 19:19-21). Elisha became a spiritual son to Elijah (2 Kings 2:12). In this relationship, he learned the teaching and ways of the LORD.

---

[122]Ben-Sasson, *A History of the Jewish People*, 206.

When Elijah was taken up to heaven, Elisha received a double portion of the mantle and anointing that had rested on Elijah (2 Kings 2:9-15) and with this mantle he carried on the ministry of Elijah. As a result, Elisha had the honor of being known as the one "who poured water on the hands of Elijah" (2 Kings 3:11).

The *Ethics of the Fathers* is careful to provide a record of the master-disciple relationships that preserved and passed on leadership in Torah knowledge to future generations:

> "Shimon the Righteous was among the last surviving members of the Great Assembly ... Antignos of Socho received the tradition from Shimon the Righteous ... Yossei the son of Yoezer of Tzreidah, and Yossei the son of Yochanan of Jerusalem, received the tradition from them ... Joshua the son of Perachia and Nitai the Arbelite received from them. ... Judah the son of Tabbai and Shimon the son of Shotach received from them ... Shmaayah and Avtalyon received from them ... Hillel and Shammai received from them."[123]

Consequently, there was an unbroken succession of masters and disciples that continued from the Great Assembly into the first century CE.

A disciple is one who is taught. Isaiah 54:13 says, "All your children will be taught [as disciples] of the LORD." The disciple was committed to learn and freely give himself to serve his master, caring for his personal needs. He was willing to sacrifice and endure hardship for the sake of learning—learning through study and through observing his master's way of life. Brad Young adds, "In rabbinic literature the disciples of the sages neglect their business and sacrifice much to acquire Torah learning. ... He listens to his master's teaching while doing menial chores to assist his mentor. The master teacher was a mentor whose purpose was to raise up disciples who would not only memorize his teachings but also live out the teachings in practical ways."[124] By following the example of his master, the disciple was to become a living expression of Torah. He was expected to not only learn, but to keep and teach what he had learned. According to Ethics of the Fathers Rabbi Ishmael would say,

---

[123]*Ethics of the Fathers* 1.1, 1.2, 1.3, 1.4, 1.6, 1.8, 1.10, 1.12.
[124]Brad H. Young, *Meet the Rabbis: Rabbinic Thought and the Teachings of Jesus* (Grand Rapids: Baker Academics, 2007), 30

"One who learns Torah in order to teach is given the opportunity to learn and teach. One who learns in order to do is given the opportunity to learn, teach, observe and do."[125]

The disciple gave up family and professional life to devote his time to his master (1 Kings 19:19-21). To become a disciple of a respected teacher represented a great honor, so the family and community often rallied to help a young man realize his aspiration.[126] The passing on of the mantle of Torah was likened to bringing the learner into a new life; so masters were often referred to as "fathers" and disciples as "sons." Hillel, one of the disciples who became a master, said, "One who acquires the words of Torah has acquired life in the World to Come."[127]

The Written and Oral Law

In Jewish tradition the LORD gave Moses both the Written Torah as well as its oral application. The belief in divine inspiration not only of the Scriptures but also of the Oral Torah is central to the religious thought of rabbinic Judaism.[128] Cohen says, "It was claimed that the Oral Torah, equally with the Written Torah, goes back to the Revelation on Sanai, if not in detail at least in principle."[129] George Robinson adds:

> "The Men of the Great Assembly believed that there had been oral interpretation of Torah almost from the moment Moses came down from Mount Sinai with the tablets in his hands. After all, was it not said that God had given the Oral Law to Moses on Sinai as well as the Torah, the Written Law? That the Almighty had whispered it into his ear by day, explained its meaning by night for forty days and nights?"[130]

Throughout the Second Temple period, the masters and disciples in the Jewish community not only studied the Written Torah, but

---

[125] *Ethics of the Fathers* 4.5.
[126] Young, *Meet the Rabbis*, 31.
[127] *Ethics of the Fathers* 2.7.
[128] John C. Johnson, "Mishnah," ed. John D. Barry et al., *The Lexham Bible Dictionary* (Bellingham, WA: Lexham Press, 2016).
[129] Cohen, *Everyman's Talmud*, 146.
[130] Robinson, *Essential Judaism*, 313.

they memorized the Oral Torah as an explanation of the Written Word. It was passed on by memory from one generation of masters and disciples to the next. A summary of contributions to the oral interpretation by each generation of masters was added to the Oral Torah. Each succeeding generation was meticulous in the way they preserved the oral traditions and acknowledged the contribution of each teacher. These contributions were considered as having come from Moses, and the memorized oral tradition was preserved verbatim as if it had been written in text.[131] This oral tradition was later referred to as the Mishnah.[132]

Leading scribes, teachers, and sages were constantly faced with the task of making the Torah applicable to life. This was important for the exiles in Babylon as well as for those who had returned to their homeland. In many cases the written commandments were made relevant using the existing oral traditions. In some cases, as new situations arose, obscure or seemingly outdated aspects of the commandments were explained and made relevant through intense study of the Torah. This intensive study of the biblical text is called midrash.[133]

A primary concern of the interpreters in the Second Temple period was to uncover the meaning of the biblical texts. In this, they sought to demonstrate how the Torah could be applied in Jewish life considering their ever-changing circumstances.[134] The process of midrash became very sophisticated during the first century BCE. It began to generate a mass of interpretations and traditions that became interwoven with the fabric of the biblical text. These interpretations and traditions were taught in synagogues, studied in schools, and passed on from masters to disciples. The resulting compilations of midrashic commentaries on the biblical texts grew considerably through the first century CE.[135]

---

[131] Young, *Meet the Rabbis*, 109.
[132] *The Mishnah* is the compiled record of Oral Torah. Around 220 CE Rabbi Judah the Prince compiled a written version of this complex body of laws (Halakah) in order to preserve them for future generations.
[133] "Midrash" refers to the act of interpreting by analyzing the meaning of words in the Torah. The purpose of Midrash is to make connections between the changing current realities of life with the biblical text. Midrash Halakhah seeks to extend a law beyond the conditions assumed in the Bible, making connections between current-life practice and the biblical text. Midrash Aggadah explores ethical ideas, biblical characters, and biblical narratives.
[134] Julius J. Scott Jr., *Jewish Backgrounds of the New Testament* (Grand Rapids: Baker Academic, 1995), 127.
[135] Young, *Meet the Rabbis*, 103.

It is worth briefly noting that during the Second Temple period, the idea of oral teaching founded on written texts was also practiced in other cultures. In these cultures, the learning of the written text was considered basic education, while learning of the oral teaching was considered advanced education. The more sophisticated oral teaching prepared one culturally for professional careers such as teaching and politics.[136]

Hillel and the Early First Century CE

Hillel and his contemporary, Shammai, were the last of a group of teachers in the transmission of the Torah called the "pairs." After the time of the Great Assembly, the Written and Oral Torah were passed on from one pair of master teachers to another. Through the early first century CE the pairs were responsible for the leadership of the Sanhedrin.[137] The Sanhedrin was a group of seventy-one sages, including teachers, priests, and scribes who presided over the spiritual life of the Jewish people. One of the pairs was called the Nasi. The Nasi served as president of the Sanhedrin. Hillel held this position later in his life.[138]

Each of the pairs added to the growing body of Oral Law but none added as distinctively as the last pair, Shammai (c. 50 BCE–c. 30 CE) and Hillel (c. 70 BCE–c. 10 CE).[139] Hillel and Shammai presided over schools for the preparation of teachers who would be educated in the Written and Oral Torah. Both men were skilled in midrash and taught their students how to intensely study and interpret the Torah. Shammai and his school were known for their more strict interpretation of the Torah. Hillel and his school were known for their more moderate approach.[140] Through their schools, both Hillel and Shammai were faithful to the admonition of the Great Assembly to raise up many disciples. During the first century CE the leaders and disciples of these two schools often debated their interpretations and resulting applications of the Torah.[141]

---

[136]Richard A. Horsley, *Scribes, Visionaries, and the Politics of Second Temple Judea* (Louisville: Westminster John Knox Press, 2007), 107-108.
[137]Robinson, *Essential Judaism*, 314.
[138]Moore, *Judaism in the First Centuries of the Christian Era*, 79.
[139]Robinson, *Essential Judaism*, 314.
[140]Moore, *Judaism in the First Centuries of the Christian Era*, 79-81.
[141]Moore, *Judaism in the First Centuries of the Christian Era*, 79-81; and Cohen, *Everyman's Talmud*, xli.

Young observes, "Judaism was far from being the monolithic legal authority that forced one view upon the people. Respect and honor were accorded to divergent opinions, and this seems to be one reason why two leaders are described in the literature; scholarship requires debate and opposing views."[142]

Hillel was an example of intense hunger and commitment to study God's Word. He moved from Babylon at the age of forty to continue his studies at the academy in Jerusalem. At that time there were schools in Babylon and in other centers of Jewish population. It is believed that Hillel had been a student in his own country before he moved to Jerusalem to sit under the most eminent teachers and expositors of the time, Shemaiah and Avtalyon.[143] Hillel left his well-to-do family in Babylon and worked daily as a woodcutter, earning a small amount of wages. Half of the wages he earned was used for his bare needs and half was used for the admission fee to the academy of Shemaiah and Avtalyon.[144]

The example of Hillel is referenced in Jewish literature to show that even poverty is not an excuse for neglecting the study of Torah. One wintry day, Hillel had not earned any money and could not pay the required admission fee. So he climbed to the roof of the academy where he could listen to the words of instruction. That day a heavy snow fell on Jerusalem. Later in the day, Hillel was found covered with snow on the skylight of the building. Because of Hillel's intense desire for Torah education, he was admitted to the academy daily and ultimately became one of the great sages of Israel.[145]

Hillel is famous for his seven rules of midrash, for his interpretation of the Scriptures and for the deduction of laws from them.[146] Halakah is the body of accepted traditions that have been derived through the intensive study of midrash and handed down by Jewish teachers. Hillel is credited with furthering the body of halachic interpretations of the Torah. George F. Moore explains, "His great significance in the history of Judaism lies in the new impulse and direction he gave the study of the law, the new spirit he infused into Pharisaism."[147]

---

[142]Young, *Meet the Rabbis*, 136.
[143]Moore, *Judaism in the First Centuries of the Christian Era*, 77.
[144]Cohen, *Everyman's Talmud*, 136.
[145]Goldman, *Life-Long Learning Among the Jews*, 48.
[146]Cohen, *Everyman's Talmud*, xli.
[147]Moore, *Judaism in the First Centuries of the Christian Era*, 81.

During the teaching ministry of Hillel, a group of midrashim called *Tannaim* began to emerge.[148] The Tannaim or "repeaters" were known for their ability to memorize and repeat the Oral Torah.[149] There were many Tannaim in the early centuries of the common era. These rabbinic sages produced a growing amount of halachic interpretations through the time when Rabbi Judah the Prince compiled the Mishnah in 220 CE. Young states, "What had been preserved in the collective memory of disciples who were living books needed to be written. The Mishnah that Rabbi Judah compiled and edited contains the opinions and sayings of sages and rabbis from about 300 BCE to 220 CE."[150]

Pharisees—Education Versus Culture

Under the kings of Babylon and Persia, conquered nations were generally allowed to keep their religious traditions. However, this policy of tolerance changed for the Jewish people when Greece conquered the Persian empire. Originally, the Greeks had a policy of non-intervention regarding the religious affairs of the people in the lands they ruled. However, over time, Greek influence began to be seen in Israel and Jerusalem, and mounting pressures for conformity were exerted by the Seleucid rulers.[151] This clash of cultures resulted in the Maccabean revolt (167 BCE) and the brief reestablishment of the kingdom of Israel under the Hasmoneans (142 BCE).[152]

Three influential schools of thought emerged during the Hasmonean rule: the Pharisees, the Sadducees, and the Essenes.[153] The Essenes established their own community in the Judean desert in order to practice a strict observance of the Torah. They attached great importance to the study of the Scriptures and are thought to be the group that assembled the Dead Sea Scrolls.[154] The Sadducees were comprised of the leading

---

[148] Cohen, *Everyman's Talmud*, xli.
[149] Drazin, *History of Jewish Education*, 36.
[150] Young, *Meet the Rabbis*, 83.
[151] Ben-Sasson, *A History of the Jewish People*, 181, 201-2015.
[152] Ben-Sasson, *A History of the Jewish People*, 206-215.
[153] Martin Goodman, "Jewish History, 331 BCE-135 CE," in *The Jewish Annotated New Testament*, ed. Amy-Jill Levine and Marc Zvi Brettler (New York: Oxford University Press, 2011), 507.
[154] Chad Brand et al., ed., "Essenes," *Holman Illustrated Bible Dictionary* (Nashville, TN: Holman Bible Publishers, 2003), 508.

priests and they controlled the Temple worship. They only recognized the Written Torah and their own application of the laws for the Temple, worship, and conduct. Many of the Sadducees were elitists who wanted to maintain the status of the priestly class, but they were also liberal in their willingness to incorporate Hellenism into their lives.[155] The Pharisees represented the common people and preached Jewish loyalty and holiness. They recognized the Oral Law as given by God to Moses at Sinai along with the Written Torah.[156] Consequently, they realized that the greatest threat to the survival of their nation was "the assimilatory trend toward Hellenism, which was rotting the very vitals of Jewish life. Jews were nullifying God's law."[157]

The Pharisee movement took control of the synagogues located throughout the communities of Judea and the Galilee, using them as a forum for religious education.[158] Israel Goldman states that by doing so, "the Pharisees stirred up a religious revival. They brought about a 'back-to-the-synagogue movement' whose chief exhortation may well have been: 'Back to the Torah!' Through such conditions in Jewish history, and through such insight and foresight of Jewish leadership, did the synagogue grow as the house of instruction in Jewish life."[159]

Education of the people in their inheritance, the Torah, was the only effective way to combat the pervasive influence of Hellenism (or any other culture). The Pharisees reinforced among the people the desire for learning and rehearsing their sacred history. They "built a fence around the Torah"[160] by instructing the people in the commands of the LORD and how to follow them. The Pharisees promoted a high regard for Torah study because "right actions require knowledge, [and] people lacking that knowledge will not know the proper way to behave. Thus, study takes precedence over action not because it is more important, but because without it, right behavior will not be maintained for long."[161]

---

[155] Moore, *Judaism in the First Centuries of the Christian Era*, 67-70.
[156] Moore, *Judaism in the First Centuries of the Christian Era*, 59-61, 66.
[157] Goldman, *Life-Long Learning Among the Jews*, 11.
[158] Charles W. Draper with Harrop Clayton, "Jewish Parties in the New Testament," ed. Chad Brand et al., *Holman Illustrated Bible Dictionary* (Nashville, TN: Holman Bible Publishers, 2003), 916-917.
[159] Goldman, *Life-Long Learning Among the Jews*, 12.
[160] *Ethics of the Fathers* 1.1.
[161] Joseph Telushkin, *Jewish Wisdom: Ethical, Spiritual, and Historical Lessons from the Great Works and Thinkers* (New York: HarperCollins e-books, 1994), 339.

The Pharisees carried on an educational trend that had its beginnings in the Persian period under Ezra and the *Soferim*.[162] Under the Pharisees and their predecessors, the study of Torah was made available for the whole of the people, and Torah scholarship now also emerged from the non-priestly classes. Ben-Sasson explains:

> "The study of Torah and the development of the halakhah, which determined the patterns of everyday life in Hasmonean Judea, attracted the [best] of the nation's intellectual and spiritual elements, who devoted their lives to it. Even in the generations preceding the [Maccabean] revolt, the study of Torah and the shaping of the nation's spiritual life had, in practice, ceased to be the exclusive affair of the priests and had become the concern of men who did not belong to the priestly caste. Whoever was willing could achieve the status of Torah scholar."[163]

As a final thought, it should be noted that most of the prominent scribes and teachers in the later Second Temple period were part of the Pharisee movement; however, the bulk of the Pharisees were not scholars.[164] Many of the Pharisees were common laborers who devoted their spare time to studying and teaching. The common people treated the Pharisees as authorized teachers.[165] It was from the Pharisee movement that Rabbinic Judaism developed in the first century CE.[166]

The Synagogue

The synagogue as an institution may have emerged as early as the Babylonian captivity. Synagogues were designated places where the Jewish communities could gather together socially, and for the dispensing of justice, and for worship and prayer.[167] The pattern for the synagogue may have evolved from various meetings that were led by

---

[162]Ben-Sasson, *A History of the Jewish People*, 235.
[163]Ben-Sasson, *A History of the Jewish People*, 234.
[164]Moore, *Judaism in the First Centuries of the Christian Era*, 66.
[165]James Bauckham, *The Book of Acts In Its First Century Setting: Volume 4, Palestinian Setting* (Grand Rapids, MI: William B. Eerdmans Publishing Company, 1995), 176.
[166]Ben-Sasson, *A History of the Jewish People*, 235.
[167]Cohen, *Everyman's Talmud*, xxxiii-xxxiv.

An Introduction to Education in Bible Times

Israel's prophets and teachers: by the prophets before the exile as they taught and conducted worship in various cities (1 Sam. 7:15-17), from instructional events where teaching priests would travel from town to town and read the Torah to the people (2 Chron. 17:5-9), and from the home assemblies of the prophets during the Babylonian exile (Ezek. 8:1; 20:1).

By the time of Ezra, the public reading of Scripture was becoming a prominent aspect of Jewish life. Every Sabbath the people assembled to hear a section of the Scripture read aloud and explained. Jewish tradition attributes the public reading of Scripture on the Sabbath to Moses. The first century Jewish historian Josephus recounts that Moses "appointed the Law to be the most excellent and necessary form of instruction, not that it should be heard once for all or twice or on several occasions, but that every week men should desert their other occupations and assemble to listen to the Law."[168] Goldman underscores the reason for this weekly emphasis on God's Word: "The Jew must know! Without knowledge he cannot truly worship God. Without mastering the contents of his people's religious literature, he cannot possibly lead the Jewish good life. From its very beginnings, therefore, one of the supreme functions of the synagogue was to serve not only as a house of prayer but also as a school of instruction."[169]

Here it is helpful to note that the synagogues of the Second Temple period were not likely the same as the ones developed after the fall of Jerusalem in 70 CE. While there is not much archaeological evidence of pre-70 CE synagogue buildings, some scholars conclude that more simple structures or rooms attached to other buildings were used for these meeting places; and that these meeting places grew more and more prominent during the Second Temple period (530 B.C.E – 70 CE), and especially by the time of the first century BCE.[170]

While the synagogue was not considered a substitute for the Temple worship, it did become integral to the spiritual life of the

---

[168] Josephus, *Against Apion* 2.17.
[169] Goldman, *Life-Long Learning Among the Jews*, 11.
[170] See Rainer Riesner, "Synagogues in Jerusalem," In *The Book of Acts In Its First Century Setting: Volume 4, Palestinian Setting*, ed. James Bauckham (Grand Rapids: Eerdmans, 1995),180-187. Also see Lee Levine, and I. Levine, "The Synagogue," in *The Jewish Annotated New Testament*, ed. Amy-Jill Levine and Marc Zvi Brettler (New York: Oxford University Press, 2011), 519-521. Also see Ben-Sasson, *A History of the Jewish People*, 285.

Jewish communities.[171] The synagogue eventually developed into an institution of public education for all people. First, Ezra increased the number of times devoted to Torah instruction each week. Goldman adds, "In addition to the readings on Sabbath mornings, he prescribed the reading on Monday and Thursday mornings and at the afternoon service on the Sabbath so that three days could never pass without some public instruction in the Torah."[172] Second, synagogues were established throughout the towns of Israel, in Judea and Galilee, and in the cities of other countries where Jews were living.[173] Third, the Pharisees used the synagogues to bring Torah education to the people.

The establishment of synagogues opened the door for universal Torah education for the Jewish people.[174] Luke, the first century writer of the book of Acts says, "Moses from ancient generations has in every city those who preach him, since he is read in the synagogues every Sabbath" (Acts 15:21). There is little doubt that by the first century CE, Torah reading was the center of the synagogue services and all adults were expected to attend and participate.[175] According to Moses Maimonides, Mishna Torah, Hilkot Talmud Torah 1:8:

> "Every person in Israel is obligated to be engaged in Torah learning, whether one is poor or wealthy, whether one is whole in body or afflicted with suffering, whether one is young or one is old and feeble, even a poor person who is supported by charity and goes from door to door seeking benevolence, even the man supporting his wife and children—everyone is required to find a set time during the day and the night to study Torah, as it was said, 'you shall go over it, again and again, day and night (Joshua 1:8).'"

Along with the reading of Scripture, sermons became an educational strategy for the synagogue services.[176] As the Scriptures were read in Hebrew, they were translated into the common language of the people. Then a sermon was employed to provide an exposition of the readings.

---

[171] Scott Jr., *Jewish Backgrounds of the New Testament*, 139.
[172] Goldman, *Life-Long Learning Among the Jews*, 16.
[173] Moore, *Judaism in the First Centuries of the Christian Era*, 283-284.
[174] R. Riesner, "Teacher," ed. Joel B. Green and Scot McKnight, *Dictionary of Jesus and the Gospels* (Downers Grove: InterVarsity Press, 1992), 808.
[175] Levine, "The Synagogue," 521.
[176] Goldman, *Life-Long Learning Among the Jews*, 18.

These expositions helped the people to study and think creatively about the meaning and application of God's Word. This pattern of reading and teaching is first seen when Ezra read the Torah to the people. The Levites "explained the law to the people while the people remained in their place. They read from the book, from the law of God, translating to give the sense so that they understood the reading" (Neh. 8:7-8). This same pattern was used by teachers in the synagogue services.[177]

As the canon of the Tanakh became more established, additional Scripture readings were added to the synagogue services. These included readings from the Prophets and prayers based on the Psalms. At a minimum, adults in the synagogues had access to the most important scrolls of Scripture (the Torah, Isaiah, and the Psalms).[178] One final development in the synagogue service was the increased involvement of the people in the Sabbath worship. In the first century CE most adult males could take part in leading prayer, reading a Scripture passage, and providing an explanation and application of the passage.[179] The educational training given to children and young adults, and the lifelong learning afforded by the synagogue services created a well-educated adult population. The Gospels give an example of this kind of participation in the synagogue services when Jesus was handed the book of Isaiah to read from.

> *And He came to Nazareth, where He had been brought up; and as was His custom, He entered the synagogue on the Sabbath, and stood up to read. And the book of the prophet Isaiah was handed to Him. And He opened the book and found the place where it was written,* **"THE SPIRIT OF THE LORD IS UPON ME, BECAUSE HE ANOINTED ME TO PREACH THE GOSPEL TO THE POOR. HE HAS SENT ME TO PROCLAIM RELEASE TO THE CAPTIVES, AND RECOVERY OF SIGHT TO THE BLIND, TO SET FREE THOSE WHO ARE OPPRESSED, TO PROCLAIM THE FAVORABLE YEAR OF THE LORD."** *And He closed the book, gave it back to the attendant and sat down; and the eyes of all in the synagogue were fixed on Him. And He began to say to them, "Today this Scripture has been fulfilled in your hearing."*

---

[177]Michael Graves, "The Public Reading of Scripture in Early Judaism." In *Journal of the Evangelical Theological Society* 50/3 (September 2007), 480-481.
[178]Riesner, "Teacher," 808.
[179]Riesner, "Teacher," 808.

And all were speaking well of Him, and wondering at the gracious words which were falling from His lips.

Luke 4:16–22

Drazin concludes, "Adult education was widespread and popular among the Jews. Every Jew knew that he was obligated by sacred Law to study Torah every day of his life. Consequently, many men, even artisans and industrial workers, reserved part of every day for study."[180] By the time of the New Testament, the synagogue was a central part of Jewish life, and synagogue schools were a vital part of Jewish communities.

Schools

The second great institution of Jewish education was the school. In some form or other, schools for teaching and learning Torah existed before synagogues.[181] Education focused primarily on the study of the Torah: to read it, memorize it, study it, interpret it, walk in it, and teach it. Certainly the priests and sages received a considerable amount of education in order to be able to carry out their religious duties and to teach the people.

Schools as a more organized institution of learning developed in the Second Temple period. By the middle of the first century CE there were colleges, secondary schools, and elementary schools in Judea and Galilee. While formalized education in schools evolved throughout this period, parents still carried the primary responsibility for instructing their children; community synagogues offered lifelong learning opportunities for adults; and sages trained disciples to pass on their mantle of Torah leadership.

Colleges

The scholars of the Great Assembly believed it was necessary to establish colleges in Jerusalem. They recognized the necessity of raising up many disciples, other sages who would be able to lead and teach future generations. However, while a master could teach a few disciples, colleges had the potential of teaching a greater number of students. According to

---
[180]Drazin, *History of Jewish Education from 515 B.C.E. to 220 C.E.*, 76.
[181]Moore, *Judaism in the First Centuries of the Christian Era*, 308.

Jewish literature, a college building was constructed in Jerusalem before the end of the Soferim period.[182] This school building was known as the *bet hamidrash*, the house of study, and was adjacent to the Temple. It housed the centralized college of higher learning at Jerusalem and continued as the main college in Jerusalem until the founding of the two rival schools of Hillel and Shammai at the beginning of the first century CE.[183]

The reason for the college being adjacent to the Temple may have been to merge the formal education with the practical administration of the Law by the Sanhedrin and with the actual service of worship in the Temple. Drazin recognizes that the Jewish scholars "felt that the sacred ceremonials and service of the Temple would have a psychological effect upon the students, influencing them to become God-fearing as well as more industrious in the pursuit of their studies."[184] In addition, being built on the Temple Mount, the college would be accessible for members of the Sanhedrin as well as for the priests and Levites serving in the Temple.

Admission fees were required for attendance in the college at Jerusalem; however, an exception to this rule included a provision of free admission for the priests and Levites, because higher education was necessary to fulfill their duties in the Temple and they typically did not earn enough to pay these fees. The practice of charging admission fees continued until Hillel was appointed as president of the college.[185]

Students who successfully completed their college education were ordained as rabbis. Drazin explains this process:

> "The master [of the college] would officially lay his hand on the head of the student and declare him ordained. This ordination, smicha in Hebrew, gave to the student the title of Rabbi, master or zaken, elder. It gave him also the authority to render decisions in questions of Jewish Law. It declared him, furthermore, to be an important link in the unbroken chain of tradition that was continuous from Moses, the law-giver of Israel. He could [also] be elected to the Sanhedrin."[186]

---

[182]The time of the Soferim is believed to have begun during the time of Ezra and continued until the time of Shimon the Righteous (about 300 BCE), who was the last of the men of the Great Assembly. Some believe that the time of the Soferim continued until about 200 BCE.
[183]Drazin, *History of Jewish Education.* 42, 57.
[184]Drazin, *History of Jewish Education*, 57.
[185]Drazin, *History of Jewish Education*, 51.
[186]Drazin, *History of Jewish Education.*, 70-71.

CHRISTOPHER J. REEVES

Secondary Schools

There were two factors that led to the establishment of secondary schools. First, the college in Jerusalem had a high entrance requirement and there were not enough qualified young students who were able to enter college studies. This highlighted a need to supplement the parental and community education that young adults were receiving. The second factor was a result of the Maccabean victories which encouraged a revival of Jewish culture. Many young adults now desired further education in Torah. However, they were not far enough advanced in their studies to gain admission to the college in Jerusalem. This growing need for young adults to become qualified to enter college precipitated the establishment of secondary schools.

During the time of the Maccabees (approximately 164 to 63 BCE), careful attention was given to education. Simon b. Shetah (120 to 40 BCE) was a scholar of the Pharisees, a teacher of Torah, and president of the Sanhedrin. In about 75 BCE under Simon's leadership, a "two-level" school system was instituted for the first time in the history of the Jewish people. This two-level system consisted of the Jerusalem college for advanced students and the free preparatory "secondary schools" which were spread throughout the lands in which Jews lived.[187] (This is evidenced by Hillel's educational preparation in Babylon before moving to Israel to attend the Jerusalem college.[188]) These secondary schools, A. W. Streane explains, "may be regarded as the first general attempt on the part of the nation to encourage rabbinical scholarship, and to draw youths of promise to professional careers."[189]

In identifying where to establish secondary schools, synagogues became the logical solution. Synagogues had already been established throughout the Jewish communities. Since synagogue services were conducted in the early mornings and late afternoons and evenings, the buildings were unoccupied during much of the midday. As a result, they quickly became utilized for housing the new secondary schools.[190] The synagogue which had been known as bet hakeneset,

---

[187] Drazin, *History of Jewish Education from 515 B.C.E. to 220 C.E.*, 43.
[188] Moore, *Judaism in the First Centuries of the Christian Era*, 321.
[189] A. W. Streane, *The Age of the Maccabees* (London: Eyre and Spottiswoode, 1898), 74.
[190] Drazin, *History of Jewish Education*, 60.

the house of assembly, now also became known as bet hamidrash, the house of study.[191]

Elementary Schools

The education of children was the responsibility of parents. Some parents were able to hire tutors or pay for private school; but since a child was taught by his parents, orphans were left without education. Simon b. Shetah established the first elementary schools in the first century BCE.[192] Shetah began the practice that "teachers of children be appointed in Jerusalem; and a father (who resided outside the city) would bring his child there and have him taught, but the orphan was again left without tuition."[193] Jewish leaders were not satisfied with the reality that elementary education for children was restricted to parents who had the ability teach them or who had the means to hire a teacher or pay tuition.[194] Without an adequate elementary education in the ancient Hebrew language and the ability to read the Torah, children would not be able to progress into the secondary schools. By the time of the New Testament, elementary schools were being made available for families.[195]

Further opportunities occurred when Joshua b. Gamala[196] realized that not all villages had elementary education and not all families were able to have their children attend. In 54 CE, he instituted a reform that established free elementary schools for all boys. The Talmud says that he "instituted that teachers should be appointed in every province and in every city, and children about the age of six or seven placed in their charge (B. B. 21a)."[197]

The training provided in the elementary school system was unique for its time. Youth were taught reading and writing from

---

[191]Moore, *Judaism in the First Centuries of the Christian Era*, 314.
[192]Robinson, *Essential Judaism*, 155.
[193]Cohen, *Everyman's Talmud*, 174.
[194]Moore, *Judaism in the First Centuries of the Christian Era*, 316.
[195]William Barclay, *Train Up A Child: Educational Ideals in the Ancient World* (Philadelphia: Westminster Press, 1959), 15.
[196]Gamala was "a high priest who officiated about 64 C.E. ... Although Joshua himself was not a scholar, he was solicitous for the instruction of the young, and provided schools in every town for children over five years of age, earning thereby the praises of posterity (B. B. 21a)." By Richard Gottheil and Samuel Krauss, "Joshua (Jesus) Ben Gamla," *Jewish Encyclopedia*, accessed January 28, 2019, http://www.jewishencyclopedia.com/articles/8912-joshua-jesus-ben-gamla.
[197]Cohen, *Everyman's Talmud*, 174.

the holy Scriptures, usually by the person who oversaw synagogue activities.[198] Parents were publicly notified and made to realize that the religious obligation of teaching their children Torah could only be properly satisfied by sending their boys to these elementary schools to receive daily instruction by fully qualified and competent teachers.[199] Eventually, throughout the villages of Judea and Galilee communities were expected to establish and maintain these elementary schools. The community was responsible for financing the education of poor or orphaned children as well.[200]

School Buildings and Class Sizes

When secondary and elementary schools started, accommodations were made in the numerous synagogues located in the larger towns of Judea and Galilee and the other lands where Jews resided in large numbers.[201] Some schools operated in special buildings and others in the teachers' own houses, but most schools were attached to a synagogue. Many synagogues provided space for both primary and secondary students. In larger towns the community was expected to provide two school buildings for reasons of commuting distance and class size.

Class sizes were expected to be around twenty-five students, with a teacher and an assistant for forty students, or two teachers for fifty students. Students sat on the ground at the teacher's feet to learn the Scriptures and Oral Law.[202] Drazin says that during the first century CE, "there were four hundred and eighty synagogues in Jerusalem and each had its own *bet sefer* and its own *bet Talmud, bet sefer* for *Mikra* (elementary education) and bet *Talmud* for *Mishnah* (secondary education)."[203]

---

[198]Riesner, "Teacher," 808.
[199]Drazin, *History of Jewish Education*, 46.
[200]Walter A. Elwell and Barry J. Beitzel, *Baker Encyclopedia of the Bible* (Grand Rapids: Baker Book House, 1988), 657–661.
[201]Drazin, *History of Jewish Education*, 60.
[202]Cohen, *Everyman's Talmud*, 176; Elwell and Beitzel, *Baker Encyclopedia of the Bible*, 657–661.
[203]Drazin, *History of Jewish Education*, 61.

An Introduction to Education in Bible Times

The Basic Educational Program

Philo notes that the Jews "from their very swaddling clothes are taught by parents and teachers and masters, and above all by their sacred laws and unwritten customs, to acknowledge one God, the father and creator of the world."[204] The Jewish educational system had as its ultimate goal the intimate knowledge of God. Education consisted of learning the Written and Oral Torah and knowing the history of the Jewish people. In their studies, students became proficient in reading Hebrew, writing, and a certain amount of arithmetic.[205] Children memorized large sections of the Torah "because the vowelless Hebrew texts could be recited error-free and with the right emphasis only through memorization."[206]

The learning of Scripture and oral traditions consisted of repetition. The mechanics of learning required the teacher to listen to the student repeat the lesson back to him verbatim. As Cohen adds:

> "Although books of reading were used and the art of writing was cultivated, materials were costly and scarce, and learning meant memorization by constant repetition. 'The teacher must keep on repeating the lesson until the pupil has learnt it' (Erub. 54b); and as for the student, 'If he learns Torah and does not go over it again and again, he is like a man who sows without reaping' (Sanh. 99a). 'One who repeats his lesson a hundred times is not like him who repeats it a hundred and one times' (Chag. 9b)."[207]

The basic educational program for children consisted of learning selected Bible texts. At a bare minimum, children were expected to master the following:

- The Shema - Deuteronomy 6:4–9, 11:13-21, and Numbers 15:37–41.
- The Hallel (praise to God) consisting of Psalms 113 through 118. These were recited during feasts, festivals, and special occasions.
- The Story of Creation

---

[204] Philo, *Embassy*, 16.115.
[205] Elwell and Beitzel, *Baker Encyclopedia of the Bible*, 657–661.
[206] Riesner, "Teacher," 809.
[207] Cohen, *Everyman's Talmud*, 176.

- The Essence of the Levitical Law
- A Personal Text

It is of interest to note that beginning in the first century CE, scholars and teachers were called Tannaim (repeaters, reciters) because of their ability to recite the oral traditions from memory.

When a young person was able to read and study the Law in more detail, instruction began with the book of Leviticus. William Barclay explains, "Even after the destruction of the Temple, when sacrifice had been rendered impossible, Leviticus remained the beginning of detailed education. As a Midrash beautifully described: 'Sacrifices are pure; and children are pure; let the pure be occupied with that which is pure.'" [208]

According to a later entry in the *Ethics of the Fathers*, "Five years is the age for the study of Scripture. Ten, for the study of Mishnah. Thirteen, for the obligation to observe the mitzvot. Fifteen, for the study of Talmud."[209] Elementary education for children ages five to ten became known as *bet sefer* for *Mikra*. Mikra emphasizes the educational focus on the written text of Torah. Then after a thorough study of the Written Torah came the study of the Oral Torah. This was based on oral teaching and involved repeating for memorization. Secondary education for youth ages ten to fifteen became known as *bet Talmud* for *Mishnah*. Mishnah means the educational focus on "that which is repeated."[210]

Afterwards, colleges built upon educational foundations of the primary and secondary schools, where students studied under one of the principle sages and developed their skills in Midrash, Halakhah, and Haggadah. Midrash refers to the act of interpreting by analyzing the meaning of words in the Torah to derive from it, or to confirm by it, the rules of the Oral Law; Halakah refers to the precisely formulated rule itself; and Haggadah refers to the study of Torah's religious, ethical, and historical teachings. Moore points out that even a moderate proficiency in Mishnah, Halakah, and Haggadah "was not to be attained without long and patient years of learning; mastery demanded unusual capacity."[211]

In conclusion, the priority of educating all the people created a unique and lasting system of universal education. The basic educational

---

[208] Barclay, *Train Up A Child*, 42–43.
[209] *Ethics of the Fathers* 5.22.
[210] Barclay, *Train Up A Child*, 39-40.
[211] Moore, *Judaism in the First Centuries of the Christian Era*, 319.

program consisted of learning to read and study the written Scripture by memorizing large portions of it. It included memorizing the Oral Torah and learning its application to life. Prayers were memorized as well as the sacred history of the Jewish people. Added to this were the daily experiences of family and community life where they studied, prayed, celebrated the Sabbaths and the feasts, and observed the commands of the LORD. Continuing education for adults was afforded by the synagogues, and individuals with the means and capacity continued their education in the colleges.

Integrating Secular with Religious Knowledge

Learning Torah was the basis of understanding the world the LORD God had created, and it taught the Jews how to successfully live in community within that world. Wisdom, understanding, and success in life's endeavors were associated with the study of Torah and its observance (Ps. 1:2-3; Prov. 3:1-26). Moses told the children of Israel, "So keep and do them, for that is your wisdom and your understanding in the sight of the peoples who will hear all these statutes and say, 'Surely this great nation is a wise and understanding people'" (Deut. 4:6). The following quote from *History of Jewish Education* describes the integration of secular knowledge with Torah study.

> "Secular knowledge was brought to the child not as separate bits of knowledge, but in relation to the Law. In studying, for example, the laws of permitted and forbidden foods, one learned directly and indirectly many facts about botany, zoology, physiology, anatomy, hygiene, and medicine as may be evidenced by the extant work, the Mishnah. To understand the Jewish calendar, the child had to be made familiar with certain elements of astronomy. So, too, in studying the laws pertaining to distances that one was permitted to walk on the Sabbath, the pupil learned certain facts of arithmetic and geometry. The narrative portions of the Bible supplied the child with certain facts of history and geography. Thus the study of Torah completely integrated life."[212]

---

[212]Drazin, *History of Jewish Education*, 14.

Apprenticeships

It is important to note at this point something about apprenticeships. One could say that almost all learning occurred through this relational method of instruction. As already noted, children were mentored in Torah education by their parents and teachers. Additionally, children learned other skills like mathematics and number sense while studying the application of Torah regulations in how their fathers measured and calculated while building, or how their mothers counted money at the market. Girls learned how to prepare food by helping their mothers and sisters. The method of learning practical skills and any Torah regulations related to them was through observing and imitating those who possessed the skills.[213]

Specialized vocational training was achieved through the method of apprenticeship.[214] Most young adults followed the trades and professions of their fathers. Upon completing formal schooling at the age of thirteen, a boy would begin apprenticeship in the family trade. Ann Spangler and Lois Tverberg continue this thought:

> "Sometimes a father would apprentice his son to another craftsman and the boy would move into his master's home for a number of years. Working all day at his mentor's side, he would perform menial chores, gradually gaining know-how as he observed the craftsman's expert hands. Learning was not so much about retaining data as it was about gaining essential skills and wisdom for living, absorbing it from those around him."[215]

The practical skills learned through apprenticeship were situated in the context of imparted wisdom through hearing and observing the mentor in the conduct of their life.

---

[213] Drazin, *History of Jewish Education*, 14-15.
[214] Drazin, *History of Jewish Education*, 14.
[215] Ann Spangler and Lois Tverberg, *Sitting at the Feet of Rabbi Jesus: How the Jewishness of Jesus Can Transform Your Faith* (Grand Rapids: Zondervan, 2009), 53.

An Introduction to Education in Bible Times

Community Teachers

The Jews maintained high regard for Moses and the earlier priests, prophets, and scribes. This high regard and the value placed on education gave great dignity to the profession of teaching. Teaching was one of life's highest callings and learning from a teacher was one of life's greatest gifts. According to Ethics of the Fathers, "Yossei the son of Yoezer of Tzreidah [one of the early Sages] would say: Let your home be a meeting place for the wise; dust yourself in the soil of their feet, and drink thirstily of their words."[216]

The person who worked as a teacher in expounding the Law was considered the most important person in the community. The rabbis reasoned that a teacher had "precedence even over a parent, 'because the parent only brings the child to the life of this world, whereas the teacher brings him to the life of the World to come' (B. M. II. I I)."[217] In the language of the Second Temple period disciples were called banim, "sons" or "children."[218] Likewise, if someone other than the father had to assume the responsibility of teaching a child, that person was considered his father.

Moses was an example to the people, and in like manner teachers were also to be examples. They were expected to walk in uprightness and preserve knowledge as messengers from the LORD (Mal. 2:7). The highest ethical qualifications were required of a teacher.[219] So in choosing a rabbi as a village teacher, the community was more concerned with his personal character than with his ability to teach. Ronald Youngblood and colleagues stated:

> "The ideal rabbi was a married man who also was industrious and serious. He would never joke with the boys, nor would he tolerate any wrongdoing. However, it was considered important that he be a patient man. Both rabbi and parents took God as their model for proper teaching. God was the Master Teacher (Is. 30:20–21), who taught by word and example (Ps. 78:1; Deut. 8:2 3)."[220]

---

[216] *Ethics of the Fathers* 1.4.
[217] Cohen, *Everyman's Talmud*, 175.
[218] Young, *Meet the Rabbis*, 31.
[219] Elwell and Beitzel, *Baker Encyclopedia of the Bible*, 657–661
[220] Ronald F. Youngblood, F. F. Bruce, and R. K. Harrison, ed., "Education," *Nelson's New Illustrated Bible Dictionary* (Nashville: Thomas Nelson, 1995).

Finally, Cohen presents the following story to express the importance of the teacher in Jewish society:

> "Rab came to a certain place where he ordained a fast because there was a drought. The precentor of the congregation conducted the service, and when he uttered the words, "He causes the wind to blow," the wind at once blew; and when he uttered the words, "He causes the rain to fall," at once the rain fell! Rab said to him, "What is your exceptional merit?" He answered, "I am an elementary teacher, and I instruct the children of the poor exactly the same as I teach the children of the rich. If anyone is unable to pay me a fee I forgo it; also I have a fish-pond, and when I find a pupil negligent in his studies, I bribe him with some of the fish so that he comes regularly to learn" (Taan. 24a)."[221]

Studying in Relationship

The process of education was accomplished in family relationships and in the relationship with a teacher and other students. This can be seen in the pattern of teaching and learning in the synagogues, community schools, or colleges, as well as with masters who would take on a group of disciples. The early rabbinic sages discussed the value of studying in relationship: "Joshua the son of Perachia would say: Assume for yourself a master, acquire for yourself a friend, and judge every man to the side of merit."[222] Additionally, "Hillel would say: Do not separate yourself from the community."[223] Further, "Rabbi Chanina son of Tradyon would say: two who sit and exchange words of Torah, the Divine Presence rests amongst them."[224] Finally, "Ben Zoma would say: Who is wise? One who learns from every man. As is stated: 'From all my teachers I have grown wise, for Your testimonials are my meditation.'"[225]

> *Then those who feared the LORD* **spoke to one another**, *and the LORD gave attention and heard it, and a book of remembrance was*

---
[221]Cohen, *Everyman's Talmud*, 139.
[222]*Ethics of the Fathers* 1.6.
[223]*Ethics of the Fathers* 2.4.
[224]*Ethics of the Fathers* 3.2.
[225]*Ethics of the Fathers* 4.1.

written before Him for those who fear the LORD and who esteem His name. "They will be Mine," says the LORD of hosts, "on the day that I prepare My own possession, and I will spare them as a man spares his own son who serves him" [emphasis added].

Malachi 3:16–17

Two key elements of biblical education are highlighted in this passage from Malachi: the fear (reverence) of the LORD which is the foundation for all learning; and learning in a community that teaches and studies the Word of God together.

The Value and Impact of Education in the First Century CE

The Jewish people knew that the Torah was given to them by God and that it was a sign of His love. Rabbi Akiva said in *Ethics of the Fathers*:

"Beloved are Israel, for they were given a precious article; it is a sign of even greater love that it has been made known to them that they were given a precious article, as it is stated: 'I have given you a good purchase; My Torah, do not forsake it' (Proverbs 4:2)."[226]

With the great gift of receiving the Torah from God came great personal and national responsibility. The well-being of their community and the well-being of creation rested on their keeping God's Word. Cohen emphasizes this concept:

"The thought that the world-order is dependent upon Torah is conveyed in this way: The Holy One, blessed be He, made a condition with the works of Creation and said to them, 'If Israel accepts the Torah you will endure; if not I will reduce you again to chaos' (Shab. 88a). That only in its atmosphere can the human being lead a wholesome, ethical existence is derived from

---

[226] *Ethics of the Fathers* 3.14.

the text, 'Thou makest men as the fishes of the sea' (Hab. 1:14): 'Why are men likened to fishes? To tell you that as the fishes in the sea immediately perish when they come up to dry land, so do men immediately perish when they separate themselves from the words of the Torah' (A. Z. 3b)."[227]

It was considered the highest duty and privilege of the Jewish people to study the Torah. The study of God's Word was considered a lifelong endeavor. They were to be diligent in their educational pursuit, making it a permanent fixture in their life.[228] The Jews continually studied to learn about God and His ways as they would "turn it (the Torah) and turn it over again, for everything is in it; and contemplate it, and wax grey and old over it; and stir not from it."[229]

Jewish education was entirely religious education with no textbook except the Scriptures and the living memory of the teachers. The goal of Jewish education was to train disciples in the ways of God based on a detailed knowledge of the Written and Oral Torah.[230] Because a detailed understanding of the Torah allowed it to influence one's life, the study of it was elevated as an important religious obligation. Cohen emphasizes, "Indeed, it was in itself part of the service of God. The words, 'To love the LORD your God and to serve Him' (Deut. xi. 13), received the comment: 'to serve' means the study of Torah (Sifre Deut. 41; 80a)."[231] The impact of this education was so great that Philo said, "For all men hold their own customs, but this is especially true of the Jewish nation. Holding that the laws are oracles vouchsafed by God and having been trained in this doctrine from their earliest years they carry the likeness of the commandments enshrined in their souls."[232]

If Torah education was highly esteemed, so also was the education of children. The command to "teach them diligently to your children" was taken very seriously (Deut. 6:7). The Jewish historian Josephus made the observation, "Above all we pride ourselves on the education of our children, and regard as the most essential task in life the observance of our laws and the pious practices, based thereupon, which we have

---

[227] Cohen, *Everyman's Talmud*, 132.
[228] *Ethics of the Fathers* 2.14, 1.15.
[229] *Ethics of the Fathers* 5.21.
[230] Barclay, *Train Up A Child*, 13.
[231] Cohen, *Everyman's Talmud*, 135-136.
[232] Philo, *Embassy to Gaius*, 31 (210).

inherited."²³³ The result was that no other nation had ever set a higher priority of educating their children than did the Jews. Barclay added, "It would not be wrong to say that for the Jew the child was the most important person in the community."²³⁴

> *Behold, children are a gift of the LORD,*
> * The fruit of the womb is a reward.*
> *Like arrows in the hand of a warrior,*
> * So are the children of one's youth.*
> *How blessed is the man whose quiver is full of them;*
> * They will not be ashamed*
> * When they speak with their enemies in the gate.*
>   Psalm 127:3–5

The priority given to education stemmed from the value of children in the Jewish family. Children were considered a great joy and reward. Children were loved by their parents. There was no greater blessing than in the relationship of parents teaching their children. A parent teaching Torah to his or her children (and even grandchildren) was considered the same as if the children had received the Torah directly from Mount Sinai.²³⁵

Teaching children was the first step in a life that would be given to learn and walk in the ways of the LORD. One of the Jewish sages observed, "One who learns Torah in his childhood, what is this comparable to? To ink inscribed on fresh paper. One who learns Torah in his old age, what is this comparable to? To ink inscribed on erased paper."²³⁶ The Jews understood the importance of beginning the teaching process at a young age and sought for all children to have this opportunity.

The concern of leading Jewish sages that all children, including orphans, receive a quality education led to the establishment of schools. Their priority of educating all children is reflected in these quotes from the Talmud, "The world only exists through the breath of schoolchildren. ... We may not suspend the instruction of the children even for the rebuilding of the Temple. ... A city in which there are no schoolchildren will suffer destruction" (Shab. 119b).

---

[233] Josephus, *Against Apion*, 1.12 (60).
[234] Barclay, *Train Up A Child*, 11.
[235] Cohen, *Everyman's Talmud, 172-173.*
[236] *Ethics of the Fathers* 4.20.

Further, Moore acknowledges that the Jewish endeavor to provide education for everyone, young and old, created "a unique system of universal education, whose very elements comprised not only reading and writing, but an ancient language and its classic literature."[237] The outcome of this education was to be the knowledge of God, the knowledge of (and keeping of) His ways, and the ability to apply God's Word to new and unique situations in life. In New Testament times, so widespread and far-reaching was this education that Barclay called it an "age of the widest literacy for [the next] eighteen hundred years to come."[238]

Finally, as Robinson points out, it is worth noting that "from the period of the fall of the Second Temple until the Haskalah in the nineteenth century, most male Jews received at least some schooling and the rate of literacy among Jewish men was considerably higher than that in the general population."[239] Historical records from various periods of time show the continued educational methods and the corresponding literacy among Jewish populations.[240] Rabbi Jonathan Sacks recognized, "The quality of education varied from country to country and from century to century, but until the modern era there was virtually no Jewish community, however small, without its own school and teachers."[241] Looking back on the sustained community life of the Jewish people, Sacks noted it was their educational methods that continued to be at the center of their resilience throughout a history in which other religions and cultures would have long since disappeared.[242]

---

[237]Moore, *Judaism in the First Centuries of the Christian Era*, 322.
[238]Barclay, *Train Up A Child*, 14.
[239]Robinson, *Essential Judaism*, 155.
[240]Ben-Sasson, *A History of the Jewish People*, 517-527.
[241]Jonathan Sacks, *Ceremony and Celebration: Introduction to the Holidays* (New Milford: Maggid Books, 2017), 281.
[242]Sacks, *Ceremony and Celebration*, 193.

Part 4

EDUCATION IN THE LIFE AND MINISTRY OF JESUS

And He began teaching in their synagogues and was praised by all.

Luke 4:15

Jesus's Early Years

Although not much is written about the early life of Jesus, we know that He grew up in a period when Torah education was emphasized.[243] The most revered religious institutions of Jewish society were the Torah and the Temple in Jerusalem. Brad Young explains, "In the countryside, away from the activities of the Temple in Jerusalem, the synagogue and bet midrash ('house of study') emerged to play lead roles in the religious lives of the people."[244] Each week in the synagogue services prayers were made, a portion of the Torah and other Scriptures were read, and sermons were delivered to engage the learners in how to walk in the laws of God. In the bet midrash (house of study) the Torah was memorized and studied. The growth of these two institutions and the abundance of teachers resulted in a Torah-centric culture in first-century Israel.

Two prominent colleges produced Torah scholars and teachers: the college of Hillel in Jerusalem and the college of Shammai.[245] Education for young adults was required to be provided in the synagogue or in an attached school building. Although parents continued to be responsible to teach their young children, formal universal education was beginning to be established for all children. It is reported that in Jerusalem alone there were four hundred and eighty synagogues each with its own house of study.[246] While scholars have considered this report to be exaggerated, it does suggest that first-century synagogues (and their study functions) were quite a prominent part of Jewish life.

Jesus grew up in the town of Nazareth in the region of Galilee. The Galilee had experienced a revival of Torah education as a result of the concentration of Pharisees in the area,[247] and therefore many of

---

[243]See Part 3, "Education from the Captivity Through the Second Temple Period."
[244]Brad H. Young, *Meet the Rabbis: Rabbinic Thought and the Teachings of Jesus* (Grand Rapids: Baker Academics, 2007) 29.
[245]George Foot Moore, *Judaism in the First Centuries of the Christian Era: The Age of the Tannaim, vol. 1* (New York: Schocken Books, 1974), 79-81.
[246]Nathan Drazin, *History of Jewish Education from 515 B.C.E. to 220 C.E. (During the Periods of the Second Commonwealth and the Tannaim)* (Baltimore: The Johns Hopkins Press, 1940), 61.
[247]Israel M. Goldman, *Life-Long Learning Among the Jews: Adult Education in Judaism from Biblical Times to the Twentieth Century* (New York: Ktav Publishing House, 1975), 12. And H. H. Ben-Sasson, *A History of the Jewish People* (Cambridge, MA: Harvard University Press, 1969), 234-235. And Sean Freyne, *Galilee From Alexander the Great to Hadrian 323 B.C.E. to 135 C.E.: A Study of Second Temple Judaism* (Notre Dame, IN: University of Notre Dame Press, 1980), 305-323. While the extent of the Pharisee movement is considered a revival or more cautiously seen as a positive influence in the area, all agree of the presence and influence on the Pharisees in early first century Galilee.

the Jewish population in the region gave attention to the study of the Written and Oral Torah. In *Meet the Rabbis*, Brad Young notes, "Torah scholarship never resided exclusively in Jerusalem. Galilee, too, was a place of great learning, where synagogues and academies were integral to community life. Academies of learning supported the religious needs of the community. Rabbinic literature mentions great scholars from the Galilee region."[248]

Jesus grew up in a household that assembled and studied in the local synagogue and made pilgrimages to the Temple in Jerusalem (Luke 2:41). They would have known the God of Israel and the history of their people. Jesus's family would have followed Torah practices,[249] kept the Sabbath each week in remembering the acts and providence of the God of Israel, and would have provided some amount of instruction in the home.[250] The town of Nazareth (in Galilee) where Jesus grew up had a local synagogue which He regularly attended (Luke 4:16). The synagogue likely had a house of study that was either attached or included in it.[251]

According to the educational program of the first century, by the age of twelve Jesus would likely have had an extensive education.[252] He would have known how to read the Scriptures in the ancient Hebrew language. He would have memorized the Shema and the other morning and evening prayers, as well as the prayers recited during sabbaths and feasts.[253] He would have memorized large portions of the Torah, started studying and memorizing the Oral Torah, and would have been able to engage and converse with the Torah teachers as well. Luke 2:46-52

---

[248] Young, *Meet the Rabbis*, 58.
[249] Amy-Jill Levine and Marc Zvi Brettler, ed., *The Jewish Annotated New Testament* (New York: Oxford University Press, 2011), 103. Luke 2:39 emphasizes the family's connection to the Torah. "When they had performed everything according to the Law of the Lord, they returned to Galilee." (Luke 2:39).
[250] Drazin, *History of Jewish Education from 515 B.C.E. to 220 C.E.*, 17-18; William Barclay, *Train Up A Child: Educational Ideals in the Ancient World* (Philadelphia: The Westminster Press, 1959), 14-17. Also see A. B. de Toit, "Life in Obedience to the Torah: Jewish Belief, Worship, and Everyday Religion in the First Century AD," in *The New Testament Milieu*, ed. A.B. du Toit, vol. 2, *Guide to the New Testament* (Orion Publishers, 1998).
[251] Moore, *Judaism in the First Centuries of the Christian Era*, 314.
[252] *Ethics of the Fathers* 5.22; Barclay, *Train Up A Child*, 39–40.
[253] See du Toit, "Life in Obedience to the Torah."

An Introduction to Education in Bible Times

provides an account of Jesus in Jerusalem at the age of twelve, engaging the teachers there.[254]

> *Then, after three days they [Jesus's parents] found Him in the temple, sitting in the midst of the teachers, both listening to them and asking them questions. And all who heard Him were amazed at His understanding and His answers. When they saw Him, they were astonished; and His mother said to Him, "Son, why have You treated us this way? Behold, Your father and I have been anxiously looking for You." And He said to them, "Why is it that you were looking for Me? Did you not know that I had to be in My Father's house? [literally "in the things of My Father"—likely the study of Torah]" But they did not understand the statement which He had made to them. And He went down with them and came to Nazareth, and He continued in subjection to them; and His mother treasured all these things in her heart. And Jesus kept increasing in wisdom and stature, and in favor with God and men.*
>
> Luke 2:46-52

Generally, teachers engaged their students, and fellow students often engaged each other and their teachers, through the use of questions and answers. This passage in the second chapter of Luke says that Jesus was listening to the teachers in Jerusalem and asking them questions. This practice of asking and answering questions was a common, effective way of learning in ancient Judaism.[255] The passage continues by saying that the teachers were amazed at His understanding and answers. According to David Flusser, "This anecdote from the childhood of Jesus has special significance. It is a story of a precocious scholar, one might almost say of a young Talmudist."[256]

In addition to Torah study at home and in the synagogue, Jesus's family went up to Jerusalem to celebrate the feasts every year (Luke

---

[254]Phillip Sigal, *The Halakhah of Jesus of Nazareth according to the Gospel of Matthew* (Atlanta: Society of Biblical Literature, 2007), 192. "During his brief ministry Jesus was a proto-rabbi whose views influenced his contemporaries and possibly entered tannaitic literature as the views of others. If there is any truth at all to the tradition at Luke 2:46, the precocious Jesus enjoyed the company of proto-rabbinic scholars and his maturation in this regard is observed at Luke 2:52."
[255]Young, *Meet the Rabbis*, 32.
[256]David Flusser, *Jesus*, 3rd ed. (Magnes Press, 2001), 29.

2:41-42). These feasts would have provided educational experiences in the history of Israel and opportunities to see the Temple, observe the sacrificial rituals, and listen to teachers of the Law.[257] Connected with these experiences, the travel from Galilee to Jerusalem would have provided Jesus's family with opportunities to recount the history of Israel as they passed through various locations highlighted in the biblical stories. Families recited the Psalms of Ascent as they made their way up the hill to Jerusalem or recited the Hallel during the feasts.[258] The family experiences of the feasts in Jerusalem and the hospitality surrounding these encounters would have had a great impact on children as they grew up.[259]

The land of Galilee was also an educational experience packed with history. From the hill of Nazareth one could see many significant areas filled with memories of the past, observations of the present, and prophecies of the future. Jesus learned the sacred history of Israel, and as He walked through its land, every part of it was a learning experience through the lens of Scripture.[260] W. M. Ramsay adds, "No education was ever so well adapted to train a thoughtful child in the appreciation of his own country, to render its past history living and real to him, to strengthen his patriotic feeling, to make every geographical name and scene full of meaning and historic truth, as the training which every Hebrew child then received."[261]

The city of Sepphoris was about an hour's walk from Jesus's home town of Nazareth. Sepphoris was a large Jewish center as well as an important Roman town. The city was destroyed by the Romans after a revolt in 4 BCE and then rebuilt as a regional center by Herod Antipas. The Jewish historian Josephus presents a picture of Sepphoris as the largest and most cosmopolitan city in the Galilee, describing it as "the ornament of all Galilee."[262] The rebuilding of Sepphoris was a project

---

[257] Barclay, *Train Up A Child*, 20-22.
[258] The Psalms of Ascent consist of Psalm 120 through Psalm 134. These Psalms were sung as Jews made their annual pilgrimage to the Temple in Jerusalem during one of the feasts. The Hallel consists of Psalm 113 to Psalm 118. The Hallel covers all of Jewish history—past, present, and future.
[259] R. H. Stein, "Entertain," ed. Geoffrey W. Bromiley, *The International Standard Bible Encyclopedia*, Revised. (Wm. B. Eerdmans, 1979–1988), 105–106.
[260] W.M. Ramsay, *The Education of Christ: Hill-side Reveries* (New York: G.P. Putnam's Sons, 1902), 45-58.
[261] Ramsay, *The Education of Christ*, 61.
[262] Josephus, *Antiquities*, 18.27.

that lasted for many years, providing work for the residents of neighboring towns like Nazareth. It is likely that as a young man Jesus would have accompanied his father to work at Sepphoris. Here Jesus would have been able to observe first-hand the influences of Greek culture and the harshness of Roman occupation. He would have also had access to many of the teachers who lived and taught in this center of Jewish culture.[263]

Like many Jewish youth of His day, Jesus had great opportunity to participate in the rich educational experiences provided by His parents and teachers. These experiences molded and shaped His life as a dedicated and observant Jew. The Jewish people understood the Scriptures as the story of their people and saw them as their own family history. They considered themselves to be as much a part of the story of Scripture as their ancestors were thousands of years before. These treasured family memories spoke directly to them, personally and as a community, about their relationship with the God of Israel.

The apostle John writes, "But when it was now the midst of the feast Jesus went up into the temple, and began to teach. The Jews then were astonished, saying, '*How has this man become learned* [emphasis added], having never been educated [in one of the colleges]?' So Jesus answered them and said, 'My teaching is not Mine, but His who sent Me'" (John 7:14-16). While Jesus did not attend either the college of Hillel or the college of Shammai to become an approved Torah scholar, David Flusser reminds us, "He was perfectly at home in both the holy scripture and in oral tradition, and he knew how to apply this scholarly heritage."[264] While Jesus grew up in a culture of Torah education, at some point He was also instructed by the Heavenly Father, the One who gave the Torah to His people. Jesus's faithfulness to learn and keep His Father's words must have created an atmosphere for the Father to continue His education.

The New Testament teaches that the Father was instrumental in instructing His Son (John 8:28; Heb. 5:7-9). Jesus recognized the Torah as His Father's words given out of a loving relationship with His people and understood that the Hebrew Scriptures revealed the way for a people to walk with God in His presence. Jesus also saw Himself in the Scriptures (Luke 4:21; 24:27,44; John 5:39). So He learned the Law of

---

[263]Michael D. Morrison, "Sepphoris," ed. John D. Barry et al., *The Lexham Bible Dictionary* (Bellingham, WA: Lexham Press, 2016).
[264]Flusser, *Jesus*, 30-32.

God in order to keep it, to teach its meaning and application, and to express it through His life and ministry. At the start of Jesus's ministry and also near the end of it, He received this commendation from the Father: "This is My beloved Son, with whom I am well-pleased" (Matt. 17:5; see also 3:17).

Jesus as a Teacher

Jesus faithfully lived the Shema prayer of Deuteronomy 6 and loved the Father with all His heart, soul, mind, and strength. God's words were continually on His heart and He taught them diligently to His disciples and to the people of Israel. He taught in the synagogues of Galilee and at the Temple in Jerusalem. He taught wherever crowds gathered: in the countryside, while He was walking from one location to another, or at home and at meals. He taught during sabbaths and feasts, early in the mornings, and at any occasion.

Luke, a well-educated physician and disciple of Paul, provides a summary of Jesus's teaching ministry saying, "The first account I composed, Theophilus, about all that Jesus began to do and teach" (Acts 1:1). Here Luke emphasizes Jesus as a teacher. Each of the Gospel accounts are full of Jesus's teachings. They also record the works that He did as signs to confirm His teaching and to reveal the Father's love for His people. These works were another powerful form of teaching.

The Gospel accounts of Jesus's ministry often refer to Him as a teacher.[265] They highlight that Jesus was acknowledged as a teacher of the Torah by the scribes, Pharisees, and teachers of His day. Some of these teachers followed Jesus and engaged Him in His teaching (Matt. 8:19-20; Luke 5:17; John 3:1-2). David Flusser observed that "External corroboration of Jesus's Jewish scholarship is provided by the fact that, although he was not an approved scribe, some were accustomed to address him as 'Rabbi,' 'my teacher/master.'"[266] In Luke's gospel account, it is primarily those other than Jesus's disciples that called Him "Rabbi"—a popular name for describing scholars and teachers of the Torah.[267]

---

[265]Matt. 8:19, 9:11, 12:38, 17:24, 19:16, 22:16, 22:24, 22:36, 26:18; Mark 5:35, 9:17, 9:38, 10:17, 10:20, 10:35, 12:14, 12:19, 12:32, 13:1, 14:14; Luke 3:12, 7:40, 8:49, 9:38, 10:25, 11:45, 12:13, 18:18, 19:39, 20:21, 20:28, 20:39, 22:11, 23:5; John 3:2, 3:10, 8:4, 18:19.
[266]Flusser, *Jesus*, 32.
[267]Flusser, *Jesus*, 32.

An Introduction to Education in Bible Times

Much of Jesus's teaching with the Jewish people occurred in the synagogue. The land of Galilee had one or more synagogues in every town (depending on the size of the town). The Gospels record Jesus's ministry as beginning with His travel throughout the towns of Galilee, teaching in their synagogues. This pattern of teaching in the synagogues of Galilee and Judea continued throughout His ministry (Matt. 4:23; 9:35; Mark 6:2; Luke 13:22).

Jesus also taught in the Temple at Jerusalem. The Temple had areas where teachers could gather people together to teach them. It appears that Jesus often taught at the Temple when He went up to Jerusalem for the annual feasts (Matt. 21:23; Luke 19:47; John 7:14; 8:2).

Like the teachers of His day, Jesus taught the people in other venues, as well as in the synagogues and the Temple. Young adds, "Rabbinic literature records that rabbis taught while seated, and their classrooms often were an orchard, vineyard, or portico of the Temple. These open-air classrooms provided subject material and excellent illustrations for the lessons."[268] Jesus taught large crowds on hillsides and in open fields, while sitting in a boat off the shore of a lake, while walking through public areas, and in houses. He often taught His own disciples privately while at meals, while walking along the road, or wherever there was an opportunity.[269]

The Jews usually offered hospitality to teachers who traveled through their villages and towns. This was a long-standing tradition promoted by the early Jewish sages: "Yossei the son of Yoezer of Tzreidah would say: Let your home be a meeting place for the wise; dust yourself in the soil of their feet, and drink thirstily of their words."[270] When Jesus sent His disciples to teach and minister in the towns of Galilee, it was expected that hospitality (food and lodging) would be willingly provided for them (Matt. 10:7-11). The Gospel of Luke has a beautiful story about this kind of hospitality.

> *Now as they were traveling along, He entered a village; and a woman named Martha welcomed Him into her home. She had a sister called Mary, who was seated at the Lord's feet, listening to His word. But Martha was distracted with all her preparations; and she came up to*

---

[268] Young, *Meet the Rabbis*, 32.
[269] Matt. 5:1-2; 13:36; 16:13; 20:17; Mark 2:13; 4:1; 6:34; 10:1; 13:1-3; Luke 5:3; 10:38-39.
[270] *Ethics of the Fathers* 1.4. For other teachings from the rabbinic sages in *Ethics of the Fathers*, see Chabad.org, https://www.chabad.org/library/article_cdo/aid/5708/jewish/Translated-Text.htm.

> Him and said, "Lord, do You not care that my sister has left me to do all the serving alone? Then tell her to help me." But the Lord answered and said to her, "Martha, Martha, you are worried and bothered about so many things; but only one thing is necessary, for Mary has chosen the good part, which shall not be taken away from her."
>
> Luke 10:38-42

In this story we see that Martha welcomed Jesus and His disciples into her home. She provided food for them and a place to rest from their travels. Her sister Mary sat with the disciples at the feet of the Teacher, drinking in His words. Jesus encouraged Martha, who had opened her home to them, to also take advantage of the opportunity to sit and undistractedly listen to His teaching.

How Jesus Taught

Jesus was well-prepared as a teacher. His education as a young child taught Him many of the prayers and historical narratives of the Jewish people, preparing Him to later read and memorize the Written Torah. As a young adult Jesus studied and memorized the Oral Torah, and most likely He also studied the midrashic ways of interpreting the Torah.[271] As an adult He regularly attended the synagogue and participated in its continuing education process of reading Scripture and expounding its meaning. The Gospels tell us that at the start of Jesus's teaching ministry, "He came to Nazareth, where He had been brought up; ***and as was His custom*** [emphasis added], He entered the synagogue on the Sabbath, and stood up to read" (Luke 4:16). Flusser notes that Josephus, looking back on Jesus's ministry as a teacher, observed that "Jesus was a wise man … [and] by these words Josephus identifies Jesus with the Jewish Sages."[272]

---

[271] "Midrash is an interpretive act, seeking the answers to religious questions (both practical and theological) by plumbing the meaning of the words of the Torah. … Midrash falls into two categories. When the subject is law and religious practice, it is called *Midrash Halacha*. *Midrash Aggadah*, on the other hand, interprets biblical narrative, exploring questions of ethics or theology, or creating homilies and parables based on the text (MJL, "What is Midrash," *My Jewish Learning*, accessed February 2, 2019, https://www.myjewishlearning.com/article/midrash-101/.)

[272] Flusser, *Jesus*, 30.

Like other teachers of the first century, Jesus employed the styles of teaching called *Halakhah* and *Aggadah*.[273] Halakhah comes from the Hebrew word "walking" and deals with the details of how one lives his life in fulfillment of Torah.[274] It focuses on each commandment and gives the knowledge and instruction of how to walk in it. Aggadah refers to the larger meaning and story of the Scriptures.[275] It deals with the eternal relationship of men and women with the Father, with other people, and with creation. The Torah contains both stories to learn from as well as the commands of the LORD. The whole of the Torah is instructional in the knowledge of the LORD, in His intimate relationship with His people, and in learning His ways to walk in them.

Parables belonged to the style of rabbinic teaching known as Aggadah. Jesus effectively used parables in His teaching ministry with many relevant illustrations to draw from in first-century Jewish life: wineskins and clothing, farming, sheep and shepherds, vineyards, day laborers, masters and servants, money lending, the rich and poor of society, kings and kingdoms, wedding feasts, the plight of widows, family life, and so on. Close to one-third of Jesus's recorded teaching is made up of parables. Young demonstrates, "The classical form of the parable, involving the king, father, landowner, tenant farmer, son, and/or servant, is found in only two bodies of writings: rabbinic literature and the New Testament."[276] Young adds, "[So] Jesus and the rabbis of old taught about God by using concrete illustrations that reached the heart through imagination. They challenged the mind on the highest intellectual level by using simple stories that made common sense out of the complexities of religious faith and human experience."[277]

Aggadah also included the teaching of ethics derived from the stories and commandments recorded in the Scriptures.[278] Centuries before the time of Jesus, the prophet Micah declared, "And what does the LORD require of you but to do justice, to love kindness, and to walk humbly

---

[273]Sigal, *The Halakhah of Jesus of Nazareth*, 187-188.
[274]MJL, "Midrash Halacha," *My Jewish Learning*, accessed February 2, 2019, https://www.myjewishlearning.com/article/midrash-halakhah/.
[275]MJL, "Midrash Aggadah," *My Jewish Learning*, accessed February 2, 2019, https://www.myjewishlearning.com/article/midrash-aggadah/.
[276]Young, *Meet the Rabbis*, 33.
[277]Brad H. Young, *The Parables, Jewish Tradition and Christian Interpretation* (Peabody, MA: Hendrickson Publishers, 1998), 3-5.
[278]MJL, "Midrash Aggadah."

with your God?" (Mic. 6:8). In like manner, Jesus confronted some of His contemporary rabbis who were overemphasizing the details of Halakhah (the ways of doing the commands) over and above Aggadah (the heart and ethics of the Torah). In teaching them He contested, "Woe to you, scribes and Pharisees, hypocrites! For you tithe mint and dill and cummin, and have neglected the weightier provisions of the law: justice and mercy and faithfulness; but these are the things you should have done without neglecting the others" (Matt. 23:23). On several other occasions the Gospels record Jesus using the method of teaching ethics from a biblical narrative. Regarding keeping the Sabbath, He used a story from the life of David: "But He said to them, 'Have you not read what David did when he became hungry, he and his companions?'" (Matt. 12:3). Regarding marriage and divorce, Jesus used the story of creation: "And He answered and said, 'Have you not read that He who created them from the beginning MADE THEM MALE AND FEMALE?'" (Matt. 19:4).

The process of asking and answering questions was one of the ways of teaching and learning in ancient Judaism. When instructing His disciples, Jesus often engaged them by asking questions and answering their questions (Matt. 6:25-28; 16:13; Luke 11:1, 11-12). He also engaged other learners and teachers in a dialogue of asking and answering questions (Matt. 21:40-42; 22:41-42; Mark 11:29; Luke 6:39; 7:24-26). At times Jesus used other teachers' questioning and criticism of His teaching and actions, even intentionally creating conflict in certain situations, to provide an opportunity to emphasize aspects of His teaching (Matt. 9:2-6; 12:1-12; 15:1-11).[279]

In *Ethics of the Fathers* the rabbis taught, "Be as careful with a minor mitzvah [commandment] as with a major one, for you do not know the rewards of the mitzvot."[280] Jesus similarly taught, "Whoever then annuls one of the least of these commandments, and teaches others to do the same, shall be called least in the kingdom of heaven; but whoever keeps and teaches them, he shall be called great in the kingdom of heaven" (Matt. 5:19). Young explains, "Through reading through their biblical text midrashically, Jesus and the sages conclude that the minor commandment is as significant as the major commandment."[281]

---

[279] Flusser, *Jesus*, 62.
[280] *Ethics of the Fathers* 2.1.
[281] Young, *Meet the Rabbis*, 45.

The rabbis often taught by linking a "minor" sin with a "major" one. This was done with the intention of "making a safety fence around the Torah."[282] By doing this they helped to ensure that the people did not violate some of the weightier commands of the LORD. In *Sifre Deuteronomy 187:11*, Jewish sages recorded this style of teaching from generations of oral tradition: "He who violates, 'Love your neighbor as yourself,' will ultimately violate, 'You shall not hate your brother in your heart,' and 'You shall not take vengeance nor bear a grudge,' until in the end he will come to shedding blood." Jesus used this rabbinic style of instruction by linking minor sins with major ones. Two examples are found in the Sermon on the Mount:

> *"You have heard that the ancients were told, 'YOU SHALL NOT COMMIT MURDER' and 'Whoever commits murder shall be liable to the court.' But I say to you that everyone who is angry with his brother shall be guilty before the court; and whoever says to his brother, 'You good-for-nothing,' shall be guilty before the supreme court; and whoever says, 'You fool,' shall be guilty enough to go into the fiery hell."*
>
> Matt. 5:21-22

> *"You have heard that it was said, 'YOU SHALL NOT COMMIT ADULTERY'; but I say to you that everyone who looks at a woman with lust for her has already committed adultery with her in his heart."*
>
> Matt. 5:27-28

Like other rabbis, Jesus took the teaching approach of presenting the ultimate aims of the Torah.[283] His goal was to teach His followers how to do the will of the Father. Jesus did this by "bringing the Torah to its greatest expression."[284] The following two passages illustrate Him teaching the ultimate aims of the Torah. In the first passage Jesus teaches about "going beyond what is written" in the Torah in order to live pleasing to God. In the second passage He teaches that love is the essence of the Torah.

---

[282]*Ethics of the Fathers* 1.1.
[283]Moshe Weinfeld, *Normative and Sectarian Judaism in the Second Temple Period* (New York: T&T Clark International, 2005), 291-293.
[284]Ann Spangler and Lois Tverberg, *Sitting at the Feet of Rabbi Jesus: How the Jewishness of Jesus Can Transform Your Faith* (Grand Rapids: Zondervan, 2009), 171.

> "You have heard that it was said, 'AN EYE FOR AN EYE, AND A TOOTH FOR A TOOTH.' But I say to you, do not resist an evil person; but whoever slaps you on your right cheek, turn the other to him also. If anyone wants to sue you and take your shirt, let him have your coat also. Whoever forces you to go one mile, go with him two. Give to him who asks of you, and do not turn away from him who wants to borrow from you. You have heard that it was said, 'YOU SHALL LOVE YOUR NEIGHBOR and hate your enemy.' But I say to you, love your enemies and pray for those who persecute you, so that you may be sons of your Father who is in heaven; for He causes His sun to rise on the evil and the good, and sends rain on the righteous and the unrighteous. For if you love those who love you, what reward do you have? Do not even the tax collectors do the same? If you greet only your brothers, what more are you doing than others? Do not even the Gentiles do the same? Therefore you are to be perfect, as your heavenly Father is perfect."
>
> Matthew 5:38-48

> One of them, a lawyer, asked Him a question, testing Him, "Teacher, which is the great commandment in the Law?" And He said to him, "'YOU SHALL LOVE THE LORD YOUR GOD WITH ALL YOUR HEART, AND WITH ALL YOUR SOUL, AND WITH ALL YOUR MIND.' This is the great and foremost commandment. The second is like it, 'YOU SHALL LOVE YOUR NEIGHBOR AS YOURSELF.' On these two commandments depend the whole Law and the Prophets."
>
> Matthew 22:35-40

Hillel once told a non-Jew about the essence of the Torah, saying: "'That which is hateful to you do not do to others.' That is all the Torah, the rest is commentary. Now go and study."[285] Jesus taught the essence of the Torah by saying, "In everything, therefore, treat people the same way you want them to treat you, for this is the Law and the Prophets" (Matt. 7:12).

Jesus had compassion for those whom He taught. Drawing from the analogy of the Hebrew Scriptures, He taught that God's

---

[285] George Robinson, *Essential Judaism: A Complete Guide to Beliefs, Customs, and Rituals* (Atria Books), 314, Kindle

shepherds were to care for His people, leading them and teaching them His ways. The Gospels record, "Jesus was going through all the cities and villages, teaching in their synagogues and proclaiming the gospel of the kingdom, and healing every kind of disease and every kind of sickness. Seeing the people, He felt compassion for them, because they were distressed and dispirited like sheep without a shepherd" (Matt. 9:35-36). As a true shepherd, Jesus was motivated by compassion to feed God's sheep and lay down His life for them (John 10:11-18).

As a teacher, Jesus was an example of being submissive and teachable. He learned and spoke only the words the Father taught Him; and He was obedient to do the works that the Father gave Him to do (John 5:19; 12:49-50; 14:7-10; Matt. 26:42). His disciples observed this obedience to the will of the Father in His life. The importance of these qualities has been beautifully summed up in the following passage:

> *So Jesus said, "When you lift up the Son of Man, then you will know that I am He, and I do nothing on My own initiative, but I speak these things as the Father taught Me. And He who sent Me is with Me; He has not left Me alone, for I always do the things that are pleasing to Him." As He spoke these things, many came to believe in Him.*
>
> John 8:28-30

Jesus was truly an example to those whom He taught of being submissive and teachable.

While Jesus's life was an example of His teaching, He also taught using specific examples. On one of the rare occasions where Jesus referred to Himself as "Teacher," He did so in order to show that being a teacher should not promote a sense of entitlement and self-importance. Instead by washing His disciples' feet He provided an example of the "teacher" humbly serving others (John 13:12-14).

Jesus's teaching was with authority and with signs confirming the words He spoke. His submission to the Word and the will of the Father gave Him authority. Matthew and Mark write in their gospel accounts:

> *Jesus was going throughout all Galilee, teaching in their synagogues and proclaiming the gospel of the kingdom, and healing every kind of disease and every kind of sickness among the people.*
>
> Matt. 4:23

> *When Jesus had finished these words, the crowds were amazed at His teaching; for He was teaching them as one having authority, and not as their scribes.*
>
> Matt. 7:28-29

> *They were all amazed, so that they debated among themselves, saying, "What is this? A new teaching with authority! He commands even the unclean spirits, and they obey Him."*
>
> Mark 1:27

These passages highlight the authority by which Jesus taught and ministered.

Finally, Jesus had the quality of being humble as a teacher. Flusser adds that Jesus rarely referred to Himself as "Rabbi" in contrast to many of the teachers of His day who desired to receive the position and respect of being recognized as "Rabbi" (Matt. 23:1-12).[286] In Judaism, Moses is referred to as *Moshe Rabbeinu* (Moses our teacher). However, the Torah says that Moses was a humble man—more than anyone else on the earth (Num. 12:3). The New Testament portrays Jesus as one who taught with humility. Jesus said to those He was teaching, "Come to Me, all who are weary and heavy-laden, and I will give you rest. Take My yoke upon you and learn from Me, for I am gentle and humble in heart, and YOU WILL FIND REST FOR YOUR SOULS" (Matt. 11:28-29).

Connecting Study and Actions

Jesus taught the inseparable connection between studying and learning God's Words and keeping them. The rabbis of the first century elevated the study of Torah as the essential task of every Jew. They

---

[286] Flusser, *Jesus*, 32.

also elevated keeping the Torah as equal to and above the study of the Torah.[287] The ultimate conclusion was that both are essential because study leads to the ability to keep the ways of the LORD. Jesus also taught the priority of learning in order to do.

Jesus constantly taught obedience to God's Word (Matt. 12:50; Luke 11:28; John 14:23-24). He compared those who heard His teachings and acted upon them to a wise man who built his house upon a solid foundation of bedrock. He likewise compared those who did not act upon the teaching they heard to a foolish man who built his house on a foundation of sand, and "the rain fell, and the floods came, and the winds blew and slammed against that house; and it fell—and great was its fall" (Matt. 7:24-27). Later Rabbi Eliezer taught, "One whose wisdom is greater than his deeds, what is he comparable to? To a tree with many branches and few roots; comes a storm and uproots it, and turns it on its face."[288]

Jesus taught parables about hearing God's Word (Matt. 13:16-23). According to the Hebrew Scriptures, "hearing" included obedient listening or diligent learning with the intent to completely obey. The Shema prayer begins with "Hear O Israel" (Deut. 6:4). The Hebrew word *šāmaʻ* means to hear, to listen (or pay attention) to, and to obey.[289] Many times in the Gospels Jesus would say, "He who has ears to hear, let him hear" (Matt. 11:15; 13:9). When Jesus talked about hearing, He included the ability to grasp what was being taught with the hearer's intention of wholeheartedly walking in the teaching. A learner needed to approach learning with the intent and desire to walk in God's ways. Jesus taught that a person's predetermined set of heart to do God's will is what gives one the ability to hear (or know) His teaching (John 7:17).

Study was not only the act of listening and memorizing God's words, it also included an intentional abiding in those words. The LORD commanded Joshua, "This book of the law shall not depart from your mouth, but you shall meditate on it day and night, so that you may be careful to do according to all that is written in it; for then you will make your way prosperous, and then you will have success" (Josh. 1:8). David called the person "blessed" who meditates on God's Word (Ps. 1:2).

---

[287] *Ethics of the Fathers* 1.17, 4.5.
[288] *Ethics of the Fathers* 3.17.
[289] Hermann J. Austel, "2412 שׁמע," ed. R. Laird Harris, Gleason L. Archer Jr., and Bruce K. Waltke, *Theological Wordbook of the Old Testament* (Chicago: Moody Press, 1999), 938.

One of the rabbis in *Ethics of Fathers* taught, "Delve and delve into it, for all is in it; see with it; grow old and worn in it; do not budge from it, for there is nothing better."[290] Another rabbi taught, "Turn it and turn it over again, for everything is in it [the Torah]; and contemplate it, and wax grey and old over it; and stir not from it. You can have no better rule than this."[291] Jesus also taught the importance of continually abiding in God's Word, saying to His disciples:

> *"Abide in Me, and I in you. As the branch cannot bear fruit of itself unless it abides in the vine, so neither can you unless you abide in Me. I am the vine, you are the branches; he who abides in Me and I in him, he bears much fruit, for apart from Me you can do nothing. If anyone does not abide in Me, he is thrown away as a branch and dries up; and they gather them, and cast them into the fire and they are burned. If you abide in Me, and My words abide in you, ask whatever you wish, and it will be done for you. My Father is glorified by this, that you bear much fruit, and so prove to be My disciples."*
>
> John 15:4-8

Jesus and His Disciples

Jesus taught His disciples through His close relationship with them. His disciples learned through following and serving Him: through listening to His teaching, through their relationships with each other, and through the experiences of being sent out to minister together. The early rabbinic sages also emphasized the value of studying in relationship, such as masters with disciples and disciples with each other.[292]

To "follow" a teacher meant more than just studying in a classroom. It involved being committed to follow the teacher's lifestyle, living with him to learn his teaching and way of life. In the first century CE, the scholar and "teacher of the law was called the *talmid* (Rabbi) and his pupils were known as *talmidim*, i.e. apprentices."[293] *Talmidim* is translated as "disciple" in the Greek text of the New Testament. The

---

[290] *Ethics of the Fathers* 5.21.
[291] *Ethics of the Fathers* 5.23.
[292] See *Ethics of the Fathers* 1.6; 2.4; 3.2.
[293] Walter C. Kaiser, "1116 דָּמַל," ed. R. Laird Harris, Gleason L. Archer Jr., and Bruce K. Waltke, *Theological Wordbook of the Old Testament* (Chicago: Moody Press, 1999), 480.

task of disciples was to learn to become like their teacher, which could only be done through the close proximity of apprenticeship—through the daily interaction of humbly serving their master.[294] According to the biblical pattern of Elijah and Elisha, the disciple gave up family and professional life to devote his entire time to serve and learn from his master (1 Kings 19:19-21).

Jesus's disciples were the product of first century Judaism. They likely had many of the educational experiences that were provided for children and youth growing up in Israel. They would have learned to read the Scriptures, memorize portions of the Oral Torah, and participated in synagogue services. Additionally, Jesus's disciples would have had apprenticeship experiences with a parent or other craftsman in learning a trade. Like others in their communities, they would have had great respect for the learned teachers of the Torah and they would have understood the sacrifice and devotion that disciples of these sages made to learn from their masters. So when Jesus called His disciples, they left all to follow Him and become His *disciples* (Matt. 19:27).

> *Now as Jesus was walking by the Sea of Galilee, He saw two brothers, Simon who was called Peter, and Andrew his brother, casting a net into the sea; for they were fishermen. And He said to them, "Follow Me, and I will make you fishers of men." Immediately they left their nets and followed Him. Going on from there He saw two other brothers, James the son of Zebedee, and John his brother, in the boat with Zebedee their father, mending their nets; and He called them. Immediately they left the boat and their father, and followed Him.*
> Matthew 4:18-22

Again, in first century Judaism, to become a disciple of a respected teacher represented a great honor, so the family and community often rallied to help a young disciple realize his aspiration.[295] Jesus called twelve disciples to study closely with Him. There were also many others who followed Him, including some who were supporting His ministry and supporting those in the master-disciple relationships. Some of these included family members of the disciples (Matt. 8:14-15; 27:55-56; Acts 1:13-15).

---

[294] Young, *Meet the Rabbis*, 30.
[295] Young, *Meet the Rabbis*, 31.

Disciples formed a close relationship with their teachers. In Jewish tradition, teachers were often referred to as a disciple's father, and disciples were referred to as a teacher's children (2 Kings 2:12). The Talmud later described this relationship as "Your father brought you into this world, but your rabbi brings [fathers] you into the world to come!" (Mishna, *Bava Metzia* 2:11). This follows the line of thinking in *Ethics of the Fathers* that says the "one who acquires the words of Torah, has acquired life in the World to Come."[296] Jesus told His disciples, "And everyone who has left houses or brothers or sisters or father or mother or children or farms for My name's sake, will receive many times as much, and will inherit eternal life" (Matt. 19:29).

Disciples served their teacher. Integral to the process of learning, they would assist their teacher by taking care of his personal needs (Exod. 24:13; 2 Kings 3:11). So Jesus's disciples entered into a relationship to serve Him as their Master (Matt. 10:24-25; 26:17-19; John 4:8). The disciples' relationship with Jesus grew as they learned through following Him, serving Him, and listening to His teaching (John 12:26). The close proximity of the disciples with Jesus allowed them to ask Him questions (Matt. 17:10; 21:20; John 9:2; 14:5-11). It also provided opportunity for Jesus to privately instruct them and to correct their thinking (Matt. 16:13-23; Luke 9:46-50, 54-55). The disciples were able to observe Jesus's way of life and learn to follow His example. They could observe and learn from His relationship with the Father, His prayer life, His devotion to the Scriptures, the way He conducted Himself in public and in private, His sacrifice, and the way He loved others. Near the end of His ministry, Jesus told His disciples, "No longer do I call you slaves, for the slave does not know what his master is doing; but I have called you friends, for all things that I have heard from My Father I have made known to you" (John 15:15).

By serving Jesus as their Master, the disciples were able to follow in His example of humbly serving the Father. This was important to the process of learning. Jesus made the statement that willingness to do God's will was an essential quality to perceiving His Word (John 7:17). The rabbis also "believed that humility was an indispensable condition for learning: 'Just as water flows away from a high point and gathers at a low point, so the Word of God only endures with the learner who is humble in his knowledge (Babylonian Talmud, Taanit 7a).'"[297]

---

[296] *Ethics of the Fathers* 5.23.
[297] Spangler and Tverberg, *Sitting at the Feet of Rabbi Jesus*, 60.

An Introduction to Education in Bible Times

Jesus loved His disciples. John writes, "Jesus knowing that His hour had come that He would depart out of this world to the Father, having loved His own who were in the world, He loved them to the end" (John 13:1). Jesus told His disciples, "Just as the Father has loved Me, I have also loved you; abide in My love" (John15:9). He used the example of His love to teach His disciples to love each other: "This is My commandment, that you love one another, just as I have loved you" (John 15:12). Finally, one of the signs of this abiding love in the lives of the disciples would be their ongoing commitment to the Teacher and His teaching. Jesus said, "If you keep My commandments, you will abide in My love; just as I have kept My Father's commandments and abide in His love" (John 15:10).

While Jesus taught the multitudes and engaged other teachers of the Torah, He also taught His disciples privately. He explained to them the meaning of His parables, helped them understand the Scriptures, and included them in His intimate relationship with the Father (Matt. 17:1-5; 26:36-38; John 17:6-8). Jesus continued to teach and instruct His disciples even after His death and resurrection (Luke 24:25-27, 44-49).

Jesus's disciples memorized His teachings. For centuries, the Oral Torah "was passed down by memory from master teacher to disciple, from one generation to the next, from Mount Sinai in the desert to the living room in the home. Jesus developed a mentoring relationship with his disciples who learned his teachings by heart and followed his example as apprentices."[298] To accomplish this, Jesus's disciples most likely devoted their time, energy, and focus on listening, learning, and memorizing the words of their Teacher. They observed His way of life. This was the way they learned His teaching and His ways. Donald Hagner noticed the parallelism and mnemonic structures recorded in the book of Matthew and realized these devices would have been in the tradition of the Second Temple period disciples; especially in how they memorized and preserved the "oral tradition very much in the form in which it was probably given by Jesus."[299]

There has been scholarly debate regarding the reliability of passing on Jesus's ministry and teaching. However, James Dunn defends the validity of the biblical authors receiving and passing on the oral tradition:

---

[298]Young, *Meet the Rabbis*, 29.
[299]Donald A. Hagner, *Word Biblical Commentary: Matthew 1–13*, vol. 33A, Bruce M. Metzger, general ed. (Dallas: Word, 1998), xlix.

"The Synoptic tradition itself illustrates how the stories about and teaching of Jesus were communicated within and among the early Christian disciple groups. A tradition which focused on the substance and gist of what was being narrated or taught and was freely expressed in varied words, in different combinations and with different emphases, looked more and more like oral tradition—the forms in which the traditions of Jesus's mission and teaching were celebrated and taught before they were written down ... a society where information would be passed from one to another by word of mouth, where teaching and story-telling would be orally communicated, is the society which we must envisage if we are talking about the earliest disciple groups in the 30s, 40s and 50s of the first century."[300]

Jesus's disciples received the oral teaching of their Master, memorizing them in order to teach them to others.

Jesus provided experiential learning opportunities for His disciples to learn how to carry on His ministry. During His time of teaching and training the disciples, Jesus gave them authority to cast out unclean spirits and to heal every kind of disease and sickness. He commissioned them to go in pairs through the towns of Israel and "as you go, preach, saying, 'The kingdom of heaven is at hand.' Heal the sick, raise the dead, cleanse the lepers, cast out demons. Freely you received, freely give" (Matt. 10:7-8). Before sending them out He gave them detailed instructions on what to do and how to think (Matt. 10). On another occasion Jesus sent out seventy of His disciples, also providing them with instruction (Luke 10:1-20). Jesus, as a wise Teacher, took advantage of every opportunity to teach His disciples as they learned to minister in His name (Matt. 17:14-20).

Jesus's Command to Teach and Make Disciples

As R.P. Meye explains, "In the rabbinic realm, the *talmid* [disciple] devoted himself to learning Scripture and the religious tradition, above all that tradition which is passed on through his teacher. A disciple was

---

[300] James D. G. Dunn, *The Oral Gospel Tradition* (Grand Rapids: William B. Eerdmans Publishing Company, 2013), 5.

himself esteemed; he would become a teacher after the proper period of listening and learning."[301] During the Second Temple period, the ultimate goal of the teaching and learning process was to educate a whole society in the knowledge of the LORD and a knowledge of His ways in order to walk pleasing to Him. This would allow God to dwell with the nation as He had done in the days of Moses, in the glory days of the tabernacle at Shiloh, and as in the days of the first Temple.

Before His ascension, Jesus commissioned His disciples to carry on His ministry of teaching and raising up disciples. The Gospel of Matthew records, "And Jesus came up and spoke to them, saying, 'All authority has been given to Me in heaven and on earth. Go therefore and make disciples of all the nations, baptizing them in the name of the Father and the Son and the Holy Spirit, teaching them to observe all that I commanded you; and lo, I am with you always, even to the end of the age'" (Matt. 28:18-20). Jesus further instructed them, saying, "You will receive power when the Holy Spirit has come upon you; and you shall be My witnesses both in Jerusalem, and in all Judea and Samaria, and even to the remotest part of the earth" (Acts 1:8). The opportunity to live under the rule of God's kingdom had been extended to all the nations. All nations would have the opportunity to recognize the LORD as their Sovereign, to learn of His ways and to walk in them.

The teaching of the Great Assembly gave top priority to the command of "establishing many pupils [disciples]."[302] And for "many disciples" to be made, there was first a need of establishing master teachers.[303] This is exactly what Jesus did. Likewise, Matthew records Jesus as saying, "Therefore, behold, I am sending you [Israel] prophets and wise men and scribes" (Matt. 23:34). In this He assured the continuance of His teaching, in both oral and written form, from those who would be considered wise teachers. Jesus's disciples would become master teachers who could take His teaching and way of life, and by the empowerment of the Holy Spirit, raise up many more disciples with the aim of making disciples of all the nations.

There are two additional aspects to consider in Jesus's commissioning of His disciples. The first is that He had been given

---

[301]R. P. Meye, "Disciple," ed. Geoffrey W. Bromiley, *The International Standard Bible Encyclopedia*, Revised (Wm. B. Eerdmans, 1979–1988), 947.
[302]*Ethics of the Fathers* 1.1.
[303]Young, *Meet the Rabbis*, 29.

all authority in heaven and earth. The second is that the same Holy Spirit that rested on Jesus would now to be given to His disciples. Because of His submission to the Father, Jesus was given all authority in heaven and on earth. And because of the disciples' submission to Him, they would be able to exercise that same authority in making disciples of the nations. Like their Master, the disciples were to teach and minister with authority (Matt. 7:29; 9:6; Luke 4:32-36).

The disciples were also to receive the mantle (anointing) that had rested on Jesus in His earthly ministry. This is similar to Joshua receiving the anointing that rested on Moses to lead Israel into the possession of the land of Canaan (Num. 27:18-23; Deut. 34:9). It was more than Moses's disciple receiving a new job to perform; it involved the impartation of the Spirit and anointing from Moses to Joshua in order to lead and teach the LORD's people. Another example is that of Elisha receiving the mantle of his mentor, Elijah (2 Kings 2:9-15). The Scriptures say that the spirit of Elijah came to rest on Elisha, and Elisha continued the ministry of Elijah to the nation of Israel. Just before His ascension, Jesus instructed His disciples that they would receive the Holy Spirit, and by the power of the Holy Spirit they would be His witnesses. The mantle of the Holy Spirit that rested on Jesus would be given to the disciples on the day of Pentecost, anointing them to carry out the ministry that Jesus prepared them for.

When Jesus began His earthly ministry *"... the Holy Spirit descended upon Him in bodily form like a dove"* and remained with Him (Luke 3:22). John the Baptist testified saying, *"I have seen the Spirit descending as a dove out of heaven, and He remained upon Him* (John 1:32).

> "THE SPIRIT OF THE LORD IS UPON ME, BECAUSE HE ANOINTED ME TO PREACH THE GOSPEL TO THE POOR. HE HAS SENT ME TO PROCLAIM RELEASE TO THE CAPTIVES, AND RECOVERY OF SIGHT TO THE BLIND, TO SET FREE THOSE WHO ARE OPPRESSED, TO PROCLAIM THE FAVORABLE YEAR OF THE LORD."
>
> Luke 4:18-19

> "BEHOLD, MY SERVANT WHOM I HAVE CHOSEN; MY BELOVED IN WHOM MY SOUL is WELL-PLEASED; I WILL

An Introduction to Education in Bible Times

PUT MY SPIRIT UPON HIM, AND HE SHALL PROCLAIM JUSTICE TO THE GENTILES [NATIONS]."

Matt. 12:18

At the day of Pentecost, the Holy Spirit fell on His disciples and they began to move in the continuance of Jesus's ministry, of all that He "began to do and teach" (Acts 1:1). They were His witnesses in Jerusalem, Judea, and Samaria, and to the nations, "even to the remotest part of the earth" (Acts 1:8).

As a final thought regarding Jesus's command to teach and make disciples in "all the nations, beginning from Jerusalem ... even to the remotest part of the earth," this command may be perceived as the direct continuation of God's purpose which began in Genesis 1:28. God's first directive to Adam and Eve was a blessing: "And God blessed them: and God said to them, 'Be fruitful and multiply, and fill the earth and subdue it.'" Joseph Shulam adds:

> "God repeats this mandate to Noah and his sons, following the flood (cf. Gen. 9:1), and again to Abraham. Through the latter He promises a blessing to the whole earth: "And in you shall all the families of the earth be blessed" (Gen. 12:3, 18:18). The New Testament texts understand this blessing to mean the transformation of the nations from being "not-My-people" into being a part of God's people."[304]

This transformation was to occur through the nations being taught and learning the ways of the LORD (Isa. 2:2-3).

A Master's Care for His Disciples

We have seen how disciples served and cared for the needs of their teacher. However, rabbis were also expected to care for their disciples. The Babylonian Talmud states, "If a disciple is sent into exile, his rabbi should go with him."[305] The thought is that even in exile, the

---
[304]Joseph Shulam with Hilary Le Cornu, *A Commentary on the Jewish Roots of Acts 1-15* (Jerusalem: Netivyah Bible Instruction Ministry, 2012), 22.
[305]Babylonian Talmud, Makkot 10a.

disciple still needs to learn from his teacher. The Talmud teaches, "A famous sage by the name of Rabbi Akiva once cared for a sick disciple, coming to his home and even performing housework until he returned to health."[306] The Gospels also show how Jesus loved and cared for His disciples. While He was with them, He kept them and guarded them (John 17:12).

An example of the Master's care for His disciples is seen in the story of Peter. Peter was from the town of Bethsaida, a fishing village on the shore of the Sea of Galilee. He operated a fishing business with his brother Andrew and with the Zebedee brothers, James and John (Mark 1:16; Luke 5:10). When Peter was called to be a disciple, he left his former way of life to follow Jesus, walking with Him, living with Him, and serving Him (Matt. 4:18; John 1:40-42; Matt. 8:14; 19:27; Luke 22:8). Peter was one of the first named of the twelve disciples that Jesus commissioned, and he was part of the three disciples (including James and John) that Jesus drew into a closer relationship with Himself (Matt. 10:2; 26:36-37). He was always learning, asking Jesus questions, and stepping out in faith at the command of the Lord (Matt. 14:28-32; 15:15; 16:21-23; 17:24-27; 18:21-22). Peter received a revelation from the Father about the divine nature of Jesus, that He was the Christ, the Son of the living God (Matt. 16:13-20). He also was one of the three disciples who witnessed the transfiguration of Jesus with Moses and Elijah on the mountain (Matt. 17:1-9).

Jesus knew that Peter would deny Him, and that Satan was seeking to destroy him. So Jesus prayed for Peter that his faith would stand.

> *"Simon, Simon, behold, Satan has demanded permission to sift you like wheat; but I have prayed for you, that your faith may not fail; and you, when once you have turned again, strengthen your brothers." But he said to Him, "Lord, with You I am ready to go both to prison and to death!" And He said, "I say to you, Peter, the rooster will not crow today until you have denied three times that you know Me."*
>
> Luke 22:31–34

---

[306]Spangler and Tverberg, *Sitting at the Feet of Rabbi Jesus*, 59.

An Introduction to Education in Bible Times

When Jesus was arrested and being condemned to death, two of his disciples, John and Peter, followed Him to the house of the High Priest. It was during this time that Peter denied the Lord just as Jesus had foretold (Matt. 26:69-75; Luke 22:54-62). The Gospels say that Peter was deeply devastated by this event and that he went out and wept bitterly. However, the Gospel accounts also clearly state that, after His resurrection, Jesus specifically appeared to Peter (Luke 24:34; 1 Cor. 15:5). Jesus's love and concern moved Him to make a special appearance to Peter. This was a profound learning experience for Peter in the transforming love and grace of God. It taught him that in his deepest failure and need, Jesus's sacrifice was for him personally. All that Peter experienced he would now be able to teach and impart to others (John 21:15-17; Acts 2:14-42). Later, during a time when the early church was experiencing various trials, Peter drew on what he had learned in this experience with the Lord as he taught God's people: "Above all, keep fervent in your love for one another, because love covers a multitude of sins" (1 Pet. 4:8).

PART 5

EDUCATION IN THE EARLY CHURCH

The things which you have heard from me in the presence of many witnesses, entrust these to faithful men who will be able to teach others also.

2 Timothy 2:2

The Holy Spirit

Before Jesus ascended to the right hand of the Father, He told His disciples, "You will be baptized with the Holy Spirit not many days from now ... [and] you will receive power when the Holy Spirit has come upon you; and you shall be My witnesses both in Jerusalem, and in all Judea and Samaria, and even to the remotest part of the earth" (Acts 1:5, 8). The disciples were to receive from the Father the same Holy Spirit that Jesus had received at the start of His earthly ministry (Matt. 3:16-17; John 1:32-33; 14:26). With the anointing of the Holy Spirit on them, they would carry on Jesus's teaching ministry, proclaiming the Word of God with authority and with confirming signs.

Jesus had told His disciples, "I will ask the Father, and He will give you another Helper, that He may be with you forever; that is the Spirit of truth, whom the world cannot receive, because it does not see Him or know Him, but you know Him because He abides with you and will be in you" (John 14:16-17). The same Holy Spirit that was with their Master would be with them. Jesus further told them, "The Helper, the Holy Spirit, whom the Father will send in My name, He will teach you all things, and bring to your remembrance all that I said to you" (John 14:26). The Holy Spirit, the Teacher, would continue to instruct them, causing them to remember all the teaching of their beloved Lord and Master and guide them into truths from God yet to be taught (John 16:12-15).

Per Jesus's instruction, His disciples gathered together in Jerusalem to wait for the promised Holy Spirit. Then on the day of the Feast of Pentecost, the Holy Spirit was given to the 120 disciples who were gathered together. In Peter's first message to the Jews who were gathered in Jerusalem, he explained the outpouring of the Holy Spirit as the fulfillment of Joel's prophecy that in the last days God would pour out His Spirit on all mankind (Joel 2:28-29). Peter went on to say:

> *"This Jesus God raised up again, to which we are all witnesses. Therefore having been exalted to the right hand of God, and having received from the Father the promise of the Holy Spirit, He has poured forth this which you both see and hear. ... Repent, and each of you be baptized in the name of Jesus Christ for the forgiveness of your sins; and you will receive the gift of the Holy Spirit. For the promise is for you and your children and for all who are far off, as many as the Lord our God will call to Himself."*
> Acts 2:32-33, 38-39

The Holy Spirit, the Teacher, the One who inspired the holy Scriptures, was being given to all.

During the Feast of Pentecost (Shavuot or Weeks) the Jews celebrated the event of the LORD God giving the Torah, His instruction to His people.[307] When God gave the Torah on Mount Sinai, "All the people perceived the thunder and the lightning flashes and the sound of the trumpet and the mountain smoking; and when the people saw it, they trembled and stood at a distance" (Exod. 20:18). The Midrash Exodus Rabbah says:

> "The Torah was given through seven voices. And the people saw the Master of the Universe revealed in every one of these voices. That's the meaning of the verse 'All the people saw the voices' (Exodus 20:18). These voices were accompanied by sparks of fire and flashes of lightening that were in the shape of the letters of the ten commandments. They saw the fiery word pouring out from the mouth of the Almighty and watched as they were inscribed on the stone tablets, as it says, 'The voice of God inscribes flames of fire' (Ps 29:4). And when the people actually saw The-One-Who-Speaks-the-World-into-Being, they fainted away. … When God's voice came forth at Mt. Sinai, it divided itself into 70 human languages, so that the whole world might understand it."[308]

The significance of "70 human languages" refers to the list of 70 nations mentioned in the tenth chapter of Genesis. This list is a representation of all the nations that were to be blessed through Abraham.[309]

During the same feast that celebrated the giving of the Torah, God gave the Holy Spirit, the Teacher, to His people. The book of Acts describes the giving of the Holy Spirit on the day of Pentecost:

---

[307] Moshe Weinfeld, *Normative and Sectarian Judaism in the Second Temple Period* (New York: T&T Clark International, 2005), 269-273.
[308] Aaron Philmus, "What Really Happened at Sinai?" *Sefaria*, "Midrash Exodus Rabbah," (3, 5), accessed February 3, 2019, https://www.sefaria.org/sheets/25573?lang=bi. Note that the reference to Psalm 29:4 in the quote from the Hebrew Scriptures is 29:7 in most English translations.
[309] Richard Bauckham, *The Bible and Mission: Christian Mission in a Postmodern World* (Grand Rapids: Baker Academic, 2003), 56-60.

An Introduction to Education in Bible Times

And suddenly there came from heaven a noise like a violent rushing wind, and it filled the whole house where they [Jesus's disciples] were sitting. And there appeared to them tongues as of fire distributing themselves, and they rested on each one of them. And they were all filled with the Holy Spirit and began to speak with other tongues, as the Spirit was giving them utterance.

Acts 2:2-4

Jews from all the surrounding countries who came to Jerusalem for the Feast of Pentecost heard Jesus's disciples speaking of the mighty deeds of God, each in his own language. Just like the events at Sinai signified, F. F. Bruce explains, "On the reputed anniversary of the law-giving, people 'from every nation under heaven' heard the praises of God, 'every man ... in his own language.'"[310] The early disciples saw this event as a second Sinai.[311] Jesus's disciples were now equipped to bring His teaching to Jerusalem, Judea, and to make disciples of the nations.

On the day of Pentecost Peter said that the promise of the Holy Spirit was for all whom the LORD would call to Himself (Acts 2:38-39). The prophecy of Joel said that the LORD God would pour out His Spirit on all mankind (Joel 2:28-29). Later, as Peter was sharing the Gospel with the Roman centurion Cornelius and his household, the Holy Spirit fell on them, signifying that God had also opened the door of salvation to the Gentiles (Acts 10:44-48). The promised Holy Spirit, the Teacher, was now available to all who believed. The Holy Spirit would be with them, in the teachers God would give to His people, and the Holy Spirit would also reside within them, teaching them and reminding them of what they learned (John 14:16-17, 26). The Holy Spirit would continue to teach and lead, causing God's people to know Him and keep His Word.

The Holy Spirit enabled the disciples of Christ to teach and proclaim the Word of the Lord with boldness, with authority, and with confirming signs. The fourth chapter of Acts tells of Peter and John being arrested because of their teaching. They were brought before the council of the chief priests and elders who threatened them and finally let them go. The apostles went back to pray with their companions, saying:

---

[310] F. F. Bruce, *Commentary on the Book of the Acts* (Grand Rapids, 1983), 59-60.
[311] Joseph Shulam with Hilary Le Cornu, *A Commentary on the Jewish Roots of Acts 1-15* (Jerusalem: Netivyah Bible Instruction Ministry, 2012), 61.

> *"And now, Lord, take note of their threats, and grant that Your bond-servants may speak Your word with all confidence, while You extend Your hand to heal, and signs and wonders take place through the name of Your holy servant Jesus." And when they had prayed, the place where they had gathered together was shaken, and they were all filled with the Holy Spirit and began to speak the word of God with boldness.*
>
> Acts 4:29-31

The book of Acts emphasizes this theme of the disciples being empowered by the Holy Spirit to teach and proclaim the Word of God.

> *And with great power the apostles were giving testimony to the resurrection of the Lord Jesus, and abundant grace was upon them all.*
>
> Acts 4:33

> *At the hands of the apostles many signs and wonders were taking place among the people; and they were all with one accord in Solomon's portico. But none of the rest dared to associate with them; however, the people held them in high esteem. And all the more believers in the Lord, multitudes of men and women, were constantly added to their number, to such an extent that they even carried the sick out into the streets and laid them on cots and pallets, so that when Peter came by at least his shadow might fall on any one of them. Also the people from the cities in the vicinity of Jerusalem were coming together, bringing people who were sick or afflicted with unclean spirits, and they were all being healed.*
>
> Acts 5:12-16

> *But the high priest rose up, along with all his associates (that is the sect of the Sadducees), and they were filled with jealousy. They laid hands on the apostles and put them in a public jail. But during the night an angel of the Lord opened the gates of the prison, and taking them out he said, "Go, stand and speak to the people in the temple the whole message of this Life." Upon hearing this, they entered into the temple about daybreak and began to teach.*
>
> Acts 5:17-20

> *After calling the apostles in, they flogged them and ordered them not to speak in the name of Jesus, and then released them. So they went on their way from the presence of the Council, rejoicing that they had been considered worthy to suffer shame for His name. And every day, in the temple and from house to house, they kept right on teaching and preaching Jesus as the Christ.*
>
> Acts 5:40-42

The book of Acts continues this theme with the Holy Spirit enabling the apostle Paul to teach and proclaim the Word of God. Acts 19 tells about Paul ministering in the city of Ephesus:

> *This took place for two years, so that all who lived in Asia heard the word of the Lord, both Jews and Greeks. God was performing extraordinary miracles by the hands of Paul, so that handkerchiefs or aprons were even carried from his body to the sick, and the diseases left them and the evil spirits went out.*
>
> Acts 19:10-12

There were great miracles and signs and wonders, but most important was the fact that they were teaching and proclaiming the Word of God. As Luke records, "So the word of the Lord was growing mightily and prevailing" (Acts 19:20).

In New Testament times, a world was changed by people who were filled with the Holy Spirit and spoke the Word of God. As a result, they altered the course of entire civilizations. Customs, seasons, times, and economies were changed or disappeared. Nothing could stop the Word they spoke. Much of the known world experienced the words that Jesus told His disciples, "You will receive power when the Holy Spirit has come upon you; and you shall be My witnesses both in Jerusalem, and in all Judea and Samaria, and even to the remotest part of the earth" (Acts 1:8).

Christopher J. Reeves

Continuing in the Apostles' Teaching

Devout Jews from many nations gathered together in Jerusalem for the Feast of Pentecost, and Jesus's disciples were among them. The Feast of Pentecost was one of the required feasts of the agricultural cycle (Lev. 23:15-21). It was a one-day feast; however, because so many devout Jews made their way to Jerusalem with their offerings, the feast could last for another six days.[312] They brought their offerings to the priests in baskets, recognizing how God had delivered them from bondage and brought them into the land of Israel and blessed them (Deut. 26:1-11).[313] It was a time of celebration and sharing, as well as reciting prayers and readings from the Torah.

Hospitality without charge was part of the way of life for the Jewish people at feast times.[314] Homes were opened up in hospitality to accommodate the thousands of people who thronged to the Feast of Pentecost in Jerusalem. People slept wherever they could, especially on rooftops where there was plenty of room, and since it was harvest time there was not much likelihood of rain. The feasts were a time of rejoicing and being altogether joyful in the Lord.

Following the outpouring of the Holy Spirit and Peter's address to those who were gathered in Jerusalem for the feast, many received the word that Peter spoke to them.

> *So then, those who had received his word were baptized; and that day there were added about three thousand souls. They were continually devoting themselves to the apostles' teaching and to fellowship, to the breaking of bread and to prayer. Everyone kept feeling a sense of awe; and many wonders and signs were taking place through the apostles. And all those who had believed were together and had all things in common; and they began selling their property and possessions and were sharing them with all, as anyone might have need. Day by day continuing with one mind in the temple, and breaking bread from house to house, they were taking their meals together with gladness*

---

[312] Shulam, *A Commentary on the Jewish Roots of Acts 1-15*, 56.
[313] Mishnah (Bikkurim 3) *Sefaria*, accessed February 4, 2019, https://www.sefaria.org/Mishnah_ Bikkurim.3?lang=bi.
[314] R.H Stein, "Entertain," in *The International Standard Bible Encyclopedia*, rev. ed., ed. Geoffrey W. Bromiley (Grand Rapids: Eerdmans, 1979–1988), 105–106.

and sincerity of heart, praising God and having favor with all the people. And the Lord was adding to their number day by day those who were being saved.

Acts 2:41–47

Those who had received Peter's word on the day of Pentecost were continually giving themselves to the teaching of the apostles (Acts 2:42). The disciples of Jesus became known as "apostles." The term *apostle* refers to one who is commissioned and sent by another.[315] The apostles were witnesses of the life, ministry, teaching, and the death and resurrection of Jesus. They were commissioned and sent by Jesus, their Lord, to be His witnesses, to teach and raise up other disciples. They had so engaged with their Master's thoughts and ways that when they began their ministry of teaching, it was evident they had been disciples of Jesus (Acts 4:1-33). As their Master had done before, the apostles were now illuminating the Scriptures for their hearers. They recounted Jesus's ministry and repeated His teachings, and the people gathered together daily at the Temple to listen as the apostles taught them.

In addition to the people devoting themselves to the apostles' teaching, they also were giving themselves to fellowship, breaking bread together, and to prayer (Acts 2:42). One of the greatest pursuits and privileges of first-century Jewish life was to study, learn, and find a teacher. It was typical in Jewish society for groups of *chaverim* (associates) to have communal meals on Sabbaths and at other times during the weekday evenings. These gatherings were dedicated to Torah study and other special events. The rabbinic sages taught, "Three who eat at one table and speak words of Torah, it is as if they have eaten at God's table."[316] And "Ten who sit together and occupy themselves with Torah, the Divine Presence rests amongst them, as is stated: 'The Almighty stands in the congregation of God.'"[317] The people were devoted to hearing the apostles teach and then they would break bread together at communal meals to talk about the teaching they had received. In this atmosphere there was a sense of awe as the Divine presence was with them.

---

[315] Karl Heinrich Rengsdorf, απποστελλω (πεμπω), εξαποστελλω, αποστολοσ, φευδαποστολοσ, αποστολοσ," in *Theological Dictionary of the New Testament*, ed. Gerhard Kittel, Geoffrey W. Bromiley, and Gerhard Friedrich (Grand Rapids: Eerdmans, 1964), 400.
[316] *Ethics of the Fathers* 3.3.
[317] *Ethics of the Fathers* 3.6.

The hunger for the apostles' teaching continued as the Word of God spread out from Jerusalem to other areas. Imagine the early gatherings of believers listening to the stories of Jesus from those who had walked with Him as disciples. And imagine these people gathering together to study the Scriptures or read a letter from one of the apostolic fathering ministries.[318] In Acts 20, Luke tells the story of the saints in Troas gathering in an upper room to break bread together; they received the Word of the Lord and continued on through the night in a teaching and learning dialogue with the visiting apostles and teachers (Acts 20:4-11).[319] From the earliest gatherings, the early church was given to continual learning, studying together, and abiding in the apostolic teaching they had received, which continued in Jerusalem after the day of Pentecost and through the expanded evangelistic ministry of Paul into other countries. This way of life was to continue, as the Scriptures commanded: "Let the word of Christ dwell in you richly in all wisdom teaching and admonishing each other" (Col. 3:16) (The Interlinear Translation of the Greek New Testament).[320]

The early church continued gathering together with the common goal of their community learning and keeping God's Word (1 Cor. 14:26; Col 3:16; Heb. 10:24-25). Lifelong biblical education was to begin with children in the home (Eph. 6:4). In many cases learning began after a person or household received Jesus Christ as Savior and Lord (Col. 2:6-7). Learning for the purpose of knowing the Lord and keeping His ways as a community of believers was to continue throughout life (2 Tim. 3:14-15). Their devotion to continuing in the apostles' teaching and the reading of Scripture produced maturity and fruitfulness and gave them wisdom and the ability to teach and impart to others (Eph. 4:11-13; Heb. 5:12; 2 Tim 2.2).

---

[318] James D. G. Dunn, *The Oral Gospel Tradition* (Grand Rapids: Eerdmans, 2013), 110
[319] Shulam with Le Cornu, *A Commentary on the Jewish Roots of Acts 16-28*, 1107. This sort of gathering is similar to the rabbinic custom of dinner clubs. These clubs were thought to be widespread during the time of the early Church. These home gatherings began with a meal and could go on into the night as the group discussed the Torah together.
[320] Thomas Newberry and George Ricker Berry, *The Interlinear Literal Translation of the Greek New Testament* (Bellingham, WA: Logos Bible Software, 2004).

An Introduction to Education in Bible Times

The Pastor-Teacher

Throughout the Hebrew Scriptures we see the great emphasis placed on the ministry of teaching. The ministry of teaching was emphasized as the LORD began His relationship with Abraham and his descendants, and when He gave the Torah (His instruction) to Israel through Moses. Teaching was also emphasized throughout the Second Temple period beginning with the ministry of Ezra. As the New Testament era opened, we also witness Jesus's ministry of teaching. One could say that teaching was essential each time God began a new era with His people. Therefore, God continued to gift His people with the ministry of teaching.

> *And He gave some as apostles, and some as prophets, and some as evangelists, and some as pastors and teachers, for the equipping of the saints for the work of service, to the building up of the body of Christ; until we all attain to the unity of the faith, and of the knowledge of the Son of God, to a mature man, to the measure of the stature which belongs to the fullness of Christ.*
>
> Ephesians 4:11–13

The apostle Paul includes teachers as one of the gift ministries of the church who bring about spiritual maturity, equipping God's people to serve Him. In this passage, Paul also groups pastors and teachers together. The word translated as pastor is actually the word *shepherd*, referring to the historical relationship of the LORD as a shepherd to His people and to those who were appointed by God to lead and teach His people. Following this imagery, Jesus referred to Himself as the Good Shepherd of God's sheep.

Pastors and teachers are joined as one group "because they both minister to the individual congregation."[321] In the Hebrew Scriptures the term *shepherd* was often applied to the priests who taught the people Torah (Jer. 3:15; 23:1-4). The purpose of teaching was to bring about an intimate knowledge of the LORD and to enable God's people to obediently walk in His ways. This purpose for teaching continued in the church as the risen Lord gave pastors and teachers.

---

[321] Joachim Jeremias, "αποιμον, αρχιποιμην, ποιμαινω, ποιμνη, ποιμνιον," in *Theological Dictionary of the New Testament*, ed. Gerhard Kittel, Geoffrey W. Bromiley, and Gerhard Friedrich (Grand Rapids: Eerdmans, 1964), 497.

The purpose of teaching to bring people into an intimate knowledge of God is conveyed through Paul, the apostle and teacher of the Gentile believers in Christ.

> *[I] do not cease giving thanks for you, while making mention of you in my prayers; that the God of our Lord Jesus Christ, the Father of glory, may give to you a spirit of wisdom and of revelation in the knowledge of Him.*
>
> Eph. 1:16–17

> *[That you] may be able to comprehend with all the saints what is the breadth and length and height and depth, and to know the love of Christ which surpasses knowledge, that you may be filled up to all the fullness of God.*
>
> Eph. 3:18-19

Paul saw the purpose of his teaching ministry was to bring people to an intimate knowledge of God.

The Holy Spirit is involved in the ministry of the teacher as well as in the individual lives of the believers. Believers are taught by the Holy Spirit through anointed teachers as they study the Scriptures, share experiences, and express the gifts of the Spirit in the church (Rom. 12:6-7; 1 Cor. 14:26; Col. 3:16). John Stevens explains that the Holy Spirit can teach God's people directly or through the ministry of teaching:

> "The Lord Jesus said we would all be taught of the Lord (John 6:45, cf. Isaiah 54:13 and Jeremiah 31:34). He also said that the Holy Spirit would come to us as a guide and lead us into all truth (John 16:12-15). The Apostle John said this anointing of the Holy Spirit would teach us all things. 1 John 2:27. We must remember, however, that while God teaches us by the Holy Spirit directly, He also teaches us through the gift ministry of the teacher. We may learn through the Holy Spirit through experiences and by revelation, but this usually takes longer. When God gives the gift ministry of the teacher, we move rapidly toward the faith that was once delivered to the saints."[322]

---

[322] John Robert Stevens, "Pastors and Teachers," in *New Testament Church Manual* (North Hollywood: Living Word Publications, 1968), 16.

The commissioned ministry of teaching was seen in many of the apostles, in the pastor-teachers who were overseeing churches, and in the local church elders. Following the first century custom of supporting local rabbis (teachers), Paul instructed that those who labored to teach in the churches were to be provided support (1 Tim. 5:17-18). They were also to be held in high regard. Paul continued, "But we request of you, brethren, that you appreciate those who diligently labor among you, and have charge over you in the Lord and give you instruction, and that you esteem them very highly in love because of their work" (1 Thess. 5:12-13).

The Preparation of Teachers

The apostles and leaders of the early church centered in Jerusalem grew up in a culture that valued the education of children and the continuing education of adults. According to the educational program of the first century, most Jews would have had an extensive education by the age of twelve. They would have known how to read the Scriptures in the ancient Hebrew language. They would have memorized the Shema and the other morning and evening prayers, as well as the prayers recited during sabbaths and feasts. They would have memorized large portions of the Torah and would have begun the study of the Oral Torah.[323] Later tradition drawing from this period states, "Five years is the age for the study of Scripture. Ten, for the study of Mishnah. Thirteen, for the obligation to observe the mitzvot. Fifteen, for the study of Talmud."[324] Most young adults would begin apprenticing in their father's trade. Some, like the apostle Paul, would go on to study at one of the colleges to become a teacher of Torah.

Further, Nathan Drazin adds, "Adult education was widespread and popular among the Jews. Every Jew knew that he was obligated by sacred Law to study Torah every day of his life. Consequently, many men, even artisans and industrial workers, reserved part of every day for study."[325] In like manner, as adults, Jesus's disciples would have continued in their

---

[323]Shulam, *A Commentary on the Jewish Roots of Acts 1-15*, 451-454.
[324]*Ethics of the Fathers* 5.22.
[325]Nathan Drazin, *History of Jewish Education from 515 B.C.E. to 220 C.E. (During the Periods of the Second Commonwealth and the Tannaim)* (Baltimore: Johns Hopkins Press, 1940), 76.

education through the regular synagogue services. They recognized Jesus as a teacher and followed Him as His disciples. They lived the life of disciples, leaving their former ways of life to follow, serve, learn, and become. Over time they came to know their teacher as the Father's beloved Son. Jesus's disciples learned through their Teacher's words and through His example—committing to memory all they had learned and observed. After Jesus's resurrection, He opened their minds and hearts to the Scriptures and illuminated what they had studied since childhood. Luke records, "Now He said to them, 'These are My words which I spoke to you while I was still with you, that all things which are written about Me in the Law of Moses and the Prophets and the Psalms must be fulfilled.' Then He opened their minds to understand the Scriptures" (Luke 24:44-45). The disciples' lifestyle of studying and learning the Scriptures had provided a foundation for the Lord to open their minds to understand them.

After the day of Pentecost the apostles continued to give themselves to being together, devoting their time to the Word of God and prayer (Acts 1:12; 6:4). Their relationship together as disciples continued as they studied the Scriptures, rehearsed Jesus's life and teaching, and prayed together; and as promised, the Holy Spirit taught them and brought to their remembrance all that Jesus had said (John 14:26).

The apostles often taught in the Temple. On one occasion the priests and Sadducees had Peter and John arrested because they had healed a man and were teaching the crowds who had gathered by proclaiming in Jesus the resurrection from the dead. So the rulers and elders and scribes who were in Jerusalem brought Peter and John into their midst to ask them questions. Peter, filled with the Holy Spirit, answered them boldly (Acts 4:1-12). Luke illustrates, "Now as they observed the confidence of Peter and John and understood that they were uneducated and untrained men, they were amazed, and began to recognize them as having been with Jesus" (Acts 4:13). Joseph Shulam adds, "This passage indicates that 'the leaders' marveling over Peter and John's confidence appears to reflect a tacit admission that Jesus's influence expressed itself in learning ... [and the apostles'] confidence may parallel the authority which people ascribed to Jesus's teaching ... as those qualified in Torah-study."[326] Jesus's disciples were prepared and equipped to carry on His ministry of teaching.

---

[326] Shulam, *A Commentary on the Jewish Roots of Acts 1-15*, 244.

An Introduction to Education in Bible Times

The apostle Paul was raised by Jewish parents and likely went through the normal stages of learning for children and young adults. As a promising student, he went on to study at the college of Hillel in Jerusalem. At that time, it was Gamaliel, grandson of Hillel, who was the master of the school. Paul received his advanced education in the Torah under Gamaliel, receiving the mantle of Torah leadership that had been passed on from generation to generation (Acts 22:3). Bruce explains that Paul's goal in his studies was to become "as proficient as possible in the ancestral traditions of his people. He claimed indeed to have outstripped his contemporaries in the knowledge and practice of the Jewish religion (Gal. 1:14)."[327] Paul understood the national and personal importance of preserving the knowledge of God and the ability to walk in His ways. Bruce continues that this ability was contained in a knowledge of the Written Torah and the Oral Law "transmitted by generations of rabbis and preserved by the School of Hillel, which interpreted those precepts and applied them in detail to every department of contemporary life."[328]

Paul was educated as a Pharisee, a teacher and keeper of Torah (Acts 22:3; 26:5; Phil. 3:5-6). After the Lord Jesus appeared to him and called him to be an apostle and teacher of the Gentiles,[329] the next few years of Paul's life were spent with teachers and prophets in the churches of Damascus and Antioch, with the Lord appearing to him, teaching him and opening his mind to the Scriptures (as He had done previously with His disciples). Lastly, Paul went up to Jerusalem to spend time with the apostles Peter and James (Gal. 1:18-24).

When Paul received the revelation of Jesus Christ, he was immediately able to proclaim and teach the gospel of Christ because of his knowledge of the Hebrew Scriptures and the oral traditions. Luke writes, "Now for several days he was with the disciples who were at Damascus, and immediately he began to proclaim Jesus in the synagogues, saying, 'He is the Son of God.' ... But Saul kept increasing in strength and confounding the Jews who lived at Damascus by proving that this Jesus is the Christ" (Acts 9:19-20, 22). Throughout his ministry, Paul continued to use his knowledge of the Hebrew Scriptures, his understanding of the oral traditions, and his skill in the process of midrash as a bridge in teaching

---

[327] F. F. Bruce, "Paul the Apostle," in *The International Standard Bible Encyclopedia*, rev., ed. Geoffrey W. Bromiley (Grand Rapids: Eerdmans, 1979–1988), 710.
[328] Bruce, "Paul the Apostle," 710
[329] Acts 9:15; 22:21; 26:17; Rom 1:5; 11:13; 15:16; Gal 1:16; Eph. 3:1, 8; 1 Tim 2:7; 2 Tim 4:17.

the claims of Jesus as the Messiah.³³⁰ However, he did not rely on his educational training alone, but he relied on the work of the Holy Spirit to reach people with the gospel of Christ (1 Cor. 2:1-5).

It was three years after his encounter with Jesus that Paul went up to Jerusalem to visit with Peter and James (Gal. 1:18-19). Bruce states, "The verb that Paul used of his visiting Peter is interesting: 'I went up,' he said, '*historesai Kēphan*'—'to get to know Cephas,' and not only to get to know the man himself, but to get to know things that Peter was especially competent to impart."³³¹ Through Peter and James, Paul received eyewitness accounts of Jesus's life, ministry, and teaching. Because of his time with Peter and James, Paul was able to fill in further details, which equipped him in greater measure to teach and impart to others what he himself had received.

Jesus's command to make disciples of the nations was founded upon the biblical culture of teaching and learning—a culture where teaching and learning was a universal responsibility. Jesus intended for His followers to continue in a devotion to lifelong learning, where learners also became teachers. The preparation of teachers with the character of the Master Teacher was to be repeated multiple times throughout the generations. Parents were to teach their children, adults were to continue in their lifelong devotion to the Word of God, and teachers were to impart what they had received (Eph. 6:4; 2 Tim. 2:2). The commitment to teach, learn, and make disciples would result in the continual preparation of those who could also teach others.³³²

The Illustration of Paul and Timothy

Throughout the Bible, God presents a lofty goal for teaching and learning. Marvin Wilson affirms, "Learning constitutes the very core of the heritage that Jewish civilization has bequeathed to the Church."³³³ Parents taught their children the ways of the Lord, and later in life

---

³³⁰Karl Heinrich Rengsdorf, "διδασκω in the NT," in *Theological Dictionary of the New Testament*, ed. Gerhard Kittel, Geoffrey W. Bromiley, and Gerhard Friedrich (Grand Rapids: Eerdmans, 1964), 136–148.
³³¹Bruce, "Paul the Apostle," 712.
³³²Marvin R. Wilson, *Our Father Abraham: Jewish Roots of the Christian Faith* (Grand Rapids: Eerdmans, 1989), 301.
³³³Wilson, *Our Father Abraham*, 278.

another teacher might become a father to the student, bringing him into a deeper relationship with God and His Word (1 Cor. 4:14-17). According to the Jewish culture in which Jesus and his followers functioned, the word *disciple* (from the Hebrew word *talmid*) meant the "student" of a master (or teacher).[334] Jesus told His disciples, whom He brought into a relationship with the Father and with His Word, to go out and make disciples of others. This means of discipleship, of teaching and learning, can be seen in the relationship between Paul and Timothy.

Timothy grew up with a Jewish mother and grandmother. He learned the Scriptures as a child and learned other aspects of the Jewish faith that his mother and grandmother taught him. Timothy would have had a good knowledge and understanding of the Scriptures when Paul took him on as his disciple. Paul taught Timothy what he received from the Lord Jesus, opening the Scriptures to him in a way that revealed the gospel of Christ. Timothy accompanied Paul during his missionary journeys and ministered to Paul's needs. Later Paul sent him to oversee churches and set them in order. Additionally, Timothy coauthored some of the letters that Paul sent to the churches.

Paul's two letters to Timothy record a spiritual father's relationship with his spiritual son. Paul's letters include tender expressions of love and concern alongside the practical admonitions that provided assistance to Timothy in his ministry. In 1 Timothy 1:18, Paul says, "This command I entrust to you, Timothy, my son ...." In 2 Timothy 1:2, Paul writes, "To Timothy, my beloved son ...," and again in 2 Timothy 2:1, "You therefore, my son, be strong in the grace that is in Christ Jesus." Even when introducing Timothy to the churches, Paul referred to him as his "beloved and faithful child in the Lord" (1 Cor. 4:17).

Timothy learned through his love and service to Paul as his spiritual father (Phil. 2:22). He faithfully accompanied and served Paul in his evangelistic travels and in the context of local church ministry (cf. 1 and 2 Timothy). Paul rehearsed, "Now you followed my teaching, conduct, purpose, faith, patience, love, perseverance, persecutions, and sufferings, such as happened to me at Antioch, at Iconium and at Lystra; what persecutions I endured, and out of them all the Lord rescued me!" (2 Tim. 3:10-11). Timothy learned from studying Paul's teachings as well as from observing his way of life. As a result, Timothy became

---

[334]Brian S. Wright, *The Great Yet Completely Misunderstood Commission of Jesus* (www.faiththink.org: Calvert Biblical Institute, 2017), 9.

one of the great ministries of the early church. Because he had learned through his close relationship with Paul, Timothy was able to further the teaching that Paul had received from the Lord. Paul instructed him, "You therefore, my son, be strong in the grace that is in Christ Jesus. The things which you have heard from me in the presence of many witnesses, entrust these to faithful men who will be able to teach others also" (2 Tim. 2:1-2).

True teaching comes from and has its expression in the life of an individual. Jesus said, "By this all men will know that you are My disciples [students], if you have love for one another" (John 13:35). It is by observing the conduct, motivation, and the expression of the Word of God in faith and action that people truly receive the teaching. Paul told Timothy, "You, however, continue in the things that you have learned and become convinced of, knowing from whom you have learned them" (2 Tim. 3:14). Teachers were to be examples. Those who learned were to witness the expression of that teaching in their teacher's motivation and the conduct of his or her life. This is the way Timothy learned from Paul and the way the other church ministries were to learn from Timothy. This ability to witness the teaching in the life of God's commissioned teachers made the early church leaders effective in their work.

Timothy experienced this same pattern of learning in his youth. He learned the Scriptures as a child while also observing the sincere faith in the life of his mother and grandmother (2 Tim. 1:5; 3:15). When the Scriptures are evidenced in the life of a parent or teacher, teaching becomes effective, and the Scriptures themselves take on greater meaning. It was this learning and knowledge of the Scriptures that made Timothy wise unto salvation through faith. Scripture was to be the starting point for Timothy as he taught by word and example. The goal of instruction was not only to impart knowledge, but to produce love from a pure heart in its expression toward God and toward others (1 Tim. 1:3-5).

> *Prescribe and teach these things. Let no one look down on your youthfulness, but rather in speech, conduct, love, faith and purity, show yourself an example of those who believe. Until I come, give attention to the public reading of Scripture, to exhortation and teaching. Do not neglect the spiritual gift within you, which was bestowed on you through prophetic utterance with the laying on of hands by the*

presbytery. Take pains with these things; be absorbed in them, so that your progress will be evident to all. Pay close attention to yourself and to your teaching; persevere in these things, for as you do this you will ensure salvation both for yourself and for those who hear you.
1 Timothy 4:11-16

Throughout his letters to Timothy, Paul emphasizes the great need for the ministry of teaching. Timothy was to continually be absorbed in the Scriptures and the teaching he had received from Paul, always ready to instruct, correct, and lead the people in a living expression of their faith in Christ Jesus. Correct teaching would bring people into the life and manner of walking that the Lord had provided for them. It also instructed them in the way to walk with each other in a manner that is pleasing to the Lord. Teaching would lay a sturdy foundation and keep God's people steadfast in the face of false doctrines and persecutions (2 Tim. 2:14-26; 3:16-4:4). As an example, Timothy was not to be quarrelsome, but kind to all, able to teach, patient when wronged, and with gentleness correcting those who were in opposition to God's truth.

Timothy was also told to stop those who taught strange doctrines and who gave themselves to fruitless speculations (1 Tim. 1:3-4). Paul warned against meaningless discussions that were promoted by those who tried to impress others with their knowledge (1 Tim. 1:6-7). Speculative teaching with empty words was to be avoided. Teaching was to be more than the mere conveying of ideas. Teaching was to be filled with the life and power of God (1 Cor. 4:17-20; Col. 3:16; 1 Pet. 4:11).

Paul's letters to Timothy (and also to Titus) include practical instructions regarding the ministry of teaching, the impartation of spiritual gifts, and the order of the church. It is in these "family" letters to Paul's spiritual sons that there are also instructions for how God's family should conduct their lives together. An example of this family teaching is in the instruction regarding elders. Elders were to be family men, those who were able to teach and lead, and those whose lives would be an example for God's people to follow (1 Tim. 3:1-7; Titus 1:5-9). The close family relationship of fathers and sons was to be repeated and duplicated in the Heavenly Father's family through His ways of teaching and learning.

To Know the LORD and Walk in His Ways

Learners coming to the knowledge of God has been a consistent theme or purpose for education in Bible times. The LORD God called Abraham to know Him and to teach His ways, as expressed through his relationship with Him and with others. Moses, the great teacher, knew the LORD and sought to teach God's people to know Him, love Him, and walk in His ways. Jesus knew the Father, revealing Him through His words and His works. Jesus faithfully imparted this knowledge to His disciples, who were raised up to teach others to love Him and keep His commandments by loving one another. The apostle Paul exemplified this quality by striving to know the Lord Jesus Christ; and he constantly prayed for the churches that he taught to also know the Lord, His love, and what the Father had prepared for them to walk in (Phil. 3:8-10). Paul writes:

> *"For this reason also, since the day we heard of [your faith], we have not ceased to pray for you and to ask that you may be filled with the knowledge of His will in all spiritual wisdom and understanding, so that you will walk in a manner worthy of the Lord, to please Him in all respects, bearing fruit in every good work and increasing in the knowledge of God."*
>
> Col. 1:9-10

The apostle Peter, who was discipled by the Great Teacher, began his second letter to the churches by expressing his faith for them to continue to grow in their knowledge of God. He also encouraged them to continue to be diligent in their faith and to walk in God's ways, reminding them of the teaching they received from the apostles and teachers who had been eyewitnesses of the Lord Jesus Christ and His glory. Peter exhorts, "So we have the prophetic word made more sure, to which you do well to pay attention as to a lamp shining in a dark place, until the day dawns and the morning star arises in your hearts" (2 Pet. 1:19). His shepherd's heart built a protective wall around the teaching to help the churches recognize false teachers: "But know this first of all, that no prophecy of Scripture is a matter of one's own interpretation, for no prophecy was ever made by an act of human will, but men moved by the Holy Spirit spoke from God" (2 Pet. 1:20-21). Peter ended his second epistle with these important words, "But grow in the grace and knowledge of our Lord and Savior Jesus Christ. To Him be the glory, both now and to the day of eternity. Amen" (2 Pet. 3:18).

Teaching – διδασκω

It is valuable to understand the New Testament definition of *teaching* to differentiate the biblical definition from other contemporary definitions. The Greek word used for *teaching* (διδασκω, διδασκειν) in the New Testament is the same word that is used in the Septuagint, the Greek version of the Hebrew Scriptures. It is based on the Hebrew word דמל meaning (1) to learn with the idea of submitting and keeping, (2) to be trained, and (3) to teach, instruct, or impart information.[335] The Septuagint word for teaching (διδασκω/διδασκειν) primarily referred to the Torah's concern with the whole man and his education in the deepest sense. As Karl Rengsdorf noted, by the time of the Second Temple "teaching" also referred to the authoritative pronouncements from scholarly decisions based on the interpretation of Scripture regarding specific halachic issues. He concluded that through the "exposition of the Law as the sum of the revealed will of God, instruction is given for the ordering of the relationship between the individual and God on the one side, and the neighbor on the other, according to the divine will."[336]

In the Gospel accounts, teaching (διδασκω, διδασκειν) was one of the most prominent functions of Jesus's ministry. Yet, the form of His teaching is not elaborated in the Gospels since their initial audiences were Jews who had grown up in the first-century culture of teaching and learning. Nevertheless, Jesus's teaching is in keeping with the historic usage of the concept of Jewish teaching, regarding God's concern for the whole man and authoritatively bringing the Torah to its highest application. Teaching was to lead people into knowing their God and into understanding and keeping His ways.

---

[335]James Swanson, דמל, in *Dictionary of Biblical Languages with Semantic Domains: Hebrew (Old Testament)* (Oak Harbor: Logos Research Systems, Inc., 1997).
[336]Karl Heinrich Rengsdorf, "διδασκω outside the NT," ed. Gerhard Kittel, Geoffrey W. Bromiley, and Gerhard Friedrich, *Theological Dictionary of the New Testament* (Grand Rapids: Eerdmans, 1964), 136–148.

With teaching and learning, there is a difference between mental knowledge acquisition and submitting to God's claims on your life. This concept marks an important distinction between teaching in the Septuagint's use of the word *teaching* (διδασκω, διδασκειν) and the secular usage of *teaching* in the Greek language. Rengsdorf clarifies:

"The idea of a total claim is not to be detected in secular Greek, where the aim is to develop talents and potentialities. In the LXX (OT), on the other hand, the concern is with the whole man and his education in the deepest sense. … A novel feature in this use [of teaching] by the Evangelists is the complete supersession of the intellectual element present in non-biblical usage. … The whole teaching of Jesus is with a view to the ordering of life with reference to God and one's neighbor (Matt. 22:37 ff. and par.; cf. 19:16ff. and par.). Thus His teaching constantly appeals to the will, calling for a practical decision either for the will of God or against it. He finds a common basis with the Rabbis and the Pharisaic community in the fact that He sees a revelation of the will of God in Scripture and especially in the Law, so that it is quite impossible for Him to surrender even a single letter (Matt. 5:17 f.)."[337]

Both the Hebrew Scriptures and the New Testament writings place a priority on the obedient response of the hearers. Here are just a few of the many passages that emphasize the desired response to God's claim on the whole man through the words of His instruction:

"Now then, if you will indeed obey My voice and keep My covenant, then you shall be My own possession among all the peoples, for all the earth is Mine.

Exod. 19:5

"And you shall again obey the LORD, and observe all His commandments which I command you today. Then the LORD your God will prosper you abundantly in all the work of your hand, in the offspring of your body and in the offspring of your cattle and in the produce of your ground, for the LORD will again rejoice over you for

---

[337] Rengsdorf, "διδασκω in the NT," 137, 140, 141

> *good, just as He rejoiced over your fathers; if you obey the LORD your God to keep His commandments and His statutes which are written in this book of the law, if you turn to the LORD your God with all your heart and soul."*
>
> Deut. 30:8–10

Samuel said:

> *"Has the LORD as much delight in burnt offerings and sacrifices*
> *As in obeying the voice of the LORD?*
> *Behold, to obey is better than sacrifice,*
> *And to heed than the fat of rams."*
>
> 1 Sam. 15:22

> *"Therefore everyone who hears these words of Mine and acts on them, may be compared to a wise man who built his house on the rock."*
>
> Matt. 7:24

> *But He said, "... blessed are those who hear the word of God and observe it."*
>
> Luke 11:28

> *So then, my beloved, just as you have always obeyed, not as in my presence only, but now much more in my absence, work out your salvation with fear and trembling; for it is God who is at work in you, both to will and to work for His good pleasure.*
>
> Phil. 2:12–13

Each of these passages illustrates the priority placed on the obedient response of the hearers.

The teaching of Jesus's disciples was bold and authoritative in proclaiming the claims of God to those who heard them. They used the Hebrew Scriptures as the starting point for teaching Jesus as Lord and Christ. Rengsdorf explains that the "whole complex of Scripture was the starting point and background for their teaching."[338] As Jesus taught them, "Therefore every scribe [*scholar and authoritative teacher*] who has

---

[338] Rengsdorf, "διδασκω in the NT," 145.

become a disciple [*one who has learned with the intent of obeying and teaching others*] of the kingdom of heaven is like a head of a household [*a father who teaches*], who brings out of his treasure things new and old" (Matt. 13:52).

Contrasts in Teaching

Abraham Cohen affirms that in biblical times "the greatest dignity [was] attached to the profession of teacher and he was held in the highest esteem. In certain matters Jewish law gives a teacher precedence over even a parent."[339] The apostle Paul recognized this relationship with those whom he taught and brought into a relationship with God through the gospel of Christ. Paul wrote to the Corinthians:

> *For if you were to have countless tutors in Christ, yet you would not have many fathers, for in Christ Jesus I became your father through the gospel. Therefore I exhort you, be imitators of me. For this reason I have sent to you Timothy, who is my beloved and faithful child in the Lord, and he will remind you of my ways which are in Christ, just as I teach everywhere in every church. Now some have become arrogant, as though I were not coming to you. But I will come to you soon, if the Lord wills, and I shall find out, not the words of those who are arrogant but their power. For the kingdom of God does not consist in words but in power."*
>
> 1 Cor. 4:15-20

David Lowery explains that when Paul taught the Corinthians "he had not depended on his own ability but on the power of the Spirit (1 Cor. 2:4-5). He would rely on this same power for discipline (2 Cor. 10:4-6). This was the authority of God's rule (cf. Acts 5:3-11). Though Paul loved the Corinthians he knew that a loving father did not shy away from discipline (cf. Heb. 12:7)."[340] Paul's commitment to rely on the teaching anointing and power of the Holy Spirit is in direct contrast

---

[339] Abraham Cohen, *Everyman's Talmud: The Major Themes of the Rabbinic Sages* (New York: Schocken Books, 1995), 175

[340] David K. Lowery, "1 Corinthians," in *The Bible Knowledge Commentary: An Exposition of the Scriptures by Dallas Seminary Faculty*, ed. John F. Walvoord and Roy B. Zuck, vol. 2 (Wheaton, IL: Victor Books, 1985), 513, LOGOS.

to those who wanted to be teachers in themselves, perhaps for a sense of self-importance (1 Cor. 4:19). Paul told the Corinthian church that he would evaluate the arrogant teachers by examining if the power of God accompanied their teaching, because God's kingdom does not consist in mere words but in the power of His Spirit. As a spiritual father, Paul's goal was not to arrogantly give his great knowledge to others. Rather, it was to bring people into God's kingdom by humbling himself and allowing the Holy Spirit to frame and confirm his teaching (1 Cor. 2—4).

During the days of the early church, some teachers ministered the Gospel for the purpose of gaining recognition and compensation; however, by contrast, Paul did not. As a spiritual father and teacher, Paul saw his role as one to provide for those whom he fathered in the Gospel (2 Cor. 12:14-18). On many occasions he supported himself while teaching and ministering and did not use his teaching ministry for personal gain (Acts 20:33-35; 2 Cor. 11:7-9; 1 Thess. 2:9). This practice was in keeping with the admonition of the sages to not expect recognition or compensation for religious teaching: "Rabbi Tzaddok would say: … Do not make the Torah a crown to magnify yourself with, or a spade with which to dig. So would Hillel say: one who makes personal use of the crown of Torah shall perish. Hence, one who benefits himself from the words of Torah, removes his life from the world."[341] While teachers were to be supported and respected, they were not to enter into a ministry of teaching for the purpose of receiving recognition or financial gain (Matt. 10:9-10; 1 Tim. 5:17).

Continuing the Patterns of Teaching and Learning

During the century that followed the early church activities recorded in the New Testament, believers continued to assemble together to listen to the readings of the Gospels and letters of the apostles, and to read portions of the Greek version of the Hebrew Scriptures.[342] The community's continual learning and growing in their faith by reading and hearing the available writings was a weekly priority through the

---
[341] *Ethics of the Fathers* 4.5.
[342] Warren Carter, "The Process of Closing the New Testament Canon," *Seven Events That Shaped the New Testament World* (Grand Rapids: Baker Academic, 2013).

middle of the second century. However, we can only guess as to how many of these available documents were recopied, read, and regularly studied. Sadly, before the start of the Middle Ages, the birthright of the Scriptures belonging to the community of believers and the biblical ministry of teaching was lost. It was not until the early 1500's that the Scriptures and the ability to study and teach them were once again becoming the inheritance of all believers in Christ.[343]

---

[343]Bruce L. Shelley, *Church History in Plain Language: Fourth Edition*, rev. by R. L. Hatchett (Nashville: Thomas Nelson, 2013), 279.

Part 6

THE EDUCATIONAL TEXT—GOD'S WORD

For the word of God is living and active.

Hebrews 4:12

Introduction

This section explores Second Temple Judaism and early Christian thought regarding the divine nature of God's Word. This topic becomes relevant when you consider that education in Bible times centered on the study of God's Word. Beginning with the time of Moses, the Jews studied the Written and Oral Torah. By the first century CE, the biblical texts also included the Law, the Prophets, and the Writings, as well as the oral traditions that were passed down from Moses to each succeeding generation. Additionally, there was a growing body of midrash and other religious writings that were not included in the canon of the Hebrew Scriptures. Following the time of Jesus's earthly ministry, the gospel accounts of His life, ministry, and teachings were also added, plus other books and letters presenting the ministry and teachings of the early apostles.

According to the biblical texts, God through the Holy Spirit is the author of Scripture (2 Pet. 1:19-21). God spoke through Moses, through the prophets, through His Son, and through the writers of the New Testament (Heb. 1:1-2, 2:3-4). God's words are divine in nature. They are creative; they reveal the Heavenly Father to His people; they impart His attributes, and they provide instruction for life. Because of this, God's words were to be meditated on, studied, and kept (Josh. 1:6-9; Ps. 1:1-3; John 15:1-11), and they would produce God's intended results within the lives of those who so treasured them.

The Divine Nature of God's Word

At the beginning of creation God "spoke" and created the heavens and the earth. Genesis records, "In the beginning God created the heavens and the earth. The earth was formless and void, and darkness was over the surface of the deep, and the Spirit of God was moving over the surface of the waters. Then God said, 'Let there be ...'" (Gen. 1:1-3). Nahum Sarna notes that in this account of creation "the divine word shatters the primal cosmic silence and signals the birth of a new cosmic order. Divine fiat [decree] is the first of the several modalities of creativity employed in this account [of creation]."[344]

---

[344]Nahum M. Sarna, *The JPS Torah Commentary: Genesis* (Philadelphia: Jewish Publication Society, 1989), 7.

The first chapter of Genesis uses the phrase "God said" (employing the Hebrew word 'āmar) some ten times. Charles Feinberg explains, "Half of these times it is 'God said, let there be' and then it happened. At other times it says, 'God said, let there be' and then God proceeded to create. This creative word of God is recognized in Psalm 33:9, 'He spoke ('āmar) and it was done; he commanded and it stood fast.'"[345] Referring back to the account of creation, the writer of Hebrews confirms that "the worlds were prepared [created] by the word of God, so that what is seen was not made out of things which are visible" (Heb. 11:3).

God's Word created the world, and His Word conveys divine revelation. The Hebrew word 'āmar is also used repeatedly by God to introduce divine revelation. Feinberg continues, "One would suppose that this usage [of 'āmar] emphasizes that God's revelation is a spoken, transmissible, propositional, definite matter. The 'word' does not make it a revelation. God gives the revelation to persons as one person imparts knowledge to another—by spoken word."[346] In the wilderness, God revealed Himself through His Word. When God spoke His commands (His instruction, the Torah) to Israel, He did not reveal Himself in the likeness of any created form, instead He revealed Himself through His Word, His divine Word through which He also made all of creation.[347]

> *"Remember the day you stood before the LORD your God at Horeb, when the LORD said to me, 'Assemble the people to Me, that I may let them hear My words so they may learn to fear Me all the days they live on the earth, and that they may teach their children.' You came near and stood at the foot of the mountain, and the mountain burned with fire to the very heart of the heavens: darkness, cloud and thick gloom. Then the LORD spoke to you from the midst of the fire; you heard the sound of words, but you saw no form—only a voice. So He declared to you His covenant which He commanded you to perform, that is, the Ten Commandments; and He wrote them on two tablets of stone. The LORD commanded me at that time to teach you statutes and judgments, that you might perform them in the land where you*

---

[345] Charles L. Feinberg, "118 רמא," in *Theological Wordbook of the Old Testament*, ed. R. Laird Harris, Gleason L. Archer Jr., and Bruce K. Waltke, (Chicago: Moody Press, 1999), 55.

[346] Feinberg, "118 רמא," in *Theological Wordbook*, 55.

[347] Abraham Cohen, *Everyman's Talmud: The Major Themes of the Rabbinic Sages* (New York: Schocken Books, 1995), 131-132.

are going over to possess it. So watch yourselves carefully, since you did not see any form on the day the LORD spoke to you at Horeb from the midst of the fire, so that you do not act corruptly and make a graven image for yourselves in the form of any figure, the likeness of male or female, the likeness of any animal that is on the earth, the likeness of any winged bird that flies in the sky, the likeness of anything that creeps on the ground, the likeness of any fish that is in the water below the earth. And beware not to lift up your eyes to heaven and see the sun and the moon and the stars, all the host of heaven, and be drawn away and worship them and serve them, those which the LORD your God has allotted to all the peoples under the whole heaven. But the LORD has taken you and brought you out of the iron furnace, from Egypt, to be a people for His own possession, as today."

Deuteronomy 4:10–20

Jonathan Sacks reminds us that it was in "the silence of the desert, Israel became the people for whom the primary religious experience was not seeing but listening and hearing: Shema Yisrael. The God of Israel revealed Himself in speech."[348] He revealed Himself to Israel through His Word. Later in Israel's history, during the time of the prophet Samuel, we also see again this significant way of God revealing Himself to His people. First Samuel records, "Thus Samuel grew and the LORD was with him and let none of his words fail. ... And the LORD appeared again at Shiloh, because the LORD revealed Himself to Samuel at Shiloh by the word of the LORD" (1 Sam. 3:19 21).

Early Rabbinic teachings make a direct connection between God's spoken Word at creation with the spoken Word at Sinai. In *Ethics of the Fathers* the sages attribute Proverbs 8:22 to the Torah, "The LORD created me [Torah] as the beginning of his way; the first of his works from the commencement."[349]

> "The LORD possessed me at the beginning of His way,
>   Before His works of old.
> "From everlasting I was established,
>   From the beginning, from the earliest times of the earth.

---

[348] Jonathan Sacks, *Essays on Ethics: A Weekly Reading of the Jewish Bible* (New Milford: Maggid Books, 2016), 218.
[349] *Ethics of the Fathers* 6.10.

> "When there were no depths I was brought forth,
>   When there were no springs abounding with water.
> "Before the mountains were settled,
>   Before the hills I was brought forth;
> While He had not yet made the earth and the fields,
>   Nor the first dust of the world.
> "When He established the heavens, I was there,
>   When He inscribed a circle on the face of the deep,
> When He made firm the skies above,
>   When the springs of the deep became fixed,
> When He set for the sea its boundary
>   So that the water would not transgress His command,
>   When He marked out the foundations of the earth;
> Then I was beside Him, as a master workman;
>   And I was daily His delight,
>   Rejoicing always before Him,
> Rejoicing in the world, His earth,
>   And having my delight in the sons of men."
>
> Proverbs 8:22-31

According to *Genesis Rabbah 1*, the Torah was the plan that God used when He created the world, much like the architectural plans a king would consult when constructing a building.[350] Abraham Cohen adds that the Torah was not only the foundation for Jewish life, "it was considered the only sure basis for the entire cosmic order. Without Torah there would be moral chaos, and for that reason Torah must have existed always, even before the creation of the world."[351] Further Cohen states:

> "According to one opinion, 'the Torah preceded creation by two thousand years' (Gen. R. VIII. 2); but another view is, 'Nine hundred and seventy-four generations before the creation of the world the Torah was written and lay in the bosom of the Holy One, blessed be He' (ARN XXXI). This is calculated based on Psalm 105:8, 'He has remembered His covenant forever, the word which He commanded to a thousand generations.'

---

[350] "Genesis Rabbah 1," Sefaria Community Translation, accessed January 25, 2019, https://www.sefaria.org/Bereishit_Rabbah.1?lang=bi
[351] Cohen, *Everyman's Talmud*, 131.

However, the Revelation occurred at the time of Moses, which was the twenty-sixth generation from Adam; therefore the Torah must have existed nine hundred and seventy-four generations before the world was created (Gen. R. XXVIII. 4)."[352]

The Torah, the Word of God, existed before creation and is the reason that creation exists.

Additionally, the *Ethics of the Fathers* contains the teaching that the Torah was the instrument by which the world was created."[353] Psalm 33:6 says, "By the word of the LORD the heavens were made, and by the breath of His mouth all their host." Daniel Boyarin explains that in Aramaic the "word of the LORD" is *Merma*. In the Targum Neofiti (an ancient Aramaic translation of the Pentateuch), the word *Merma* is used in Genesis 1:3. "And the *Merma* of H' (a form for the abbreviation for the Divine Name, the Tetragrammaton) said, 'Let there be light' and there was light by his *Merma*."[354] According to ancient tradition, it was the Word of God (Merma of H') that created the world. In the Aramaic Targum, the Merma of H' also appears to Abraham in Genesis 18:1, at the destruction of Sodom and Gomorrah in Genesis 19:24, in the pillar of cloud while leading Israel in the wilderness in Exodus 13:21, and as a promise to redeem Israel.[355]

The Gospel of John begins with the revelation of God's Word—the Word that was with God at the creation of the world. The apostle writes, "In the beginning was the Word, and the Word was with God, and the Word was God. He was in the beginning with God. All things came into being through Him, and apart from Him nothing came into being that has come into being" (John 1:1-3). Some biblical scholars have discouraged any connection between this passage at the beginning of John's Gospel and the beginning of Genesis. Others have considered John's prologue to be a revelation that is new to Christianity. However, the first five verses of John are most likely a midrash of the beginning of Genesis—interpreting Genesis in light of Proverbs 8:22-30.[356] Eliyahu Lizorkin-Eyzenberg adds:

---

[352]Cohen, *Everyman's Talmud*, 132.
[353]See *Ethics of the Fathers* 3.14.
[354]Targum Neofiti
[355]Daniel Boyarin, "*Logos*, a Jewish Word: John's Prologue as Midrash," In *The Jewish Annotated New Testament*, ed. Amy-Jill Levine and Marc Zvi Brettler (New York: Oxford University Press, 2011), 547
[356]Boyarin, "*Logos*, a Jewish Word," 548.

"For a long time it has been mistakenly thought that the ideas expressed in these verses of John's prologue are unique to Christianity. It was erroneously believed that this statement constituted nothing less than a ground-breaking departure from Judaism. However, nothing could be further from the truth. In fact, it is not until verse 14 "and the Word became flesh," that an innovative idea, though not contradictory to Judaism, was first introduced."[357]

The Greek word for "Word" used by the apostle John in his prologue is "Logos." Further Boyarin states:

"In the first centuries of the Christian era, the idea of the Word (Gk Logos) was known in some Greek philosophical circles as the link connecting the Transcendent/the Divine with humanity/the terrestrial. For Jews, the idea of this link between heaven and earth, whether called by the Greek Logos or Sophia ("wisdom") or by the Aramaic Memra ("word"), permeated first- and second-century thought. Although monotheistic, Jews nevertheless recognized other supernatural beings who communicated the divine will. The use of the Logos in John's Gospel ("In the Beginning was the Word/Logos, and the Word was with God, and the Word was God" [John 1:1]) is thus a thoroughly Jewish usage. It is even possible that the beginning of the idea of the Trinity occurred precisely in pre-Christian Jewish accounts of the second and visible God that we find in many early Jewish writings."[358]

The author of the letter to the Hebrews was most likely familiar with this first century Jewish teaching and thought.[359] He highlights the divine nature of God's Word in the beginning of his letter: "God, after He spoke long ago to the fathers in the prophets in many portions and in many ways, in these last days has spoken to us in His Son, whom He

---

[357] Eliyahu Lizorkin-Eyzenberg, *The Jewish Gospel of John: Discovering Jesus, King of All Israel* (www.israelstudycenter.com, 2015), 2.
[358] Boyarin, "*Logos*, a Jewish Word," 546.
[359] Zane C. Hodges, "Hebrews," in *The Bible Knowledge Commentary: An Exposition of the Scriptures*, ed. J. F. Walvoord and R. B. Zuck, vol. 2 (Wheaton, IL: Victor Books, 1985), 776–777. LOGOS.

appointed heir of all things, through whom also He made the world. And He is the radiance of His glory and the exact representation of His nature, and upholds all things by the word of His power" (Heb. 1:1–3a). The New Testament writers make it clear that at the appointed time God spoke to man through His Son, through whom He made the world, and by His Son all creation exists.

The New Testament identified Jesus as God's divine Word incarnate. John writes, "And the Word became flesh, and dwelt among us" (John 1:14). Jesus fulfilled, taught, revealed, and exemplified God's instruction. During His earthly ministry, Jesus made the point very clear that the words He taught and proclaimed were not His own, but they were the Father's words. It was the Father speaking through Him (John 3:34, 7:17, 8:28, 12:49-50, 14:10). Jesus emphasized that He only spoke and ministered in His Father's name. This was in keeping with what God spoke through Moses, "I will raise up a prophet from among their countrymen like you, and I will put My words in his mouth, and he shall speak to them all that I command him. It shall come about that whoever will not listen to My words which he shall speak in My name, I Myself will require it of him" (Deut. 18:18-19).

The LORD spoke through the prophet Isaiah about the divine nature of His Word saying, "For as the rain and the snow come down from heaven, and do not return there without watering the earth and making it bear and sprout, and furnishing seed to the sower and bread to the eater; so will My word be which goes forth from My mouth; it will not return to Me empty, without accomplishing what I desire, and without succeeding in the matter for which I sent it" (Isa. 55:10-11). Jesus also declared the unalterable and creative nature of the Word of God when He stated, "Do not think that I came to abolish the Law or the Prophets; I did not come to abolish but to fulfill. For truly I say to you, until heaven and earth pass away, not the smallest letter or stroke shall pass from the Law until all is accomplished" (Matt. 5:17-18). God's divine Word is creative and will not pass away until everything spoken by God is accomplished.

The divine nature of God's Word requires us to pay close attention to it. The Gospels record an event where Jesus took some of His disciples (Peter, James, and John) to a mountain where He was transfigured as He spoke with Moses and Elijah. Then "while He [Jesus] was still speaking, a bright cloud overshadowed them, and behold, a voice out of the cloud said, 'This is My beloved Son, with whom I am well-pleased; listen to Him!'" (Matt. 17:5). Years later, Peter wrote to the churches of the divine origin and nature of the Word that they were taught, reminding them of the need to pay close attention to it:

> *For we did not follow cleverly devised tales when we made known to you the power and coming of our Lord Jesus Christ, but we were eyewitnesses of His majesty. For when He received honor and glory from God the Father, such an utterance as this was made to Him by the Majestic Glory, "This is My beloved Son with whom I am well-pleased"—and we ourselves heard this utterance made from heaven when we were with Him on the holy mountain. So we have the prophetic word made more sure, to which you do well to pay attention as to a lamp shining in a dark place, until the day dawns and the morning star arises in your hearts. But know this first of all, that no prophecy of Scripture is a matter of one's own interpretation, for no prophecy was ever made by an act of human will, but men moved by the Holy Spirit spoke from God.*
>
> 2 Pet. 1:16-21

The Scriptures confirm that the Word God has given to His people with its instruction and teaching has its divine origin in Him.

Moses recounted to the people at the end of the wilderness journey, "He humbled you and let you be hungry, and fed you with manna which you did not know, nor did your fathers know, that He might make you understand that man does not live by bread alone, but **man lives** [emphasis added] by everything that proceeds out of the mouth of the LORD" (Deut. 8:3). Jesus also quoted this Scripture when facing His temptation in the wilderness (Matt. 4:4). And at the end of a dialogue referring back to the time that God sustained Israel in the wilderness, Jesus said, "It is the Spirit who gives life; … the words that I have spoken to you are spirit and are life" (John 6:63). Jesus Christ was sent by the Father as the Word of God made flesh and "in Him [the Word of God] was life, and the life was the Light of men" (John 1:4). With God's promise of life, Jesus encouraged His generation to go deeper in their love and devotion to the divine Word that God had given them—the Word which God had given as an expression of His love for Israel. You can sense the longing of God for His people as Jesus spoke to them, "You search the Scriptures because you think that in them you have eternal life; it is these that testify about Me; and you are unwilling to come to Me so that you may have life" (John 5:39-40).

The Word of God is creative and life-giving to God's people. The Scriptures say, "He sent His word and healed them" (Ps. 107:20a), and "For they are life to those who find them and health to their body" (Prov. 4:22). The apostle Peter highlighted the creative power of God's Word in the life of a believer in this way: "He has granted to us His precious and magnificent promises, so that by them you may become partakers of the divine nature" (2 Pet. 1:4).

The writer of the book of Hebrews emphasized the living, creative nature of God's Word: "For the word of God is living and active and sharper than any two-edged sword, and piercing as far as the division of soul and spirit, of both joints and marrow, and able to judge the thoughts and intentions of the heart" (Heb. 4:12). Through the "living and active" Word, God intends to imprint His teaching in the lives of His people.[360] Through the divine Word and work of the Holy Spirit, God's people are to become living Scripture to be known and read by all men (2 Cor. 3:2-3).

Our attitude toward God's divine, creative Word is addressed in the following passage from the book of Hebrews as it highlights the connection between the spoken revelation of God through history with the Word that He revealed in His Son:

For this reason we must pay much closer attention to what we have heard, so that we do not drift away from it. For if the word spoken through angels proved unalterable, and every transgression and disobedience received a just penalty, how will we escape if we neglect so great a salvation? After it was at the first spoken through the Lord, it was confirmed to us by those who heard, God also testifying with them, both by signs and wonders and by various miracles and by gifts of the Holy Spirit according to His own will.

Heb. 2:1-4

---

[360]Marvin R. Wilson, *Our Father Abraham: Jewish Roots of the Christian Faith* (Grand Rapids: Eerdmans, 1989), 296.

Considering how God has transmitted and confirmed His Word through history, the writer of Hebrews is emphasizing the "close attention" that should be given the hearing of God's Word and keeping it.

Our Approach to God's Divine Word

If the Word of God is divine, what should this mean for teachers and learners in their approach to the Scriptures? In previous chapters we have seen examples through biblical history of the deep devotion in the Jews and early Church to study, keep, and teach God's Word. Now we will look to some examples of contemporary teachers highlighting their approach to the Scriptures as God's divine communication.

Abraham Cohen

The Rabbis, whose teachings comprise the Talmud, would have denied that they were originators of Jewish thought. All they would have admitted was they were excavators in the inexhaustible mine of the divine Revelation contained in the Scriptures and brought to light treasures that lay hidden beneath the surface. ... To study the inspired Writings, to meditate on them, to extract from them all they could be made to produce was, accordingly, the chief privilege as it was the greatest duty of the Jew.[361]

Rabbi Joseph Telushkin

As Harold Kushner has written: "Jews read the Bible the way a person reads a love letter. When you read a love letter, you don't just read it for content. You try and squeeze every last little bit of meaning out of it, e.g., Why did he sign it 'Yours' instead of 'Love'? (To Life, page 40). ... Among Eastern European Jews, a very devoted student of Torah was called a masmid. Although the term normally was applied to one who studied ten or more hours a day, Rabbi Israel Salanter argued that this usage was erroneous: "A masmid is not one who studies continuously, but one who studies [the Torah] every day."[362]

---

[361] Cohen, *Everyman's Talmud*, 125
[362] Joseph Telushkin, *Jewish Wisdom: Ethical, Spiritual, and Historical Lessons from the Great Works and Thinkers* (New York: HarperCollins e-books, 1994), 337, 342.

An Introduction to Education in Bible Times

Rabbi Benjamin Blech

[The revelation of the LORD at Sinai] meant that God gave us a portion of Himself. Torah, the mystics teach us, is the rearrangement of the names of God. On a deeper sense, this implies that all of Torah is His essence. To study Torah in future generations is therefore to be given the opportunity once more to know Him as did the Jews at Sinai. To immerse ourselves in the Five Books is to merge with Him. Belief is the automatic consequence of sincere Torah study. We thereby recapture the moment when God made Himself "visible," leaving no room for doubt. Study enables us to regain the certainty of His being, which we enjoyed when we stood at Sinai. Perhaps that too is why "the study of Torah is equal to all other mitzvot."[363]

Rabbi Wayne Dosick

Today we "drown" in paper; we are "Xeroxed to death." Everyone with a pencil, a sheet of paper, and a copy machine calls himself an author. In ancient times, however, writing was rare and precious. Anything that was written down had to be useful or important; anything that was purposely preserved was precious and valuable. Torah is like that: preserved and cherished, because of its importance and veracity. If Torah had been lost 2,500 years ago, and if tomorrow archaeologists discovered a complete Torah Scroll under the sands of the desert, it would be immediately hailed as definitive history and sacred writ. That we have had Torah for all this time—though it has been subject to our constant critical analysis and all too often taken for granted—makes it no less deserving of our acclaim and affection as historically accurate and spiritually uplifting.[364]

Dr. Derek Prince

In the Sermon on the Mount Christ said: "...For assuredly, I say to you, till heaven and earth pass away, one jot or tittle will by no means pass away from the law till all is fulfilled" (Matt. 5:18). The word *jot* is the English form of the name of the smallest letter in the Hebrew alphabet, roughly corresponding in size and shape to an inverted comma in modern English script. The word *tittle* indicates a little curl or horn, smaller in

---

[363] Benjamin Blech, *Understanding Judaism: The Basics of Deed and Creed* (Northvale: Jason Aronson, 1992), 261.
[364] Wayne D. Dosick, *Living Judaism: The Complete Guide to Jewish Belief, Tradition, and Practice*, 86-87.

size than a comma, added to the corner of certain letters in the Hebrew alphabet to distinguish them from other letters very similar in shape.

Thus, what Christ is saying, in effect, is that the original text of the Hebrew Scripture is so accurate and authoritative that not even one portion of the script smaller than the size than a comma can be altered or removed. It is scarcely possible to conceive how Christ could have used any form of speech that would have more thoroughly endorsed the absolute accuracy and authority of the Old Testament Scriptures.

Not merely did Christ accept the absolute accuracy of the Old Testament Scriptures in all His teaching, He also acknowledged their absolute authority and control over the whole course of His own earthly life. From His birth to His death and resurrection there was one supreme, controlling principle, which was expressed in the phrase "that it might be fulfilled."

[Regarding the continuation of the Scriptures in the New Testament writings] Jesus made all necessary provisions for the absolute accuracy of all that He intended His disciples to put down in writing, for He promised the Holy Spirit to them for this purpose (John 14:26).

A further, similar promise is contained in John 16:13-15. Notice that in these words Christ made provision both for past and for future, that is, both for accurate recording of those things that the disciples had already seen and heard and also for the accurate imparting of the new truths that the Holy Spirit would thereafter reveal to them. The past is provided for in the phrase, "He will ... bring to your remembrance all things that I have said to you" (John 14:26). The future is provided for us in the phrase, "He will teach you all things" (v26) and again, in John 16:13, "He will guide you into all truth."

We see, therefore, that the accuracy and authority of the new Testament, like that of the Old Testament, depend not [solely] upon human observation, memory, or understanding, but upon the teaching, guidance, and control of the Holy Spirit. For this reason, the Apostle Paul says, "All scripture [Hebrew Scriptures and New Testament alike] is given by inspiration of God" (2 Tim. 3:16).[365]

---

[365] Derek Prince, *Foundational Truths for Christian Living* (Lake Mary, FL: Charisma House, 2006), 21-25.

John Wesley

The Spirit of God not only once inspired those who wrote it, but continually inspires, supernaturally assists, those that read it with earnest prayer. Hence it is so profitable for doctrine, for instruction of the ignorant, for the reproof or conviction of them that are in error or sin, for the correction or amendment of whatever is amiss, and for instructing or training up the children of God in all righteousness.[366]

Smith Wigglesworth

Never compare this Book with other books. Comparisons are dangerous. Never think or never say that this Book contains the Word of God. It is the Word of God. It is supernatural in origin, eternal in duration, inexpressible in value, infinite in scope, regenerative in power, infallible in authority, universal in interest, personal in application, inspired in totality. Read it through. Write it down. Pray it in. Work it out. And then pass it on.[367]

---

[366] John Wesley, *Notes on the New Testament: 1 Corinthians—Revelation*, in The Wesleyan Heritage Library Commentary, Electronic ed. (Wesleyan Heritage Publications, 2002), 260.

[367] Smith Wigglesworth, "Like Precious Faith," in *Faith That Prevails* (Radford, VA: Wilder Publications, 2018), 13.

Part 7

Some Overarching Educational Themes

The LORD Our God as Father and Teacher

From the revelation of God (Elohim) as LORD (YHWH) to the revelation of Him as our Heavenly Father, the Scriptures portray Him as One who is intimately involved in the lives of His people. This was His intended relationship with mankind as seen in both the Hebrew Scriptures and in the New Testament writings. As a Father, God cares for and instructs His children. He teaches them so they may grow in His likeness and learn how to truly live together with Him in His creation.

In the first chapter of Genesis, in the account of creation, the name Elohim is used. Elohim refers to God's majesty and sovereignty and refers to God as Creator.[368] In the second chapter of Genesis, in the recounting of the creation of Adam and Eve, God is referred to as the LORD God (Gen. 2:7). This is a combination of the personal divine name *YHWH* with the more general name of Elohim. Once God created man, He began to reveal Himself as the LORD (YHWH), the ever-present personal God who shows concern for the needs of human beings.[369] In this personal relationship as a Father, He began to provide instruction to Adam and Eve and their descendants (Gen. 2).

God, the creator of all mankind, revealed Himself as LORD to Noah, giving him instruction on how to save a godly remnant of the human race and instruction on how to live in His creation after the flood. He revealed Himself as LORD to the Patriarchs as they accepted a relationship with Him and entered into a covenant walk with Him. Hundreds of years later, He revealed Himself as LORD (YHWH) to the children of Israel as He brought them out of Egypt to Himself. According to Jewish thought:

> "The selection of Israel was no arbitrary choice, and to avoid the imputation of favoritism to God, a tradition related that the Torah [God's instruction] was offered to all the nations, but Israel alone agreed to accept it ... Even the seven commandments which the sons of Noah had accepted [the nations] were unable to preserve, but rejected and gave them to Israel."[370]

---

[368] Jack B. Scott, "93 אלה," ed. R. Laird Harris, Gleason L. Archer Jr., and Bruce K. Waltke, *Theological Wordbook of the Old Testament* (Chicago: Moody Press, 1999), 44.
[369] Nahum M. Sarna, *The JPS Torah Commentary: Genesis* (Philadelphia: Jewish Publication Society, 1989), 17.
[370] Abraham Cohen, *Everyman's Talmud: The Major Themes of the Rabbinic Sages* (New York: Schocken Books, 1995), 61.

God had always been looking to be a Father to, and instruct the peoples of the nations; however, only one nation entered into this relationship with Him. The LORD God referred to Israel as "My firstborn son," denoting His relationship to them as a Father. The LORD told Moses to speak these words to Pharaoh, "Thus says the LORD, Israel is My son, My firstborn. So I said to you, 'Let My son go that he may serve Me'" (Exod. 4:22-23). Nahum Sarna in *The JPS Torah Commentary* makes the following observation regarding this verse: "All peoples are recognized as being under the universal fatherhood of God, but Israel has the singular status of being the first to acknowledge YHVH and to enter into a special relationship with Him."[371] Forty years later at the end of the wilderness wanderings, the LORD rehearsed these words to Israel, "You are the sons (children) of the LORD your God. ... For you are a holy people to the LORD your God, and the LORD has chosen you to be a people for His own possession out of all the peoples who are on the face of the earth" (Deut. 14:1-2).

Abraham Cohen reveals, "Throughout the utterances of the Talmudic Sages, the relationship that exists between the Creator and His creatures is conceived under the image of Father and children."[372] In the sayings captured in *Ethics of the Fathers*, Rabbi Akiva said:

> "Beloved is man, for he was created in the image [of G-d]; it is a sign of even greater love that it has been made known to him that he was created in the image, as it says, "For in the image of G-d, He made man' (Genesis 9:6). Beloved are Israel, for they are called children of G-d; it is a sign of even greater love that it has been made known to them that they are called children of G-d, as it is stated: "You are children of the L-rd your G-d' (Deuteronomy 14:1)."[373]

It is interesting to note that in this discussion of the relationship of God and His children, Rabbi Akiva goes on to talk about how the Torah (God's instruction) was given to Israel. He says:

---

[371] Nahum M. Sarna, *The JPS Torah Commentary: Exodus* (Philadelphia: Jewish Publication Society, 1991), 24.
[372] Cohen, *Everyman's Talmud*, 20.
[373] *Ethics of the Fathers* 3.14.

"Beloved are Israel, for they were given a precious article; it is a sign of even greater love that it has been made known to them that they were given a precious article, as it is stated: 'I have given you a good purchase; My Torah, do not forsake it' (Proverbs 4:2)."[374]

It was in a "Father and children relationship" that the LORD gave His people the Torah through Moses and said, "So you shall observe to do just as the LORD your God has commanded you; you shall not turn aside to the right or to the left. You shall walk in all the way which the LORD your God has commanded you, that you may live and that it may be well with you, and that you may prolong your days in the land which you will possess" (Deut. 5:32-33). As a Father, the LORD was teaching Israel how to live as His people, as His sons and daughters. He continued this relationship with His children, as it says in Psalm 32, "I will instruct you and teach you in the way which you should go; I will counsel you with My eye upon you" (Ps. 32:8).

In the covenant that the LORD made with King David their relationship is described as that of a father and son. The Psalmist records, "He will cry to Me, 'You are my Father, My God, and the rock of my salvation.' I also shall make him My firstborn, the highest of the kings of the earth. My lovingkindness I will keep for him forever, and My covenant shall be confirmed to him" (Ps. 89:26-28). In this same psalm the LORD goes on to talk about David's children:

> *"So I will establish his descendants forever and his throne as the days of heaven. If his sons forsake My law and do not walk in My judgments, if they violate My statutes and do not keep My commandments, then I will punish their transgression with the rod and their iniquity with stripes. But I will not break off My lovingkindness from him, nor deal falsely in My faithfulness."*
>
> Ps. 89:29-33

Later in David's life, the LORD made a promise regarding his son, Solomon: "I will be a father to him and he will be a son to Me; when he commits iniquity, I will correct him with the rod of men and the strokes of the sons of men, but My lovingkindness shall not depart

---

[374] *Ethics of the Fathers* 3.14.

from him, as I took it away from Saul, whom I removed from before you" (2 Sam. 7:14-15).

Solomon, in the book of Proverbs, describes the LORD as a father and teacher: "My son, do not reject the discipline (instruction) of the LORD or loathe His reproof, for whom the LORD loves He reproves, even as a father corrects the son in whom he delights" (Prov. 3:11-12). During the times of the LORD disciplining Israel, Isaiah spoke of God hearing their cry, turning to them, and teaching them—opening their ears to hear His instruction. The prophet Isaiah encourages:

> *O people in Zion, inhabitant in Jerusalem, you will weep no longer. He will surely be gracious to you at the sound of your cry; when He hears it, He will answer you. Although the LORD has given you bread of privation and water of oppression, He, your Teacher will no longer hide Himself, but your eyes will behold your Teacher. Your ears will hear a word behind you, "This is the way, walk in it," whenever you turn to the right or to the left.*
>
> Isa. 30:19-21

Jesus also referred to the Heavenly Father as Israel's teacher saying, "It is written in the prophets, 'and they shall all be taught of God.' Everyone who has heard and learned from the Father, comes to Me" (John 6:45).

During the Second Temple and Tannaim periods, sages taught that in the Bible pupils were called children and the teacher their father. Nathan Drazin adds, "Hence they interpreted the biblical precept, 'thou shalt teach them diligently unto thy children,' to mean that the teacher was obligated to take good care of his profession."[375] However, teachers needed to be aware that they were working for the LORD in teaching His children. Cohen continues this line of thought, "Despite the supreme value which was attached to studying and imparting instruction, they who are engaged in this great work should not be filled with undue pride. They are only laborers in God's sight, just the same as the men who are engaged on manual toil."[376] For example, Moses, the great teacher, was a humble man, more than any other person on the face

---

[375] Nathan Drazin, *History of Jewish Education from 515 B.C.E. to 220 C.E.* (*During the Periods of the Second Commonwealth and the Tannaim*), (Baltimore: Johns Hopkins Press, 1940), 19.
[376] Cohen, *Everyman's Talmud*, 140.

of the earth (Num. 12:3). In his humility, Moses recognized the LORD God as Israel's Teacher and Law Giver.

Additionally, the teacher was a messenger from the LORD (Mal. 2:7) of whom was required the highest ethical religious qualifications.[377] In the twenty-third chapter of Matthew, Jesus chastised some of the Pharisees and scribes for their feelings of self-importance as teachers of the Torah. He then told His disciples, "But do not be called Rabbi; for One is your Teacher, and you are all brothers [companions or fellow students]. Do not call anyone on earth your father; for One is your Father, He who is in heaven. Do not be called leaders [instructors]; for One is your Leader [Instructor], that is, Christ" (Matt. 23:8-10). He was reminding them that the Heavenly Father is also their Teacher, and that God's intention has always been to have this teaching relationship with His children.

The Heavenly Father is intimately involved in the lives of His people. Jesus taught this reality and also taught how to engage the Father in a daily walk with Him as His children (Matt. 6-7). The apostle Paul referred to God as "Father" throughout his letters to Jewish and Gentile believers in Christ.[378] The apostle John also emphasized that God is a Father to His children and that God's children are those who have learned to keep His commandments in loving Him and loving each other (1 John 3).

The writer of the book of Hebrews describes the role of the Heavenly Father in disciplining (providing instruction for) His children:

And you have forgotten the exhortation which is addressed to you as sons:

"MY SON, DO NOT REGARD LIGHTLY THE DISCIPLINE
OF THE LORD,
NOR FAINT WHEN YOU ARE REPROVED BY HIM;

FOR THOSE WHOM THE LORD LOVES HE DISCIPLINES,
AND HE SCOURGES EVERY SON WHOM HE RECEIVES."

---

[377]Walter A. Elwell and Barry J. Beitzel, *Baker Encyclopedia of the Bible* (Grand Rapids: Baker Book House, 1988), 657–661.
[378]Rom. 1:7, 8:15; 1 Cor. 1:3, 8:6; 2 Cor. 1:2-3; Gal. 1:1-4, 4:6; Eph. 1:2-3, 2:18, 3:14; 4:6, 5:21; Phil 1:2; Col. 1:2-3; 1 Thess. 1:1-3; 2 Thess. 1: 1-2; 1 Tim. 1:2; 2 Tim. 1:2, Titus 1:4; Philem. 3

> *It is for discipline that you endure; God deals with you as with sons; for what son is there whom his father does not discipline? But if you are without discipline, of which all have become partakers, then you are illegitimate children and not sons. Furthermore, we had earthly fathers to discipline us, and we respected them; shall we not much rather be subject to the Father of spirits, and live? For they disciplined us for a short time as seemed best to them, but He disciplines us for our good, so that we may share His holiness.*
>
> Heb. 12:5-10

In keeping with the idea that God called a people out from the nations that had refused to receive His instruction, Paul exhorts believers in Christ to come out from their association with the ungodly.

> *For we are the temple of the living God; just as God said:*
>
> *"I WILL DWELL IN THEM AND WALK AMONG THEM; AND I WILL BE THEIR GOD, AND THEY SHALL BE MY PEOPLE.*
> *"Therefore, COME OUT FROM THEIR MIDST AND BE SEPARATE," says the Lord.*
> *"AND DO NOT TOUCH WHAT IS UNCLEAN;*
> *And I will welcome you.*
>
> *"And I will be a father to you,*
> *And you shall be sons and daughters to Me,"*
> *Says the Lord Almighty.*
>
> 2 Cor. 6:16-18

God's people were to leave an old way of life, culture, and thought and come to the Father as His children to learn. The Father would guide and discipline His children; He would give them His Word for instruction, and He would give them teachers to help them.

An Introduction to Education in Bible Times

Love and Discipline

The New Testament Scriptures teach us that God is love (1 John 4:16) and that God, the Father, so loved the world that He sent His son to reconcile mankind back to Himself (John 3:16). He gives all those whom He has redeemed the right (and choice) to become His sons (John 1:12). Our response is to leave an old lifestyle influenced by surrounding cultures and enter into a relationship with God as our Father. It is in this relationship that the Heavenly Father begins to treat us as His children by providing us with His instruction—instruction with the goal of sharing in His nature of holiness.

According to the Scriptures, parents are to love and discipline their children and raise them in the knowledge of the LORD. Also a good teacher is to love his students and bring instruction (discipline, knowledge, and understanding) to them. Both parents and teachers are to follow the example of their Heavenly Father, for the Scriptures teach us that God disciplines those that He loves (Heb. 12:6).

Furthermore, Paul Gilchrist encourages us that the discipline of "Yahweh is his mighty activity in covenant history by which he reveals himself. The discipline of Yahweh is not to be taken negatively, for [example] the hardships in the wilderness were balanced by his miraculous provisions both designed to test 'what was in your heart, whether you would keep his commandments or not'" (Deut. 8:2).[379] Regarding the time in the wilderness, Moses told the children of Israel, "Thus you are to know in your heart that the LORD your God was disciplining you just as a man disciplines his son" (Deut. 8:5), so that they would learn to revere Him and walk in His ways. Moses went on to tell them, "Know this day that I am not speaking with your sons who have not known and who have not seen the discipline [instruction] of the LORD your God—His greatness, His mighty hand and His outstretched arm ... but your own eyes have seen all the great work of the LORD which He did. You shall therefore keep every commandment which I am commanding you today" (Deut. 11:2, 7-8). Proverbs and other wisdom literature speak of discipline with an emphasis on instruction. The passage in Hebrews 12 draws from the

---

[379] Paul R. Gilchrist, "877 רָסַי," in *Theological Wordbook of the Old Testament*, ed. R. Laird Harris, Gleason L. Archer Jr., and Bruce K. Waltke (Chicago: Moody Press, 1999), 387.

third chapter of Proverbs, "My son, do not reject the discipline of the LORD or loathe His reproof, for whom the LORD loves He reproves, even as a father corrects the son in whom he delights" (Prov. 3:11-12). The Hebrew word for *discipline* includes discipline, chastening, and instruction which emphasize the idea of education—the changing of ideas, attitudes, and behaviors. Within the loving relationship of parents and children, discipline is to be given (Prov. 19:18; 22:15; 23:13). Biblical discipline could be administered with the "rod of correction" (Prov. 22:15) or through oral instruction.[380] As a spiritual father, the apostle Paul drew upon this idea when he brought correction to the Corinthian church. In the middle of his words of correction he wrote, "What do you desire? Shall I come to you with a rod, or with love and a spirit of gentleness?" (1 Cor. 4:21).

Jesus brought words of correction to many of the spiritual leaders of His day. Some of the words He spoke seemed harsh—words of discipline and instruction. However, behind the correction was the love and yearning of the Father for His children. This love and yearning are expressed in Jesus's words, "Jerusalem, Jerusalem, who kills the prophets and stones those who are sent to her! How often I wanted to gather your children together, the way a hen gathers her chicks under her wings, and you were unwilling" (Matt. 23:37).

The LORD God in His love must instruct and discipline His children. History has shown that without God's instruction and discipline mankind tends to devolve into a society with relative values, morals that are not fixed, and eventual violence against others. It is only through the discipline of learning and keeping His ways that men and women can relate positively with their fellow human beings. Our Heavenly Father understands how we learn. So in His unfailing lovingkindness, God is committed to discipline His children.

Learning and the Heart

The Torah connected study with the heart. The prelude to the command to study and teach is the command to "love the LORD your God with all your heart and with all your soul and with all your might"

---

[380]Gilchrist, "877 רסַיִ," in *Theological Wordbook*, 387.

An Introduction to Education in Bible Times

and "these words, which I am commanding you today, shall be on your heart" (Deut. 6:5-6). Jesus recounted these words in Luke 10:27 and added that we are to also love the Lord with all our mind. The heart and mind are included in totally loving God. James Swanson clarifies that the human mind refers to "mind, reasoning, understanding, thinking, way of thinking, disposition, manner of thought, the content of what one is thinking, to be ready to learn, and prepare for action."[381] Study is connected with the heart because learning was to be with the intent of acting on what was learned.

God's people were to learn with the intent of their heart to obey (Deut. 6:4). "Hear, O Israel!" implies attention with the intent of obedience in the hearer. The heart is involved with the intent to be obedient in what is learned. Because of this, the LORD said, "Oh that they had such a heart in them, that they would fear Me and keep all My commandments always, that it may be well with them and with their sons forever!" (Deut. 5:29). The book of Jeremiah tells of a new covenant that the LORD would make with His people; a covenant where His Word is written on their hearts. A covenant where each person would not need to teach his neighbor to know the LORD, for all would know Him and walk with Him (Jer. 31:31-34).

The Scriptures teach that it is the willingness of heart that determines the ability to truly learn. King David in the Psalms described the value of having a willing heart as he wrote, "Sacrifice and meal offering You have not desired; my ears You have opened; burnt offering and sin offering You have not required. Then I said, 'Behold, I come; In the scroll of the book it is written of me. I delight to do Your will, O my God; Your Law is within my heart'" (Ps. 40:6–8). God has always desired for His people to have a willing heart.

Recall that the purpose of biblical education is to know the LORD and to walk in His ways. This takes the combination of a heart inclined toward God and a mind that is filled with His instruction. Moses's heart was inclined toward the LORD as he prayed, "Now therefore, I pray You, if I have found favor in Your sight, let me know Your ways that I may know You, so that I may find favor in Your sight" (Exod. 33:13). David also said, "O God, You are my God; I shall seek You earnestly"

---

[381] James Swanson, "1379 διανοια," *Dictionary of Biblical Languages with Semantic Domains: Greek (New Testament)* (Oak Harbor: Logos Research Systems, 1997).

(Ps. 63:1), and "I shall delight in Your statutes; I shall not forget Your word" (Ps. 119:16). Jesus connected the willingness of heart to learning by declaring, "My teaching is not Mine, but His who sent Me. If anyone is willing to do His will, he will know of the teaching, whether it is of God or whether I speak from Myself" (John 7:16–17). The willingness of heart is the key that takes what is learned and unlocks the knowledge of God and the understanding of His ways.

Jesus told His Jewish audience, "Let your light shine before men in such a way that they may see your good works and glorify your Father who is in heaven. Do not think that I came to abolish the Law or the Prophets; I did not come to abolish but to fulfill" (Matt. 5:16–17). The word *fulfill* has the meaning of "rich fullness," "accomplish," and "confirm."[382] God chose the Jewish people to be His light to the nations (Isa. 42:6). So He revealed Himself to them and gave them the Torah. They were to be an example of a people with a willing heart who studied and learned God's ways and walked in them.

The Jewish leaders understood that the pathway to being "a light to the nations" was to walk in the blessings that came through obedience to the LORD their God, through observing the words of the Torah. Many of the Pharisees of Jesus's day saw the value in the Great Assembly's admonition to "build a fence" around the Torah to keep the people from inadvertently breaking one of God's commands.[383] However, according to Jesus, this led to traditions that eventually were in excess of the Torah's requirements, to traditions that countered the "heart" of the Torah (Matt. 12:7, 15:3, 22:36-40, 23:2-3, 23). One example of this excess is the definition of what was considered "work" to be avoided on the Sabbath. Abraham Heschel explains that the ancient teachers correctly discerned:

> "The Sabbath demands all of man's attention, the service and single-minded devotion of total love. [However] the logic of such a conception compelled them to enlarge constantly the system of laws and rules of observance. ... Yet law and love, discipline and delight, were not always fused [together]. In their illustrious fear

---

[382] Gerhard Delling, "πληρης, πληροω, πληρωμα, αναπληροω, ανταναπληροω, εκπληροω, εκπληρψσις, Συμπληροω, Πληροφοροω, Πληροφορια," in *Theological Dictionary of the New Testament*, ed. Gerhard Kittel, Geoffrey W. Bromiley, and Gerhard Friedrich (Grand Rapids: Eerdmans, 1964), 285.
[383] *Ethics of the Fathers* 1.1.

of desecrating the spirit of the day, the ancient rabbis established a level of observance which is within the reach of exalted souls but not infrequently beyond the grasp of ordinary men."[384]

The twelfth chapter of Matthew records two incidents surrounding the Sabbath day.[385] These incidents directly follow a statement by Jesus about finding the Sabbath rest in Him (Matt. 11:28–29). In the first incident Jesus and His disciples were walking through a grain field, likely on their way to a synagogue in order to observe the Sabbath. The disciples were hungry and plucked some grain, removed the husk, and ate some of the grain. Because of this, some of the Pharisees confronted Jesus about His disciples breaking the prescribed Sabbath regulations. Jesus responded with a story from the Scriptures which illustrated God's higher principle of compassion and taking care of the needs of His people. He concluded with quoting Hosea 6:6 and saying, "But if you had known what this means, 'I desire compassion [mercy], and not a sacrifice,' you would not have condemned the innocent" (Matt. 12:7).

Jesus referred to the words of the prophet Hosea, "For I delight in loyalty rather than sacrifice, and in the knowledge of God rather than burnt offerings" (Hos. 6:6). The word for "loyalty" is *checed* which means loyal love, loving-kindness, and mercy.[386] The word "knowledge" implies the knowledge of God that comes from study of the Scriptures by one who is seeking to know Him and walk in His ways. This passage in Hosea follows the complaint by God, "What shall I do with you, O Ephraim? What shall I do with you, O Judah? For your loyalty [*checed*, loyal love] is like a morning cloud and like the dew which goes away early" (Hos. 6:4). Isaiah also identified the tendency to drift from loving and serving God with all of one's heart by saying, "This people draw near with their words and honor Me with their lip service, but they remove their hearts far from Me, and their reverence for Me consists of tradition

---

[384]Abraham Joshua Heschel, *The Sabbath: Its Meaning for Modern Man* (FSG Classics) (New York: Farrar, Straus and Giroux, 2005), Locations 314-318. Kindle.
[385]See Phillip Sigal, *The Halakhah of Jesus of Nazareth according to the Gospel of Matthew* (Atlanta: Society of Biblical Literature, 2007), 145-186. In the chapter "The Matthean Jesus and the Sabbath Halakhah," Sigal concludes, "On the halakhah index between the Pentateuch and the Mishnah, Jesus was the vanguard of the Mishnaic teachers in a studied effort to relax the growing complexity and restrictiveness of Sabbath halakhah."
[386]James Strong, *A Concise Dictionary of the Words in the Greek Testament and The Hebrew Bible* (Bellingham, WA: Logos Bible Software, 2009), 41.

learned by rote" (Isa. 29:13). When the heart disconnects from the teaching, then keeping God's commands becomes a "form of godliness" instead of a walk of sons and daughters with their Heavenly Father.

Continuing in Matthew 12, the author presents a second Sabbath example. Jesus was attending a synagogue when the Pharisees confronted Him with a strict ruling about keeping the Sabbath and asked if it was lawful to heal a person during the Sabbath. Jesus responded by healing the sick person and teaching, "What man is there among you who has a sheep, and if it falls into a pit on the Sabbath, will he not take hold of it and lift it out? How much more valuable then is a man than a sheep! So then, it is lawful to do good on the Sabbath" (Matt. 12:11–12). Jesus was elevating the teaching on the Sabbath back to the heart and intention of the Torah and the Prophets. One of the other Gospel accounts adds this statement: "The Sabbath was made for man, and not man for the Sabbath" (Mark 2:27).

Later in time the ancient rabbis also ruled, "The Sabbath is given to you, not you to the Sabbath."[387] They realized that excessive piety may endanger fulfillment of the essence of the Torah.[388] George Robinson explains:

> "The rabbis of the Gaonic period (sixth to twelfth centuries) cautioned: "There is nothing more important, according to the Torah, than to preserve human life. … Even when there is the *slightest possibility* [emphasis added] that a life may be at stake one may disregard every prohibition of the law." This doctrine, called pikuakh nefesh/saving a soul applies to the laws governing Shabbat and the festivals; [for example] a doctor must act to save another person, even though it means she is "working" on the Sabbath."[389]

From this discussion we see that study leads to the knowledge and ability to keep God's commands, and that some level of interpretation and application is necessary to understand how to apply God's commandments to the current realities of life. However, the head and the heart must remain connected. Learning and actions must come from a heart that loves and honors God and loves one's neighbor—from a

---

[387] Mekilta to 31:13.
[388] Heschel, *The Sabbath*, Location 314.
[389] George Robinson, *Essential Judaism: A Complete Guide to Beliefs, Customs and Rituals* (New York: Atria Books, 2016), 81-92. Kindle.

heart that is willing to do His will in keeping His righteousness and justice and by honoring life.

Relationships in Teaching and Learning

Throughout this study of education in biblical times, learning in the context of relationships has been a consistent theme. Teaching and learning begin with the relationship of the Heavenly Father's love and His children loving Him in return with all their hearts. Parents were to love and teach their children, the communities learned together in synagogues and at other gatherings, and master teachers taught disciples who lived and studied together. Again, Philo observed that the Jewish people "from their very swaddling clothes are taught by parents and teachers and masters."[390]

Adam and Eve were created to exist in a relationship with the LORD their Creator. Learning was to take place within the context of their relationship with the LORD. When Eve sought to learn and become wise outside of her relationship with the LORD, and convinced Adam to do the same, that knowledge turned into shame and separation from God. Later in history we find Abraham teaching his children to walk with God and observe His ways. After God called Israel out of Egypt, He gave them the Torah, His instruction, and commanded them: "These words, which I am commanding you today, shall be on your heart. You shall teach them diligently to your sons and shall talk of them when you sit in your house and when you walk by the way and when you lie down and when you rise up" (Deut. 6:6-7).

As a result, the home was a child's first classroom. Parents were commanded to teach their children. Drazin adds:

> "Jewish religion, furthermore, invested education with sacredness and importance. The Rabbis interpreted the Biblical words, "and ye shall teach them to your children," to mean that every male adult was obligated to study Torah and to teach it to his sons. Although theoretically this obligation could be discharged with the reading of certain Biblical verses morning and evening, that

---

[390] Philo, *On the Embassy to Gaius* 16 (115), in Early Christian Writings, accessed February 10, 2019, http://www.earlychristianwritings.com/yonge/book40.html.

was not the case in practice. To observe all the laws of his faith, the Jew had to be highly educated."[391]

The priority given to education also stemmed from the value of children in the Jewish family. Children were considered a great joy and reward. Children were loved by their parents, and there was no greater blessing than in the relationship of parents teaching their children.[392] As Cohen highlights, this biblical paradigm was deeply rooted in the heart of Jewish families:

"'He who rears his children in the Torah is among those who enjoy the fruit in this world while the capital remains for him in the World to come' (Shab.127a). 'Whoever has a son labouring in the Torah is as though he never dies' (Gen. R. XLIX. 4). 'Whoever teaches his son Torah, Scripture imputes it to him as though he had received it from Mount Horeb; as it is said, "Thou shalt make them known to thy children and thy children's children"' (Deut. iv. 9)."[393]

The concern for teaching children the ways of the Lord in the context of family and community relationships was also addressed by John Wesley in the 1700s. Gayle Felton notes:

"Wesley realized that the home influenced the lives of children even before the church, and that parents were, for good or evil, the first religious teachers of their children. The foundations for subsequent spiritual development must be appropriately constructed in the context of family life. ... [And] If children are to mature as faithful Christians, their nurture must continue in the Christian community."[394]

Educational studies have shown that the atmosphere in which a child grows and matures has great implications for learning. Susan Ambrose realized, "A negative climate may impede learning and performance, but

---

[391] Drazin, *History of Jewish Education from 515 B.C.E. to 220 C.E.*, 17.
[392] Cohen, *Everyman's Talmud*, 172-173.
[393] Cohen, *Everyman's Talmud*, 173.
[394] Gayle C. Felton, "John Wesley and the Teaching Ministry: Ramifications for Education in the Church Today," *Religious Education* 92, no. 1 (Winter 1997), 96.

An Introduction to Education in Bible Times

a positive climate can energize students' learning."[395] Effective learning takes place in a positive environment and with learning experiences that are relevant to a child's life, interests, and experiences.[396] So children first learn in the loving atmosphere and security of the home and community. In the Jewish community, children learned the biblical stories as their cultural history, as their own family stories. They memorized portions of Scripture and to some degree learned to not only read Hebrew, but to write it.[397] They learned from their parents the personal significance of God's commands and about the weekly Sabbath and the annual feast celebrations. Learning and the content of that learning had its greatest significance in the context of their family and community relationships.

Research emphasizes the effectiveness of learning that builds upon prior knowledge.[398] Judy Willis also noticed the effectiveness of "the brain's processing of information by patterning. When teaching is geared to help students find meaning and patterns in the material they study and the relevance of that information to their lives and world, their brains respond by successful pattern formation and information storage in long-term memory."[399] Building on the foundation of what a Jewish child received in the home, community elementary schools taught children to read and memorize large portions of the Written Torah. Next, in secondary schools, children learned the Oral Torah through memorization, analysis, and discussion. Each learning experience from the home through the secondary schools built upon a child's prior learning, provided the important context of a shared family history, and gave the relevance of the requirements of a walk with God as His people.

All phases of learning were relevant in the context of a shared relationship as the LORD's people. Drazin clarifies, "For the Jews, the religious motive was the dominating factor of education. All Jews were required to know the Law and to observe it in practice. Their education was hence thoroughly practical. It was integrated with all the activities of life."[400]

---

[395] Susan A. Ambrose, *How Learning Works: Seven Research-Based Principles for Smart Teaching* (San Francisco: Jossey-Bass, 2010), 157.
[396] Judy Willis, *Research-Based Strategies to Ignite Student Learning: Insights from a Neurologist and Classroom Teacher* (Association for Supervision & Curriculum Development, 2006), Locations 1070-1071. Kindle.
[397] Drazin, *History of Jewish Education from 515 B.C.E. to 220 C.E.*, 85.
[398] Ambrose, *How Learning Works*, 13.
[399] Willis, *Research-Based Strategies to Ignite Student Learning*, Locations 1052-1055.
[400] Drazin, *History of Jewish Education from 515 B.C.E. to 220 C.E.*, 138.

Learning also involved observation. Studying in relationship allowed the learner to observe the life of his teacher. Children and youth would learn how to conduct their lives by observing their parents and instructors. For this reason, great importance was placed on the qualities of a teacher, for teaching involves both the passing on of knowledge and the modeling of behavior. Paul exhorted those he taught to imitate his faith and conduct (1 Cor. 11:1). The writer of the book of Hebrews likewise said, "Remember those who led you, who spoke the word of God to you; and considering the result of their conduct, imitate their faith" (Heb. 13:7).

The passing on of the Word of God from one person to another, from one generation to the next, was facilitated through relationships. In a primarily oral culture, much of the learning needed to be passed on from one person to another. Teachers were living textbooks who passed on their knowledge and love of God's instruction. They passed on their wisdom from a lifetime of applying God's instruction to life. Learning in relationships provided the atmosphere, motivation, examples, and relevance for learning. It provided the wisdom for what a child or young adult would encounter in life. It equipped them to be able to walk in the world and not be of it. Finally, it formed the character of love for God and love for others and faithfulness to His instruction.

Education as an Exodus

After Israel's deliverance from Egypt, the LORD had to provide a way to teach them to live as His people. The children of Israel had lived in slavery for four hundred years in Egypt, one of the longest-lived empires of the world. Egypt became powerful through conquest, through the use of slavery, and through the use of resources—not for the benefit of people, but to build an empire. So why is education an exodus? God's people were not to be like the cruel and inhumane empires of the world. They would not follow their systems of hierarchy, governance, and control. The former slaves of Egypt needed to learn a new way of life, so education became the next step in their exodus from Egypt.

To do this, the children of Israel had to learn about the LORD their God. They had to learn to think and live as His people. They had to become an example of a nation that lived under God's care and righteous rule. So God gave them the Torah, His instruction. In addition, the LORD kept putting in context their learning and the keeping of His commandments by reminding them that they were once slaves in Egypt (Deut. 5:15, 6:21, 16:12). Remembering that the LORD had delivered them from the slavery of Egypt would help them choose to remain faithful to His instruction and to create a society that treated others with dignity. The purpose of education in family, school, and synagogue was to transform the Jewish people from being enslaved to other influences into a people who could choose to follow the LORD as His kingdom of priests, a holy people (Exod. 19:4-8).

Education can be seen an exodus from imposed slavery into the ability to choose.[401] As slaves in Egypt Israel had no right to choose, but only to obey the commands of their taskmasters. As His people, God taught them and gave them the *choice* to love and serve Him. Because of their time of education in the wilderness, the LORD could say to Israel, "So choose life in order that you may live, you and your descendants, by loving the LORD your God, by obeying [hearing and responding to] His voice, and by holding fast to Him" (Deut. 30:19-20). Education gave the former slaves the ability to choose another way of life.

The New Testament speaks about the exodus from imposed slavery to the spiritual kingdoms and forces that rule this world. "For He [God] rescued us from the domain of darkness, and transferred us to the kingdom of His beloved Son" (Col. 1:13). Here again, education follows deliverance. As those who have been delivered from oppressive slavery, God's people must learn to think, live, and walk as those who are now citizens of His kingdom. The apostle Paul aptly describes this in his letter to the Ephesians.

> *So this I say, and affirm together with the Lord, that you walk no longer just as the Gentiles also walk, in the futility of their mind, being darkened in their understanding, excluded from the life of God because of the ignorance that is in them, because of the hardness of their heart; and they, having become callous, have given themselves over to sensuality for the practice of every kind of impurity with greediness. But you did not learn Christ in this way, if indeed you have heard*

---

[401] Jonathan Sacks, *Ceremony and Celebration: Introduction to the Holidays* (New Milford: Maggid Books, 2017), 191-192.

> *Him and have been taught in Him, just as truth is in Jesus, that, in reference to your former manner of life, you lay aside the old self, which is being corrupted in accordance with the lusts of deceit, and that you be renewed in the spirit of your mind, and put on the new self, which in the likeness of God has been created in righteousness and holiness of the truth.*
>
> Ephesians 4:17-24

God has given the Scriptures and has also given teaching ministries in order to lead His people out of the bondage of a "darkened understanding" to be equipped to live effectively in the knowledge of God and the knowledge of His ways (Eph. 4:11-16; 2 Tim. 3:14-17). Therefore, education is an exodus out of the bondage of ignorance and into the freedom of understanding. It is in this freedom of understanding that a person can choose to love God, to hear and respond to His voice, and to hold fast to Him (Deut. 30:19-20).

The Purpose of Teaching and Learning

The intimate knowledge of God was the primary objective for education.[402] This meant that each person would also come to know of his or her shared history with all of God's people, and understand God's claims, requirements, and blessings on each life. It should be emphasized again that this "knowing" was not merely intended for the sake of gaining knowledge. The LORD spoke through the prophet Jeremiah that to do justice and righteousness, and to be concerned for the cause of those in need is to intimately know the LORD (Jer. 22:16). Thus to know God included an equipping to faithfully walk in His ways.[403] Paul also described the intended result of instruction as the knowledge of God, knowledge that is evidenced by love from a pure heart (Eph. 4:11-13; 1 Tim. 1:5).

Educational research has defined learning as a process that leads to change. Learning involves change in knowledge, beliefs, attitudes, or

---
[402]R. Laird Harris, Gleason L. Archer Jr., and Bruce K. Waltke, ed., *Theological Wordbook of the Old Testament* (Chicago: Moody Press, 1999), 366.
[403]Marvin R. Wilson, *Our Father Abraham: Jewish Roots of the Christian Faith* (Grand Rapids: Eerdmans, 1989), 287-289.

behaviors. This change unfolds over time and has a lasting impact on how learners think and act.[404] It is God who created in man the capacity to learn. Therefore He constantly emphasizes in the Scriptures the importance of what is learned. We are told to continually rehearse God's words, to meditate on them to the exclusion of other influences (Ps. 1:1-3), and to continually abide in the teaching we have received (John 15:1-11). Because there is the pressure of competing influences to teach other ways of thinking and living, the apostle Paul wrote, "Pay close attention to yourself and to your teaching; persevere in these things, for as you do this you will ensure salvation both for yourself and for those who hear you" (1 Tim. 4:16).

Further Paul states, "As a result, we are no longer to be children, tossed here and there by waves and carried about by every wind of doctrine [teaching—what is taught], by the trickery of men, by craftiness in deceitful scheming; but speaking the truth [rehearsing God's Word] in love, we are to grow up in all aspects into Him who is the head, even Christ" (Eph. 4:14-15). Through continuing in God's instruction, we are to mature as His family, no longer moved by other teachings, but able to live in the fullness of Christ.

The many "winds of doctrine" Paul describes in Ephesians 4:14 are constantly competing for the opportunity to exert influence over the minds and formation of individuals. For example, educational researchers have been studying the impact of modern-day culture on the education and identity formation of children and young adults. Their growing engagement with popular culture and social media has empowered these influences to become a growing force in their identity formation, even beyond what they learn in schools. According to Peter Demerath and Allison Mattheis, children are becoming one of the most prized targets of marketing; and it is the market that "supplies the most attractive and useable symbolic and expressive forms that are now consumed by teenagers and early adults."[405]

According to the Scriptures, one of Satan's tactics against the people of God has been to influence them to compromise regarding God's instruction and adopt other cultural practices (Num. 31:16). The book

---

[404] Ambrose, *How Learning Works*, 3.
[405] Peter Demerath and Allison Mattheis, "Toward Common Ground: The Uses of Educational Anthropology in Multicultural Education," in *International Journal of Multicultural Education* 14, no. 3 (2012), 10.

of Revelation picks up this thought in the message to the churches of Pergamum and Thyatira (Rev. 2:12-19). Here the Lord Jesus confronts these churches for tolerating those who introduced the teaching of Balaam and the teaching of Jezebel. Balaam taught the sons of Moab to invite the children of Israel to share in their culture, thereby bringing God's judgment on many of them (Num. 31:16). Jezebel taught her culture of idolatry and immorality to the northern tribes of Israel (1 Kings 16:30-33; 21:25). The northern tribes of Israel never recovered from this and were eventually conquered and disbursed by the Assyrians. The Lord instructed the churches to no longer allow the accepted cultural teachings of idolatry and immorality in their midst.

After years of teaching the children of Israel in the wilderness, God warned them to not be influenced by the teaching of the surrounding cultures; instead *they* were to influence and be a light to the nations (Deut. 4:6-8; 12:29-32; 26:16-19). Jesus came into the world as God's light, fulfilling all of God's instruction (John 1:9). Jesus taught that God's people were also to be a light to the world (Matt. 5:13-16). God's intent was for a people to know Him and walk with Him, men and women who would have a positive influence on the world around them. They were not to be influenced by the surrounding culture, but they were to continually keep His instruction in their hearts as the absolute truth.

Research published by the Barna Group in May 2017 has pointed to a progressive shifting of worldview among many Christians who now embrace ideals of pluralism and relativism. Many competing worldviews have similarities to Christian teachings, causing some to latch on to these ideas.[406] While biblical education can adapt to changing times and environments, God never intended for it to become relativistic (the belief that there is no absolute truth; that cultures can determine what is moral or immoral). However, according to Scripture, God's Word is absolute truth and has relevance to all aspects of life.

In his book *Christ and Culture*, H. Richard Niebuhr discusses various ways the Church has embraced, withdrawn from, or confronted culture over the centuries. Niebuhr presents the danger of becoming relativistic in beliefs as a result of the changing world around us and writes, "Relative justice becomes relativistic when some relative value is substituted for the

---

[406]See "Competing Worldviews Influence Today's Christians," in *Barna*: Research Releases in Culture and Media (May 9, 2017), https://www.barna.com/research/competing-worldviews-influence-todays-christians/.

truly absolute one; as when a man's worth for his state or his class or his biological race is accepted as his final value" rather than acknowledging the truth that man was created in the image of God.[407] Niebuhr concludes that on too many occasions we forget the value to God of our neighbors and fellow creatures, and because of that we make choices based on relative values without referencing the absolute value-relation of God's Word.

Paul in his letters reminded believers to continue abiding in the teaching of God's Word and to no longer be influenced by culture: "So this I say, and affirm together with the Lord, that you walk no longer just as the Gentiles also walk, in the futility of their mind" (Eph. 4:17). Instead, God's purpose for teaching and learning is to bring us to the knowledge of Himself and His ways. There are many influences continually competing for people's attention; but there is one God and Father of all, Who in His great love has redeemed us to Himself and has made a way for us to know Him. He gives teaching and teachers so that we can mature into a life that is pleasing to Him—a life that is fruitful and constructive in its expression in the world. Ultimately, as the Father sent Christ into the world, so we are also sent as living epistles (God's instruction) to be known and read by all men (2 Cor. 3:2-3).

Christ Our Wisdom

The New Testament contrasts God's wisdom with man's wisdom (1 Cor. 1:18-2:16; Col. 1:9-2:23). It is only through God's wisdom that we come to the knowledge of salvation (2 Tim. 3:15) and learn to live a life that is pleasing to Him. The apostle James adds:

Who among you is wise and understanding? Let him show by his good behavior his deeds in the gentleness of wisdom. But if you have bitter jealousy and selfish ambition in your heart, do not be arrogant and so lie against the truth. This wisdom is not that which comes down from above, but is earthly, natural, demonic. For where jealousy and selfish ambition exist, there is disorder and every evil thing. But the wisdom from above is first pure, then peaceable, gentle, reasonable, full of mercy and good fruits, unwavering, without hypocrisy.

James 3:13-17

---

[407]H. Richard Niebuhr, Christ and Culture (San Francisco: HarperCollins, 1975), 241.

The Scriptures teach that God is the One who gives true wisdom (Prov. 2:6-7). We can receive God's wisdom through the knowledge of His Word, and by desiring it (Prov. 2:3-9) and by asking for it. As James encourages, "If any of you lacks wisdom, let him ask of God, who gives to all generously and without reproach, and it will be given to him" (James 1:5).

Wisdom is always linked to the learning and keeping of God's Word. We can clearly see this in Moses's exhortation to the children of Israel. He reminded the children of Israel that he taught them all the statues and judgments that God had commanded they learn, and that keeping them would be their wisdom and understanding "in the sight of the peoples who will hear all these statutes and say, 'Surely this great nation is a wise and understanding people'" (Deut. 4:6). Further Warren Wiersbe adds:

> "Wisdom was important to the Jewish people. They realized that it was not enough to have knowledge; you had to have wisdom to be able to use that knowledge correctly. All of us know people who are very intelligent, perhaps almost geniuses, and yet who seemingly are unable to carry out the simplest tasks of life ... wisdom enables us to put things together and relate God's truth to daily life."[408]

Wisdom for life was directly connected with biblical teaching and learning.

In the introduction to his Exodus commentary, Dennis Prager makes an observation about the lack of wisdom in modern life. He states, "We live in an age that not only has little wisdom, it doesn't even have many people who value it. People greatly value knowledge and intelligence, but not wisdom. And the lack of wisdom—certainly in America and the rest of the West—is directly related to the decline in biblical literacy."[409] It is through a path of lifelong learning and keeping God's Word that we gain the wisdom to evaluate all life from God's perspective. We acquire His wisdom that serves as a guide for how to conduct all the affairs of our lives (e.g., relationships, education, business), including how to navigate new situations that may develop.

---

[408] Warren W. Wiersbe, *The Bible Exposition Commentary*, vol. 2 (Wheaton, IL: Victor Books, 1996), 362.
[409] Dennis Prager, "Exodus: God, Slavery, and Freedom," in *The Rational Bible* (Washington DC: Regnery Faith, 2018), xvi-xvii.

God's wisdom is the context for all other learning and gaining of knowledge. Without this context, all other instruction and knowledge can become self-serving and eventually, even with the best intentions, harmful. Derek Prince concludes, "So it is with secular education. It is a wonderful thing, but it can be misused. Divorced from the illumination of God's Word, it can become extremely dangerous. A nation or civilization that concentrates on secular education but gives no place to God's Word is simply forging instruments for its own destruction."[410]

Paul taught believers to not be wise in their own estimation (Rom. 12:16). He imparted that in Christ we can find "all the treasures of wisdom and knowledge" (Col. 2:3). It was through wisdom that God created the world. And it has been our Heavenly Father's intention to impart His wisdom that we might understand how to live in and steward His creation. Gaining knowledge *without* God's wisdom has contributed to many of the destructive events and trends throughout history. However, it is God's wisdom that teaches us how to creatively use knowledge to accomplish His purposes. It is the "fear of the LORD" and biblical teaching and learning that are the foundation of God's wisdom for all of life (Ps. 111:10; Prov. 2:1-8).

Using Stories in Teaching and Learning

Most of the Bible is written in narrative form, the telling of stories. The apostle Paul recognized the educational value of stories when he wrote: "Now these things happened to them as an example, and they were written for our instruction" (1 Cor. 10:11). God gave us stories throughout the Scriptures that young and old can relate to and learn from. This is important because "faith is much more about recognition than cognition. The hearers recognize themselves in the juxtaposition of stories and see the implication for their own lives."[411]

In a discussion regarding the value of stories in Christian education, Fraser Hannam offers the following observation, "Divorced from its [narrative] context, the data with which we populate our teaching

---

[410]Derek Prince, *Foundational Truths for Christian Living* (Lake Mary, FL: Charisma House, 2006), 43.
[411]Richard A. Jensen, *Envisioning the Word: The Use of Visual Images in Preaching* (Minneapolis, MN: Fortress Press, 2005), 127.

programs render our lessons informative at best."[412] Hannam continues that as human beings, we have …

> "… an indescribable attraction to narrative. Something that will make the most-unruly junior school class sit quietly at the promise of a story. Teenagers may not have a preference for subjects, but they will always have a favorite movie or book. How might this natural attraction be exploited for teacher and learning? More importantly, how might God's story, be brought into our classrooms? When we anchor ourselves in the Biblical narrative and discern meaning, purpose and vision as individuals and as living communities how might the gospel transform our methodology, practices, policies and curriculum?"[413]

The narrative stories of the Scriptures should always be linked to its other teachings.

A walk with God is the continued unfolding story of God in His relationship with men and women. It is more than a set of creeds, doctrines, and beliefs. However, Marty Michelson explains:

> "As the separation between Judaism and emerging Christianity grew, Christian theologians wrote fewer stories. Within Christian tradition, the focus turned to 'believing' or 'thinking' right things about God.[414] … It is in the Jewish and Christian stories of God's intricate and intimate relationships—not primarily God's labels or titles—that we discern the greatest depth, wonder, and mystery about our relationship with God."[415]

For this reason God gave commands at Sinai for Israel to set aside time as families and communities to remember the stories of the great things that God had done for them.

---

[412] Fraser D. Hannam, "Teaching Through Narrative," *Forum on Public Policy Online* (Urbana: Oxford Round Table, 2015): 2, https://files.eric.ed.gov/fulltext/EJ1091524.pdf.
[413] Hannam, "Teaching Through Narrative," 1.
[414] Marty Alan Michelson, "Jewish-Christian Dialogue," in *Relational Theology: A Contemporary Introduction* (Point Loma Press, 2016), 105.
[415] Michelson, "Jewish-Christian Dialogue," 106.

God commanded His people to keep the Sabbath (Exod. 20:9-11; 31:13-16). They were to work for six days and then rest in their homes on the seventh day. On the Sabbath they were to remember the stories of their history. Moses said, "You shall remember that you were a slave in the land of Egypt, and the LORD your God brought you out of there by a mighty hand and by an outstretched arm; therefore, the LORD your God commanded you to observe the sabbath day" (Deut. 5:15).

At some point in history, the Sabbath evening Shabbat meal was established. Here again, the telling of the story is emphasized. As Mark Glenn explains:

> "Shabbat centered around the home, the table, and the family, and focused on telling the story of the faith to everyone gathered together. There was one table for the whole extended family. From the moment you were born, you had a place at that table. There was no children's table—only one table from infants to elders. ... The charge of each generation is to re-tell the story, to celebrate and welcome the youngest and newest members around the table and invite them to join in and become a part of that never-ending story, a story that told them who they were."[416]

The annual feasts and festivals also were times to relive their timeless stories. At Passover the Jewish people were to retell the story of the Passover and their deliverance from the slavery of Egypt. At Pentecost they remembered the awesome experience of God revealing Himself in speech as they received the Law. At other feast times significant events and their meanings were recalled: living in tents in the wilderness with God's presence dwelling with them, the heroism of Queen Esther and their deliverance from the decree of death, and the miracle of God's provision of the oil at Hanukkah.

In like manner, the Gospel stories became the centerpiece for early Christianity. When Jesus instituted the new covenant, He included with it a remembrance of Himself (Luke 22:19). Paul records this in his letter to the Corinthians, "And when He [Jesus] had given thanks, He broke the bread and said, 'This is My body, which is for you; do this in remembrance of Me.' In the same way He took the cup also after supper,

---

[416]Mark Glenn, "Pastor's Pen" (Sept. 21, 2018).

saying, 'This cup is the new covenant in My blood; do this, as often as you drink it, in remembrance of Me'" (1 Cor. 11:24-25). What are we to remember? The story of Jesus's life and ministry, the story of His sacrificial death, the story of His resurrection, and the story of His ascension, His Lordship, and His continuing intercession for us. The early church was constantly devoted to listening, learning, and retelling the stories of Jesus.[417]

God's stories are to have a timeless-living quality.[418] When Christ said, "This do in remembrance of Me," He did not mean that we should only remember an historical event; rather, that the event should become a living memory, bringing the reality of it into the present moment. For this reason, the words of God are described as "living" (Heb. 4:12). Learning and continually rehearsing the stories of Jesus allows the Holy Spirit to inscribe them on our hearts and to bring them to our remembrance (John 14:26; 2 Cor. 3:3). Our Lord and Savior was never to be an historical figure of the past, but He is an ever-present relationship Who is the same yesterday, today, and forever (Heb. 13:8).

Lifelong Learning

Learning in Bible times was a lifelong endeavor that centered on God's Word. It began as a child in the home and in school, and it continued into adulthood in the synagogue and community. To study God's words, to meditate upon them, and to draw out of them all the meaning and experience they could be made to yield was one's greatest privilege and duty.[419] Many of the sages of the Second Temple period emphasized the importance of lifelong learning. Here it is worth repeating again a few excerpts from the *Ethics of the Fathers* that express this emphasis on continued study and learning:

> "Let your home be a meeting place for the wise [in Torah]; dust yourself [sit] in the soil of their feet, and drink thirstily of their words (1:4)."

---

[417] James D. G. Dunn, *The Oral Gospel Tradition* (Grand Rapids: Eerdmans, 2013), 110.
[418] Benjamin Blech, *Understanding Judaism: The Basics of Deed and Creed* (Northvale: Jason Aronson, 1992), 261.
[419] Cohen, *Everyman's Talmud*, 125.

An Introduction to Education in Bible Times

"Assume for yourself a master, acquire for yourself a friend [to study with] (1:6)."

"Make your Torah study a permanent fixture of your life (1:15)."

"One who increases Torah, increases life; one who increases study, increases wisdom (2:7)."

"If you have learned much Torah, do not take credit for yourself—it is for this that you have been formed (2:8)."

"Delve and delve into it, for all is in it; see with it; grow old and worn in it; do not budge from it, for there is nothing better (5:21)."

Lifelong learning was valued in the Jewish community. As Drazin states, "Adult education was widespread and popular among the Jews. Every Jew knew that he was obligated by sacred Law to study Torah every day of his life. Consequently, many men, even artisans and industrial workers, reserved part of every day for study."[420] This emphasis on continuing education found expression in the synagogue and through the Jewish dinner clubs where members of a community would set aside additional time during the week to have a meal together and study Scripture throughout the evening.[421]

At the birth of the early church, the apostles continually gave themselves to the Word of God and prayer. Likewise, believers in the early church would find suitable meeting places at the Temple, in an upper room, or in private homes where they could study the Scriptures together and continue in the apostles' teaching (Acts 2:42, 46; 20:7). Believers were exhorted to be faithful in their study of God's Word and to continue in their times of meeting together (Col. 3:16; 2 Pet. 1:19; Heb. 10:25).

Paul encouraged Timothy, who himself was an established teacher, to remain diligent in his study (2 Tim. 2:15; 3:14-17). And after a lifetime of learning and teaching others, Paul continued in his own faithful devotion to the Word of God. Near the end of his life, during

---

[420]Drazin, *History of Jewish Education from 515 B.C.E. to 220 C.E.*, 6.
[421]Joseph Shulam with Hilary Le Cornu, *A Commentary on the Jewish Roots of Acts 16-28* (Jerusalem: Netivyah Bible Instruction Ministry, 2012), 1107-1108.

his final imprisonment in Rome, Paul wrote to Timothy to bring him the books that he had left with one of the believers at Troas (generally believed to be referring to one or more books of the Hebrew Scriptures).[422] Paul, one of the greatest teachers of the early church, was also a devoted lifelong learner.

Lifelong learning is of great value. Scripture encourages us to grow in the grace and knowledge of God, and there are always new encounters in life where God's teaching needs to be applied. For this purpose God has given us His Words and His Spirit to teach and guide us. He has gifted us teachers and companions to learn with, and He equips us as continual learners who can teach others also (2 Tim. 2:2).

Lifelong learning is not a discipline; it is a choice to be made in one's personal and community relationship with the Lord. It begins with encountering God in a personal way through family, or as did Abraham, the children of Israel in the wilderness, the first disciples with Jesus, the apostle Paul, and the many churches of the New Testament. Our choice to love Him with all our heart and all our mind comes from experiencing Him as the LORD, our Heavenly Father, our Redeemer who reconciled us to Himself through Christ. As a loving Father, He has given us His Word as an unfolding revelation of Himself, as a communication of His ways, as wisdom for life, and as a creative force that will accomplish His purpose in and through our lives.

---

[422]George W. Knight III, *New International Greek Testament Commentary: The Pastoral Epistles*, ed. I. Howard Marshall and W. Ward Gasque (Grand Rapids: Eerdmans, 1992), 467.

CONCLUSION

In this book we have traced the history of God's ways of educating His people. From the creation of man through the creation of the nation of Israel, teaching and learning God's ways have been a centerpiece for the Jewish people. Throughout the biblical history of the nation of Israel, including from the Second Temple period to the time of Jesus Christ, and through the brief history of Jesus's ministry and the early church, we see the recurring themes of *the priority, the means, and the impact* of biblical education.

In general, education means (1) "the action or process of educating or of being educated," and (2) "the knowledge and development resulting from the process of being educated."[423] The action or process of educating includes:

- to provide schooling
- to train by formal instruction and supervised practice
- to develop mentally, morally, or aesthetically especially by instruction
- to provide with information
- to persuade or condition to feel, believe, or act in a desired way

Education is a powerful tool to shape the minds and hearts of people and to equip them for life. Therefore, biblical education has always been concerned with the focus and content of teaching and learning and the impact it has on one's life. The Shema prayer captures this concern, "You shall love the LORD your God. ... These words, which I am commanding you today, shall be on your heart [continually]. You shall teach them diligently..." (Deut. 6:5-7).

Jesus's final command to "make disciples of the nations" also involved a commitment to a lifestyle of continually learning and teaching others. The biblical patterns of teaching and learning were to be part of the daily life of families and communities. Adults were to be well educated so they could teach their children. Disciples were to learn well so they could disciple and teach others. Everyone was to be filled with the "knowledge of the Lord" so they could bring a teaching or have an answer ready for anyone who asked. The result was to have people called out of every nation who would know the Lord and walk in His ways.

---

[423] "Education," *Merriam-Webster*, https://www.merriam-webster.com/dictionary/education.

As a conclusion to this study, it seems valuable to consider some important questions.

- If God is unchangeable, are His requirements for teaching and learning unchanged? What place should study have in the life of God's people?
- Is loving God and a willing heart the foundation for all biblical teaching and learning?
- What should biblical teaching and learning look like today? In the home, in the church community, and in the school?
- What role should loving relationships have in the teaching of children?
- How can a home or church create an environment for teaching and learning?
- Should popular culture be introduced to children? When is it appropriate? What foundation is necessary to be in the world and not of it—to be a person who impacts culture rather than being influenced by it?
- What impact can a culture of biblical teaching and learning have on the church and on society?
- Is the knowledge of God and keeping His ways still the purpose of biblical teaching and learning? Is the result of teaching and learning to be evidenced in loving God and others?
- Should the knowledge of God and His ways be the foundation for all other learning? Is this still valid today? Is it more valid today?
- Is God's wisdom necessary for God's people today? How can it be attained?
- How should individuals and churches approach lifelong learning? How can everyone be equipped as a learner and as a teacher?

It is my hope that exploring the origin, purpose, and means of education in biblical times will foster a deeper understanding of God's consistent plan for education. I also hope that this book will stir appropriate actions from thoughtful consideration and form the basis of additional study and research—that it will inspire further questions, discussion, and roadmaps for the biblical education of children and youth, and for the continuing education of adults.

GLOSSARY

Aggadah: Telling (or narrative). Non-halakhic content in the Talmud and Midrash. Aggadah includes folklore, legend, theology/theosophy, scriptural interpretations, biography, etc.; also spelled Haggadah.

Banim: A name given to disciples meaning "sons" or "children."

BCE: Before Common (or Christian) Era. Used in place of B.C.

Bet Hamidrash: The house of study which was adjacent to the Temple.

Bet Knesset: House of assembly; a synagogue.

Bet Midrash: House of study. A place set aside for study of sacred texts such as the Torah, generally a part of the synagogue or attached to it.

Bet Sefer: For the study of Mirka; referring to elementary education.

Bet Talmud: For the study of Mishnah; referring to secondary education.

CE: Common (or Christian) Era. Used in place of A.D.

Chaverim (haverim): Members or friends (who study together).

Commandments: According to rabbinic Jewish tradition, there are 613 religious commandments referred to in the Torah (and elaborated upon by the rabbinic sages). Of these, 248 are positive commandments and 365 are negative. See also Mitzvah.

Darash: To inquire.

Decalogue: A Greek term referring to the Ten Commandments received by Moses on Mount Sinai according to Hebrew Scriptures (Exodus 20:1–17; Deuteronomy 5:1–21).

Deuteronomy: From the Greek, meaning the second telling of the Law. Refers to the fifth book of the Pentateuch.

Diaspora: The dispersion of Jews throughout the world after the fall of the Second Temple in 70 CE. Refers to all Jews living outside of Israel.

Eretz Yisrael: A Hebrew term for the Land of Israel. A special term for the land that was promised to the Jewish people by God in the covenant with Abraham.

Essenes: The name of a Jewish subgroup in the first century CE according to Josephus, Philo, and other sources. The Essenes sought to live a life in fulfillment of the Law by forming separate communities.

Ethics of the Fathers: Also referred to as Abbot or Pirkei Avot. A compilation of oral traditions that covers the time of the Great Assembly through the time of the Mishnah, around 220 CE. The first five chapters were written before the Mishnah, and they reflect the way oral teachings were preserved by studying and memorizing them and passing them on from one generation of spiritual leaders to the next. The Ethics of the Fathers begins with a statement of the chain of transmission of the Torah from the original revelation at Sinai through the men of the Great Assembly, to the disciples of these original teachers, and on through the generations of teachers who followed. By placing themselves in a line of transmission that began at Sinai, their interpretations carried the same authority as the laws that were given by God to Moses.

Exodus: From the Greek, meaning to exit or go out. Refers to the event of the Israelites leaving Egypt and to the biblical book that tells of that event. Refers to the second book of the Pentateuch.

First Temple: Built in Jerusalem by Solomon and destroyed by the Babylonians in 586 BCE. The First Temple housed the Ark of the Covenant and was the site of all the most important religious rites of Judaism.

Gemara: A Hebrew term meaning "completion." Popularly applied to the Jewish Talmud as a whole, to discussions by rabbinic teachers on Mishnah, and to decisions reached in these discussions.

Great Assembly: Thought to have been a panel of 120 prophets, scribes, and sages (wise men) including Ezra, Nehemiah, Mordecai, Daniel, Simeon the Righteous and the prophets Haggai, Zechariah, and Malachi. This Assembly was the ultimate religious authority at the onset of the Second Temple period. They are credited with institutionalizing many important liturgical practices (reading of Torah on Shabbat, festivals, Mondays, and Thursdays; recitation of the Amidah two times daily; blessings before meals, etc.) and the foundations of halakhah.

Haggadah: See Aggadah

Halakhah: Any normative Jewish law, custom, practice, or rite—or the entire body of Jewish law. It is laws established or customs ratified by authoritative rabbinic jurists and teachers. The word halakhah is usually translated as "Jewish Law," although a more literal translation might be "the path that one walks."

Hallel: A portion of the service for certain Jewish festivals, consisting of Psalms 113–118 (the Hallel Psalms).

Hasmoneans: Descendants of Hashmon. A Jewish family that included the Maccabees and the high priests and kings who ruled Judea from 142 to 63 BCE.

Haverim: See Chaverim

Hillel: Hillel was a Jewish religious leader during the time of king Herod. He is considered one of the most important figures in Jewish history. He is associated with the development of the Mishnah and the Talmud. Founder of the House of Hillel, school for Tannaïm. His carefully applied exegetical principles came to be called the Seven Rules of Hillel.

Joshua b. Gamala: A high priest who officiated about 64 CE. Although Joshua himself was not considered a scholar, he was concerned for the instruction of the young and provided schools in every town for children over five years of age.

Ketuvim: (Hebrew, "writings") The third and last division of the Jewish Bible, including Psalms, Proverbs, and Job, as well as other writings (Song of Songs, Ruth, Lamentations, Ecclesiastes, Esther, Daniel, Ezra-Nehemiah, and Chronicles).

Knesset: Assembly.

Knesset Ha-Gadol: See Great Assembly.

Levite: A descendant of the tribe of Levi, dedicated to the service of the Temple and assisting the priests (the kohanim).

Maccabees: A group of Jewish rebel warriors who took control of Judea, which at the time was under the rule of the Seleucid Empire. They founded the Hasmonean dynasty, which ruled from 167 BCE to 37 BCE, being a fully independent kingdom from about 110 to 63 BCE.

Mezuzah: A parchment scroll with selected Torah verses (Deuteronomy 6:4–9; 11:13–21) placed in a container and affixed to the exterior doorposts (at the right side of the entrance) of Jewish homes (see Deuteronomy 6:1–4), and sometimes also to interior doorposts of rooms.

Midrash: From the Hebrew word darash, "to inquire," referring to the exposition of Scripture. It also refers to the "commentary" literature developed in classical Judaism that attempts to interpret Jewish Scriptures in a thorough manner. Midrash is founded on the premise of the oneness and self-interpreting nature of the Scriptures. Literary Midrash may focus either on Halakhah or on Aggadah.

Midrash Aggadah: Explores biblical passages with ethical ideas, biblical characters, and biblical narratives. It deals with theological ideas, ethical teachings, popular philosophy, imaginative exposition, legend, allegory, animal fables, etc.

Midrash Halacha: Seeks to extend a law beyond the conditions assumed in the Bible, making connections between current-life practice and the biblical text. It directs the Jew to specific patterns of religious practice.

Mikra: Elementary education for children ages 5 through 10 that focused on the written text of the Torah.

Mishnah: (Hebrew, "teaching") The digest of the recommended Jewish oral halakhah as it existed at the end of the second century (around 200 CE) and was collated, edited, and revised by Rabbi Judah Ha-Nasi. The compiled work is the authoritative legal tradition of the early sages and is the basis for the legal discussions of the Talmud.

Mitzvah: (pl. mitzvot) Obligation or commandment. In general, a mitzvah refers to any act of religious duty or obligation; colloquially, a mitzvah refers to a "good deed."

Nasi: (lit. "prince") The presiding officer of the Sanhedrin.

Navi: (pl. nevi'im) A prophet.

Oral Law: In traditional Pharisaic/Rabbinic thought, God reveals instructions for living through both the written Scriptures (the Torah) and through a parallel process of orally transmitted traditions. Critics of this approach within Judaism included the Sadducees.

Pentateuch: (from Greek for "five books/scrolls") The five books attributed to Moses: Genesis, Exodus, Leviticus, Numbers, and Deuteronomy; known in Jewish tradition as the Torah.

Pharisees: The name given to a group or movement in early Judaism whose origin is unclear. Many scholars identify them with the later sages and rabbis who taught the oral and written law. According to Josephus, the Pharisees believed in the immortality of souls and resurrection of the dead, in a balance between predestination and free will, in angels as active divine agents, and in authoritative oral law. In the early Christian materials, Pharisees are often depicted as leading opponents of Jesus and his followers. Most of the notable scribes and teachers were part of the Pharisee movement. However, many of the Pharisees were also common laborers who devoted their spare time to study and teaching. In the first century CE, Rabbinic Judaism developed from the Pharisees.

Psalms of Ascent: Psalms 120-134 which were sung as Jews made their way up to the Temple in Jerusalem during the annual feasts.

Rabbi: ("my teacher" or "my master") An ordained expert in Jewish worship and law, and an authorized teacher of the classical Jewish tradition after the fall of the Second Temple in 70 CE.

Rabbinic Judaism: A general term encompassing all movements of Judaism descended from Pharisaic Judaism.

Revelation: A general term for the self-disclosure of God that He reveals to humans, which is often considered to be focused in the revealed Scriptures.

Sadducees: Sect of the Second Temple period, allied with the priestly caste in opposition to the Pharisees.

Sanhedrin: (from Greek for "assembly") A legislative and judicial body from the period of early Judaism and into rabbinic times. Traditionally composed of 71 members.

Second Temple: The temple that was rebuilt after the Babylonian Exile. The Temple stood in Jerusalem until it was destroyed by the Romans in 70 CE.

Sepphoris: Josephus called Sepphoris "the ornament of all Galilee." Herod Antipas chose this site in 4 BC. as the capital of his government. The city became a large building project employing workers from neighboring towns, like Nazareth. Sepphoris was possibly the largest city in Galilee and an exceptionally strong fortress at the time of the First Revolt in 66 AD.

Septuagint: Originally referred to the ancient Greek translation of the Hebrew Pentateuch, probably made around 250 BCE. Subsequently, Greek translations of other portions of the Jewish Scriptures came to be added to the corpus, and the term Septuagint was applied to the entire collection. Such collections served as the "scriptures" for Greek-speaking Jews and Christians.

Sh'ma: (Hebrew, "hear") Title of the fundamental, monotheistic statement of Judaism, found in Deuteronomy 6:4. "Hear, O Israel, the LORD is our God, the LORD is One"; Shema Yisrael.

Shammai: A Jewish scholar of the 1st century, and an important figure in Judaism's core work of rabbinic literature, the Mishnah. Shammai was elected vice-president of the Sanhedrin while Hillel was its president. He also founded a school of his own, which differed fundamentally from that of Hillel.

Sofer: (pl. sopherim, "scribe") Used as a general designation for scholars and copyists in both Talmudic and later literature; a "scholastic," a learned researcher whose vocation was the study and teaching of the tradition. In early times the sofer was a scholar. By the first century CE, he was no longer a scholar but an official and teacher of children. Today it usually refers to one who writes a Torah scroll.

Soferim: A class of scholars like Ezra who interpreted and taught the Torah and its application. The time of the Soferim is believed to have begun during the time of Ezra and continued until the time of Shimon the Righteous (about 300 BCE), who was the last of the men of the Great Assembly. Some believe that the time of the Soferim continued until about 200 BCE.

Synagogue: (Greek for "gathering"). The central institution of Jewish communal worship and study since antiquity, and by extension, a term used for the place of gathering. The structure of such buildings has changed, though in all cases the ark containing the Torah scrolls faces the ancient Temple site in Jerusalem.

Talmud: (Hebrew, "study" or "learning") Rabbinic Judaism produced two Talmuds: the one known as "Babylonian" is the most famous in the western world. It was completed around the fifth century CE. The other is known as the "Palestinian" or "Jerusalem" Talmud. Both Talmuds have as their common core the Mishnah collection of the tannaim, to which are added commentary and discussion (Gemara) by the later teachers.

Talmîd: A disciple who devoted himself to learning Scripture and the religious tradition, and the tradition which was passed on through his teacher. Can also refer to a recognized scholar and teacher who has learned the religious tradition, and the tradition which was passed on through his teacher. The ultimate purpose of being a disciple was to also be able to keep the teaching and raise up other disciples.

Tanakh: (TaNaKh) A relatively modern acronym for the Jewish Bible, made up of the names of the three parts: Torah (Pentateuch or Law), Nevi'im (Prophets), and Ketuvim (Writings).

Tanna: (Hebrew, "repeater, reciter"; pl. tannaim) A Jewish sage from the period of Hillel to the compilation of the Mishnah (around 200 CE). Tannaim were primarily scholars and teachers. The Mishnah, Tosefta, and halakhic midrashim were among their literary achievements.

Targum: The Aramaic translation of the Hebrew Bible. It forms a part of the Jewish traditional literature, and in its inception was as early as the time of the Second Temple.

Tefillin: Usually translated as "phylacteries." Box-like appurtenances that accompany prayer, worn by adult males (and now some females as well) at the weekday morning services. The boxes have leather thongs attached and contain scriptural excerpts. One box (with four sections) is placed on the head, the other (with one section) is placed (customarily) on the left arm, near the heart. The biblical passages emphasize the unity of God and the duty to love God and be mindful of Him with "all one's heart and mind" (e.g., Exod. 13:1–10, 11–16; Deut. 6:4–9, 11:13–21).

Torah: (Hebrew, "teaching, instruction") In general, Torah refers to study of the whole gamut of Jewish tradition or to some aspect thereof. In its special sense, "the Torah" refers to the "five books of Moses" in the Hebrew Scriptures.

BIBLIOGRAPHY

Ambrose, Susan A., Michael W. Bridges, Michele DiPietro, Marsha C. Lovett, Marie K. Norman. *How Learning Works: Seven Research-Based Principles for Smart Teaching*. San Francisco: Jossey-Bass, 2010.

Barclay, William. *Train Up A Child: Educational Ideals in the Ancient World*. Philadelphia: Westminster Press, 1959.

Barton, J. *Isaiah 1–39*. London: T&T Clark, 1995.

Bauckham, Richard. *The Bible and Mission: Christian Mission in a Postmodern World*. Grand Rapids: Baker Academic, 2003.

Ben-Sasson, H. H. *A History of the Jewish People*. Cambridge, MA: Harvard University Press, 1969.

"Bereishit–Genesis–Chapter 18." In *The Complete Jewish Bible with Rashi Commentary*, accessed on January 19, 2019, https://www.chabad.org/library/bible_cdo/aid/8213/jewish/Chapter-18.htm#showrashi=true&lt=primary.

Blech, Benjamin. *Understanding Judaism: The Basics of Deed and Creed*. Northvale: Jason Aronson, 1992.

Blizzard, Roy, B. *Mishna and the Words of Jesus*. Austin: Bible Scholars, 2013.

Boyarin, Daniel. "Logos, a Jewish Word: John's Prologue as Midrash." In *The Jewish Annotated New Testament*, edited by Amy-Jill Levine and Marc Zvi Brettler. New York: Oxford University Press, 2011.

Brand, Chad, Charles W. Draper, Archie English, and Holman and Broadman Staff, eds. "Essenes." In *Holman Illustrated Bible Dictionary*. Nashville: Broadman & Holman Bible Publishers, 2003.

Bruce, F. F. *Commentary on the Book of the Acts*. Grand Rapids: Eerdmans, 1983.

Bruce, F. F. "Paul the Apostle." In T*he International Standard Bible Encyclopedia*, rev., edited by Geoffrey W. Bromiley. Grand Rapids: Eerdmans, 1979–1988.

Cahill, Thomas. *The Gifts of the Jews: How a Tribe of Desert Nomads Changed the Way Everyone Thinks and Feels*. New York: Anchor Books, 1999.

Carter, Warren. *Seven Events That Shaped the New Testament World*. Baker Publishing Group. Kindle.

Cohen, Abraham. *Everyman's Talmud: The Major Themes of the Rabbinic Sages*. New York: Schocken Books, 1995.

Culver, Robert D. "1277 אָבֵד." In *Theological Wordbook of the Old Testament*, edited by R. Laird Harris, Gleason L. Archer Jr., and Bruce K. Waltke. Chicago: Moody Press, 1999.

Delling, Gerhard. "Πληρης, Πληροω, Πληρωμα, Αναπληροω, Ανταναπληροω, Εκπληροω, Εκπληρωσις, Συμπληροω, Πληροφοροω, Πληροφορια." In *Theological Dictionary of the New Testament*, edited by Gerhard Kittel, Geoffrey W. Bromiley, and Gerhard Friedrich. Grand Rapids: Eerdmans, 1964.

Demerath, Peter, and Allison Mattheis. "Toward Common Ground: The Uses of Educational Anthropology in Multicultural Education." In *International Journal of Multicultural Education* 14, no. 3, 2012.

Dosick, Wayne. *Living Judaism: The Complete Guide to Jewish Belief, Tradition, and Practice*. HarperCollins e-books, 2007.

Draper, Charles W., and Harrop Clayton. "Jewish Parties in the New Testament." In *Holman Illustrated Bible Dictionary*, edited by Chad Brand, Charles W. Draper, Archie English, and Holman and Broadman Staff. Nashville: Broadman & Holman Bible Publishers, 2003.

Drazin, Nathan. *History of Jewish Education from 515 B.C.E. to 220 C.E. (During the Periods of the Second Commonwealth and the Tannaim)*. Baltimore: Johns Hopkins Press, 1940.

du Toit, A. B. "Life in Obedience to the Torah: Jewish Belief, Worship, and Everyday Religion in the First Century AD." In *The New Testament Milieu*, ed. A.B. du Toit, vol. 2, *Guide to the New Testament*. Halfway House: Orion Publishers, 1998.

Dunn, James D.G. *The Oral Gospel Tradition*. Grand Rapids: Eerdmans, 2013.

Edersheim, Alfred. *The Life and Times of Jesus the Messiah: Complete and Unabridged in One Volume*. Hendrickson Publishing, 1993.

Eisenberg, Joyce, and Ellen Scolnic. *Dictionary of Jewish Words*. Philadelphia: Jewish Publication Society, 2001.

Elwell, Walter A., and Barry J. Beitzel. *Baker Encyclopedia of the Bible*. Grand Rapids: Baker Book House, 1988.

Elwell, Walter A., and Robert W. Yarbrough. *Readings From the First-Century World*. Grand Rapids: Baker Books, 1998.

Ethics of the Fathers (*Pirkei Avot*) by the leading rabbinic scholars of various generations.

Felton, Gayle C. "John Wesley and the Teaching Ministry: Ramifications for Education in the Church Today." *Religious Education* 92, no. 1, Winter 1997.

Foster, Richard J. *Celebration of Discipline: The Path to Spiritual Growth*. New York: HarperOne, 2003.

Flusser, David. *Jesus*, 3rd edition. Magnes Press, 2001.

Fraade, Steven D. "The Early Rabbinic Sage." In *The Sage in Israel and the Ancient Near East*, edited by John G. Gammie and Leo G. Perdue. Winona Lake, IN: Eisenbrauns, 1990.

Freyne, Sean. *Galilee From Alexander the Great to Hadrian 323 B.C.E. to 135 C.E.: A Study of Second Temple Judaism*. Notre Dame, IN: University of Notre Dame Press, 1980.

Gilchrist, Paul R. "877 רָסִי." In *Theological Wordbook of the Old Testament*, edited by R. Laird Harris, Gleason L. Archer Jr., and Bruce K. Waltke. Chicago: Moody Press, 1999.

Ginzberg, Louis. *Legends of the Jews*. Global Grey, 2017.

Goldman, Israel M. *Life-Long Learning Among the Jews: Adult Education in Judaism from Biblical Times to the Twentieth Century*. New York: Ktav Publishing House, 1975.

Goodman, Martin. "Jewish History, 331 BCE-135 CE." In *The Jewish Annotated New Testament*, edited by Amy-Jill Levine and Marc Zvi Brettler. New York: Oxford University Press, 2011.

Graves, Michael. "The Public Reading of Scripture in Early Judaism." In *Journal of the Evangelical Theological Society* 50/3 (September 2007), 467-87.

Greenberg, Irving. *The Jewish Way: Living the Holidays*. New York: Simon & Schuster, 1988.

Guiterrez, Juan Marcos B. *Forgotten Origins: The Lost Jewish History of Jesus and Early Christianity*. Grand Prairie, Yaron Publishing, 2017.

Hagner, Donald A. "Matthew 1–13, vol. 33A." *Word Biblical Commentary*. Dallas: Word, 1998.

Hannam, Fraser D. "Teaching Through Narrative." *Forum on Public Policy Online*. Urbana: Oxford Round Table, 2015. https://files.eric.ed.gov/fulltext/EJ1091524.pdf.

Harris, Laird R., Gleason L. Archer Jr., and Bruce K. Waltke, eds. *Theological Wordbook of the Old Testament*. Chicago: Moody Press, 1999.

Heschel, Abraham Joshua. *The Sabbath: Its Meaning for Modern Man* (FSG Classics). New York: Farrar, Straus and Giroux, 2005. Kindle.

Hodges, Zane C. "Hebrews." In *The Bible Knowledge Commentary: An Exposition of the Scriptures*, edited by J. F. Walvoord and R. B. Zuck, vol. 2. Wheaton, IL: Victor Books, 1985.

Horsley, Richard A. *Scribes, Visionaries, and the Politics of Second Temple Judea*. Louisville: Westminster John Knox Press, 2007.

Jamieson, Robert, A. R. Fausset, and David Brown. *Commentary Critical and Explanatory on the Whole Bible, vol. 1*. Oak Harbor, WA: Logos Research Systems, 1997.

Jensen, Richard A. *Envisioning the Word: The Use of Visual Images in Preaching*. Minneapolis: Fortress Press, 2005.

Jeremias, Joachim. "Ποιμην, Αρχιποιμην, Ποιμαινω, Ποιμνη, Ποιμνιον." In *Theological Dictionary of the New Testament*, edited by Gerhard Kittel, Geoffrey W. Bromiley, and Gerhard Friedrich. Grand Rapids: Eerdmans, 1964.

Johnson, John C. "Mishnah." In *The Lexham Bible Dictionary*, edited by John D. Barry et al. Bellingham, WA: Lexham Press, 2016.

Josephus, Flavius. Josephus, *The Complete Works*. Translated by William Whiston. Nashville, TN: Thomas Nelson, 1998.

Kaufman, Stephen A., ed. in chief. *Targum Neofiti to the Pentateuch*. From the files of the Comprehensive Aramaic Lexicon Project. Hebrew Union College, 2005. LOGOS.

Kierspel, Lars. *Charts on the Life, Letters, and Theology of Paul*. Grand Rapids: Kregel Publications, 2012.

Knight III, George W. *New International Greek Testament Commentary: The Pastoral Epistles*, edited by I. Howard Marshall and W. Ward Gasque. Grand Rapids: Eerdmans, 1992.

Levine, Amy-Jill. *The Misunderstood Jew: The Church and the Scandal of the Jewish Jesus*. HarperCollins e-books, 2007.

Levine, Amy-Jill and Marc Zvi Brettler, eds. *The Jewish Annotated New Testament*. New York: Oxford University Press, 2011.

Levine, Lee, and I. Levine. "The Synagogue." In *The Jewish Annotated New Testament*, edited by Amy-Jill Levine and Marc Zvi Brettler. New York: Oxford University Press, 2011.

Lizorkin-Eyzenberg, Eliyahu. *The Jewish Gospel of John: Discovering Jesus, King of All Israel*. www.israelstudycenter.com, 2015.

Lowery, David K. "1 Corinthians." In *The Bible Knowledge Commentary: An Exposition of the Scriptures*, edited by J. F. Walvoord and R. B. Zuck, vol. 2. Wheaton, IL: Victor Books, 1985.

Mason, Steve. "Chief Priests, Sadducees, Pharisees and Sanhedrin in Acts." *The Book of Acts In Its First Century Setting: Volume 4, Palestinian Setting*, edited by James Bauckham. Grand Rapids: Eerdmans, 1995.

McClintock, John, and James Strong. "Prophets, Schools of The." In *Cyclopædia of Biblical, Theological, and Ecclesiastical Literature*, vol. 8. New York: Harper & Brothers, 1894.

McComiskey, Thomas E. "1990 שָׁדַק." In *Theological Wordbook of the Old Testament*, edited by R. Laird Harris, Gleason L. Archer Jr., and Bruce K. Waltke. Chicago: Moody Press, 1999.

Meye, R. P. "Disciple." In *The International Standard Bible Encyclopedia*, rev., edited by Geoffrey W. Bromiley. Grand Rapids: Eerdmans, 1979–1988.

Michelson, Marty A. "Jewish-Christian Dialog." In *Relational Theology: A Contemporary Introduction*. Point Loma Press, 2016.

Moore, George Foot. *Judaism in the First Centuries of the Christian Era: The Age of the Tannaim, Volume I*. New York: Schocken Books, 1974.

———. *Judaism in the First Centuries of the Christian Era: The Age of the Tannaim, Volumes II & III*. Peabody: Hendrickson Publishers, 1997.

Morrison, Michael D. "Sepphoris." In *The Lexham Bible Dictionary*, edited by John D. Barry et al. Bellingham, WA: Lexham Press, 2016.

Neusner, Jacob. *Judaism in the Beginning of Christianity*. Minneapolis: Fortress Press, 1984.

Newberry, Thomas, and George Ricker Berry. *The Interlinear Literal Translation of the Greek New Testament*. Bellingham, WA: Logos Bible Software, 2004.

Niebuhr, H. Richard. *Christ and Culture*. San Francisco: HarperCollins, 1975.

Packer, J. I., and M. C. Tenny. *Illustrated Manners and Customs of the Bible*. Nashville, TN: Thomas Nelson Publishers, 1980.

Payne, J. Barton. "484 הָוָה." In *Theological Wordbook of the Old Testament*, edited by R. Laird Harris, Gleason L. Archer Jr., and Bruce K. Waltke. Chicago: Moody Press, 1999.

Philo Judaeus. *The Works of Philo Judaeus: The contemporary of Josephus, translated from the Greek by Charles Duke Yonge. London, H. G. Bohn, 1854-1890*. Grand Rapids: Christian Classics Ethereal Library.

Prager, Dennis. "Exodus: God, Slavery, and Freedom." In *The Rational Bible*. Washington, DC: Regnery Faith, 2018.

Prince, Derek. *Foundational Truths for Christian Living*. Lake Mary, FL: Charisma House, 2006.

Ramsay, W.M. *The Education of Christ: Hill-side Reveries*. New York: G.P. Putnam's Sons, 1902.

Redditt, Paul, L. "Prophecy, History of." In *Dictionary of the Old Testament Prophets*, edited by Mark Boda and J. Gordon McConnvile. Downers Grove: IVP Academic, 2012.

Rengstorf, Karl Heinrich. "Αποστελλω (πιμπω), Εξαποστολλω, Αποστολος, Ψευδαποστολος, Αποστολη." In *Theological Dictionary of the New Testament*, edited by Gerhard Kittel, Geoffrey W. Bromiley, and Gerhard Friedrich. Grand Rapids: Eerdmans, 1964.

———. "διδασκω in the NT." In *Theological Dictionary of the New Testament*, edited by Gerhard Kittel, Geoffrey W. Bromiley, and Gerhard Friedrich. Grand Rapids: Eerdmans, 1964.

———. "διδασκω outside the NT." In *Theological Dictionary of the New Testament*, edited by Gerhard Kittel, Geoffrey W. Bromiley, and Gerhard Friedrich. Grand Rapids: Eerdmans, 1964.

Reyes, Rhea. "The Genesis Apocryphon: A More Divine Abraham." In *Prandium—The Journal of Historical Studies* 2, no. 1 (Spring, 2013). The Department of Historical Studies, University of Toronto Mississauga.

Riesner, R. "Teacher." In *Dictionary of Jesus and the Gospels*, edited by Joel B. Green and Scot McKnight. Downers Grove: InterVarsity Press, 1992.

Riesner, Rainer. "Synagogues in Jerusalem." In *The Book of Acts In Its First Century Setting: Volume 4, Palestinian Setting*, edited by James Bauckham. Grand Rapids: Eerdmans, 1995.

Robinson, George. *Essential Judaism: A Complete Guide to Beliefs, Customs and Rituals*. New York: Atria Books, 2000. Kindle.

Ryle, Herbert E. *The Book of Genesis in the Revised Version with Introduction and Notes*. The Cambridge Bible for Schools and Colleges. Cambridge: Cambridge University Press, 1921.

Sacks, Jonathan. *Ceremony and Celebration: Introduction to the Holidays*. New Milford: Maggid Books, 2017.

———. *Essays on Ethics: A Weekly Reading of the Jewish Bible*. New Milford: Maggid Books, 2016.

Sarna, Nahum M. *The JPS Torah Commentary: Exodus*. Philadelphia: Jewish Publication Society, 1991.

———. *The JPS Torah Commentary: Genesis*. Philadelphia: Jewish Publication Society, 1989.

Schürer, Emil. *The History of the Jewish People in the Age of Jesus Christ*, edited by Geza Vermes, Fergus Millar, and Matthew Black, 3 vols. Edinburgh: T&T Clark, 1973-87.

Scott Jr., Julius J. *Jewish Backgrounds of the New Testament*. Grand Rapids: Baker Academic, 1995.

Shelley, Bruce L. *Church History in Plain Language*, 4th ed. Nashville: Thomas Nelson, 2013.

Shiffman, Lawrence H., ed. *Texts and Traditions: A Source reader for the Study of Second Temple and Rabbinic Judaism*. Hoboken: Ktav Publishing House, 1998.

Shulam, Joseph, with Hilary Le Cornu. *A Commentary on the Jewish Roots of Acts 1-15*. Jerusalem: Netivyah Bible Instruction Ministry, 2012.

———. *A Commentary on the Jewish Roots of Acts 16-28*. Jerusalem: Netivyah Bible Instruction Ministry, 2012.

Sigal, Phillip. *The Halakhah of Jesus of Nazareth according to the Gospel of Matthew*. Atlanta: Society of Biblical Literature, 2007.

Spangler, Ann, and Lois Tverberg. *Sitting at the Feet of Rabbi Jesus: How the Jewishness of Jesus Can Transform Your Faith*. Grand Rapids: Zondervan, 2009.

Stein, R. H. "Entertain," *The International Standard Bible Encyclopedia*, rev. ed., edited by Geoffrey W. Bromiley. Grand Rapids: Eerdmans, 1979–1988.

Stern, David H. *Jewish New Testament Commentary*. Clarksville, MD: Jewish New Testament Publications, 1992.

Stern, Frank. *A Rabbi Looks at Jesus' Parables*. Lanham, MD: Rowman & Littlefield Publishers, 2006.

Stevens, John Robert. "Pastors and Teachers." In *The New Testament Church Manual*. North Hollywood: Living Word Publications, 1968.

Streane, A. J. *The Age of the Maccabees*. London: Eyre and Spottiswoode, 1898.

Stuart, Douglas. *Word Biblical Commentary: Hosea–Jonah. Vol. 31*, edited by Bruce M. Metzger, David A. Hubbard, and Glenn W. Barker. Dallas: Word Books, 2002.

Swanson, James. "דמל." In *Dictionary of Biblical Languages with Semantic Domains: Hebrew (Old Testament)*. Oak Harbor: Logos Research Systems, 1997.

Telushkin, Joseph. *Jewish Wisdom: Ethical, Spiritual, and Historical Lessons from the Great Works and Thinkers*. New York: HarperCollins e-books, 1994.

———. *Jewish Literacy: The Most Important Things to Know About the Jewish Religion, Its People, and Its History*. New York: HarperCollins, 2008.

Tigay, Jeffrey H. *The JPS Torah Commentary: Deuteronomy*. Philadelphia: Jewish Publication Society, 1989.

"Torah," *Orthodox Union* (June 21, 2006), https://www.ou.org/judaism-101/glossary/torah/.

Yoder, Christine Roy. *Wisdom as a Woman of Substance*. New York: Walter de Gruyter, 2001.

Young, Brad H. *Meet the Rabbis: Rabbinic Thought and the Teachings of Jesus.* Grand Rapids: Baker Academics, 2007.

———. *The Parables, Jewish Tradition and Christian Interpretation.* Peabody, MA: Hendrickson Publishers, 1998.

Youngblood, Ronald, F. F. Bruce, and R. K. Harrison, eds., *Nelson's New Illustrated Bible Dictionary.* Nashville, TN: Thomas Nelson, 1995.

Weinfeld, Moshe. *Normative and Sectarian Judaism in the Second Temple Period.* New York: T&T Clark International, 2005.

Wiersbe, Warren W. *The Bible Exposition Commentary. Vol. 2.* Wheaton, IL: Victor Books, 1996.

Wesley, John. "Notes on the New Testament: 1 Corinthians—Revelation." In *The Wesleyan Heritage Library Commentary*, Electronic ed. Wesleyan Heritage Publications, 2002.

Wigglesworth, Smith. "Like Precious Faith." In *Faith That Prevails.* Radford, VA: Wilder Publications, 2018.

Willis, Judith. *Research-Based Strategies to Ignite Student Learning: Insights from a Neurologist and Classroom Teacher.* Association for Supervision & Curriculum Development, 2006. Kindle.

Wilson, Marvin R. *Our Father Abraham: Jewish Roots of the Christian Faith.* Grand Rapids: Eerdmans, 1989.

Wright, Brian. *The Great Yet Completely Misunderstood Commission of Jesus: The Original Hebrew Understanding of Discipleship.* Calvert Biblical Institute for the Study of Religion and Society, 2017. Kindle.

ABOUT THE AUTHOR

Christopher J. Reeves, M.Ed., is President of Shiloh University. A highly respected leader and educator, Chris has been a pioneer in online Christian education with a cross-cultural and non-denominational perspective. Chris has also devoted his energies to the deepening of Christian understanding of the Bible through the teaching of its Jewish context. His love of Scripture has resulted in this study of the Jewish-Christian paradigm of education in Bible times.

www.ingramcontent.com/pod-product-compliance
Lightning Source LLC
Chambersburg PA
CBHW062206080426
42734CB00010B/1805